The Rough Guide to Muhammad

Ali

"Muhammad Ali was a god" Sugar Ray Leonard

Muhammad Ali cannot be defined. Like all the 20th century's most enduring icons, his influence and impact are too great to fit a single word. Describing Ali as a boxer would be like calling **Elvis Presley** a singer and **Marilyn Monroe** an actress. To understand Ali is to hear the voice of the boxer, the political figure and the man, and to understand the times that shaped him.

Throughout his life, Ali borrowed from others. The egotistical showmanship was inspired by a wrestler called **Gorgeous George**. The poetry was often written with the help of his entourage – it was cornerman Drew 'Bundini' Brown who coined his famous phrase "float like a butterfly, sting like a bee". The politics came from **Elijah Muhammad** and the trademark magic tricks came straight from the local five-and-dime store, but ultimately, as F. Scott Fitzgerald said of **Jay Gatsby**, Muhammad Ali sprang from his own conception of himself.

For all the borrowing, Ali's finest hours belonged to him and him alone. At the press conference after the first **Liston** fight, with the world at his feet, he allied himself with the **Nation of Islam**. He forfeited his heavyweight title rather than be drafted, and with the words "I ain't got no quarrel with them **Viet Cong**", gave the anti-war movement its best soundbite. He recaptured the heavyweight title with tactics that bewildered even his own trainer, and 20 years later, through his public battle with the symptoms of Parkinson's, recaptured a few hearts, too.

As well as tracing the story of Ali's life, this *Rough Guide* examines the fights which proved first that there was **substance** to the self-promotion and then to his great comeback. There are 101 quotes to show why Ali was the **Louisville Lip**, the **ephemera** – from the clothes he wore to the music he listened to – and, yes, the photographs. To be an icon, you have to **photograph** well. The images of Ali that endure are those that show a complicated individual at his most basic – glistening with sweat as he pounds a punchbag, or alive, alert and volatile in the ring.

Yet to remember Ali simply as a beautiful boxer is to forget why he was so **dangerous**, and why his description of himself as "the Elvis of boxing" was so apt. Both caused white America to sit up and take notice, both rewrote the rules and both changed the world. This *Rough Guide* rescues Ali from the distance of history and shows him in all his complexity. The Muhammad Ali in these pages might combine the sporting mastery of a **Michael Jordan**, the righteous anger of **Malcolm X** and the smart mouth of **Lenny Bruce**, but he's entirely Muhammad Ali. Impossible to define, but by whatever criteria you apply, **The Greatest**.

Credits

Text editors Ann Oliver, Paul Simpson
Contributors Wayne Cyrus, Frank Foster, Jon Hotten, Richard Pendleton
Production Ian Cranna, Chris Hughes, Stephanie Jones
Picture editors Dominique campbell, Jenny Quiggin
Design Frank Foster
Thanks to Sir Henry Cooper, Emmanuel Steward, Derek Williams, Steve Farhood, Brian Ganz, Kevin Mitchell, Andy Hall, Anthony Gee, Rodney Hinds, Ron Shillingford, Colin Hart, Ken Jones, Hugh McIlvanney, Simon Kanter, Sharon O'Connor
Special merit department Michaela Bushell, Helen Rodiss
Printed in Italy by LegoPrint S.p.A
Dedicated to Hugo Butler and family

Pic credits Andy Clark/Reuters; Associated Press; Baltimore Sun Photo; Bettmann/Corbis; Allsport, Hulton Archive, Bob Gomel/Time Life Pictures, Brian Hamill, Central Press, Dirck Halstead/Liaison, Fox Photos, Harry Benson, Keystone, L. Trievnor/Express, Three Lions / Getty Images; Luisita Pacheco; PA Photos; Popperfoto.com; The Courier-Journal; CSU Archv, Dan Herrick/DMI, Everett Collection, Fotos International, Juergen Hasenkopf, Media Press, Peter Brooker, Sipa Press, Snap, Steve Connolly / Rex Features; The Andy Warhol Foundationfor the Visual Arts, Inc./ARS, NY and DACS London 2004/Art Resource/Scala, Florence; Carl Fischer GOAT/TASCHEN; Flip Schulke GOAT/TASHEN; TASCHEN 2003 GOAT / TASCHEN; VinMag Archive

Special thanks to Jason Timson and Glen Marks from Rex Features, Amy Inskeep from The Courier-Journal and Nigel Gibson from Associated Press and Getty Images

Publishing info This edition published in September 2004 was prepared by Haymarket Customer Publishing for Rough Guides Ltd, 80 Strand, London, WC2R ORL

Distributed by The Penguin Group
Penguin Books Ltd, 80 Strand, London WC2R 0RL

A catalogue record for this book is available from the British Library
ISBN 1-84353-385-5

Contents

Contents

Muhammad
Ali
The life

His family, his background, his political struggle:
here's how the world's greatest fighter was made

"THIS IS THE LEGEND OF CASSIUS CLAY
THE MOST BEAUTIFUL FIGHTER IN THE WORLD TODAY
THIS BRASH YOUNG BOXER IS SOMETHING TO SEE
AND THE HEAVYWEIGHT CHAMPIONSHIP IS HIS DESTINY"
Muhammad Ali, 1963

A Kentucky childhood

L ouisville, Kentucky. The city is known as **The Gateway to the South** and there's still something of **Old Dixie** about the white clapboard mansions that line its leafy boulevards and the plantation houses that skirt its limits. 1940s **Louisville** also possessed an edge that other Southern cities didn't: in an area of America where many states are filled with "dry" counties, it had 15 whiskey distilleries within its boundaries, and a large chunk of the domestic tobacco industry was resident there too. To go with the drinking and smoking, Louisville could add gambling to its list of attractions. Each year it hosted one of America's most epic sporting occasions, **the Kentucky Derby**.

The man whose fame would come to eclipse that of the Derby, whose name would resound in the heads of people who had barely heard of America, let alone Louisville, Kentucky, was born there on 17 January 1942. He grew up in the West End, at 3302 Grand Avenue, with his father, **Cassius Clay Snr**, a signwriter and part-time painter, his mother **Odessa** and, from 1944, with his younger brother **Rudolph**. By all measures of the time, **Cassius Marcellus Clay II** was not raised as a hungry fighter, the criteria that drove men like **Sonny Liston, Joe Frazier** and **George Foreman** to the ring. The Clay family were members of the black middle class, which, as the writer **Toni Morrison** pointed out, was nothing like being members of the white middle class, but was one step removed from the abject poverty endured by many black families.

The Clays owned their home on Grand Avenue, bought at the price of $4,200. Cassius and Rudolph enjoyed none of the luxuries of the white middle classes, but they did not go short of clothes or food, or of their parents' love. They were raised as church-going baptists by Odessa, who had grown up in a broken home, and who was determined that her boys would not do the same.

Cassius Clay, the name shared by father and son, came with some history attached. When the man who would become **Muhammad Ali** referred to it as his "slave name" when he gave it up shortly after winning the world heavyweight title in 1964, he was right.

Yet the original **Cassius Clay** had been one of Kentucky's first abolitionists, a fearsome and extraordinary white plantation farmer and soldier born in 1810. Clay freed all of his 40 slaves during the 1840s, and edited an anti-slavery newspaper called **The True American. Abraham Lincoln** thought so highly of him that he sent Clay to **Russia** as an ambassador on behalf of the **US**

government. It was this Cassius Clay who freed Cassius Clay Snr's grandfather, and the name was passed on through the former slave's family line.

Odessa's side of the family tree was more complex. One of her grandfathers was a white Irishman named **Abe Grady**, who left **County Clare** for **Kentucky** and married a black girl there. Odessa's other grandfather was of mixed race, the child of a white man and a black slave.

This heritage bore one precious gift for young Cassius: his genetics. By lineage, by birth, by fluke, he had been touched by the gods. He was handsome, strong and athletic, sublimely talented. Cassius Clay was one in four billion.

Cassius's childhood was uncomplicated. The darkest moments came during Cassius Clay Snr's brushes with the law. He was arrested four times for reckless driving, a couple more for assault and battery, twice for disorderly conduct and once for disposing of mortgaged property. He was sometimes drunk, and when he was drunk he could be violent towards Odessa. His signs hung on the streets and shops around old Louisville's black areas, but while his signwriting provided the family with a living, Cassius Snr's real desire was to paint. He produced a series of religious murals and landscape canvases but they failed to earn him enough to quit his day job.

At home he spoke often of how he had been forced to leave school at 14 because of the limited opportunities afforded to black people. He was distrustful of the white establishment, and with justification. The South was still **segregated**, the hated **Jim Crow** laws still in force. Black people were treated as second class citizens. They could not sit with white people on public transport and were barred from certain restaurants and venues. They were sent to different schools and lived in different streets to whites. At the cinema, they had to sit in the balcony seats. Parks and public spaces were either "black," "white" or "mixed". Other places, like the grand country clubs and the upmarket areas of the city, remained unattainable to them by opportunity, by circumstance and by law.

Cassius and **Rudolph** would grow up having the word "nigger" directed at them. Rudy told **Thomas Hauser**: "It wasn't like the **Deep South**, but people would call us nigger and tell us to get out if we were someplace we didn't belong."

Two childhood incidents would shape the life of Cassius Clay Jnr. The first, much mythologised, involved the theft of his bicycle, a brand new red and white Schwin that cost his parents $60. Cassius and a friend cycled to the **Columbia Auditorium** to see an exhibition called the **Louisville Home Show**. When the time came to go home, Cassius discovered that his bicycle had been stolen. In tears, he wandered back into the auditorium, walking downstairs into a boxing gym run by a local cop, a white policeman called **Joe Martin**.

He told Joe Martin that he wanted to "whup whoever stole my bike." Martin

PROFILE **Ali's hometown** 1940s LOUISVILLE, KENTUCKY

Racial segregation was a way of life in Louisville in the 1940s, and reminders of the "ugly etiquette" were everywhere. As Cassius Clay grew up, he went to a segregated school and quickly got to know the areas of the city in which he was not welcome. He would sit at the back of buses and see his mother refused a glass of water at an all-white diner.

Louisville, home of the Kentucky Derby, aka 'the Gateway to the South', still retained many of the South's more obnoxious rules and customs. The Jim Crow laws – over 400 pieces of legislation that kept white and black communities segregated – were still in force, and their slow repeal would not gain pace until 1952, when the Supreme Court ruled that segregation on inter-state trains was unconstitutional. The landmark case – Brown versus Board of Education, which declared segregation in schools unconstitutional – came in 1954.

But even in 1960, after returning from Rome with an Olympic gold medal, Cassius Clay was refused service in a white restaurant, causing him, he later claimed, to throw his medal into a river.

took a look at the sobbing, scrawny 12-year-old and replied that he'd better learn to fight before he went looking for anyone to whup. Thus did the future three-time heavyweight champion connect with his fate.

The second incident involved a crime far more awful than the theft of a bicycle. In the summer of 1955, a 14-year-old black boy named **Emmett Till**, a native of **Chicago** who spent his vacations with family in the town of **Money, Mississippi**, was murdered by a white shopkeeper and his half-brother. Till was shot in the head and his body was thrown into the **Tallahatchie River**. His crime had been to talk to the white girl who operated the till inside the store.

An all-white jury acquitted the shopkeeper and his brother after deliberating for just one hour. The black newspapers, which had run pictures of Till's mutilated body, were outraged. **Cassius Clay Snr** showed his sons the images of Emmett Till and told them about the terrible injustice that he had suffered. It hit Cassius Jnr, who was just a year younger than the murdered boy, especially hard. He would lie in his bed and cry, wondering why his people had to suffer in such a way. He began to see boxing as the only way that he might make an impression on such a divided society.

Cassius Clay's beginnings in boxing weren't particularly auspicious. He had his first fight six weeks after joining **Joe Martin's gym**. Weighing 89lbs (6st 4lbs) he won a split decision over one **Ronnie O'Keefe**, another first-timer.

Joe Martin did not see Cassius Clay as a prodigy, at least not at first. Cassius was fast and neat; what marked him out was not his skill but his dedication. "He was religious about learning," Martin remembered. "He trained every day and he was easily the hardest-working kid at the gym."

Cassius stayed with Joe Martin for most of his amateur career, alternating periodically between the policeman and **Fred Stoner**, a trainer at the **Grace-Hope Community Centre**.

Martin and Stoner were contrasting characters, each shaped by their times. Martin was a white cop, an establishment figure, paid to uphold the status quo. Fred Stoner was a slim, nervy black man who had trained Louisville boxers for two decades. Both Martin and Stoner have claimed – and been awarded – varying amounts of credit for starting the enthusiastic amateur on the road to greatness.

For a year or so, Cassius didn't appear exceptional in anything other than his work rate, but as his talent flowered, it became obvious to his trainers that much of what he had could never be taught. He was lithe and athletic, gifted with lightning reflexes and a seemingly perfect sense of balance that let him fight in an unorthodox fashion. He kept his hands low and his head up, often rocking backwards from a punch rather than ducking, slipping or moving laterally. He began to win lots of amateur contests and they further fired his passion for the sport.

Kentucky raised: Cassius Clay and little brother Rudolph look past the camera

Many years later, **Ali** would remember sitting in the school classroom, drawing pictures of himself wearing a robe that said "**Golden Gloves Champion**" (the Golden Gloves title remains the high point for a national amateur boxer), or imagining that he might someday command a purse of $4,000 on a Saturday night fight card.

Cassius made several appearances on a TV programme called **Champions of Tomorrow**, for which Martin helped select fighters. Then, in 1956, at the age of 14, he won the first major title of his career, a novice Golden Gloves championship. Fighting as a light heavyweight, young Clay quickly became recognised as a major prospect. His ascent was briefly marred by the diagnosis of a heart murmur during a pre-fight physical before he was to compete for his first **National Golden**

Gloves title in 1957, but after four months of anxious inactivity, Cassius's symptoms disappeared entirely.

A year later he took the **Louisville Golden Gloves Light Heavyweight** title, advancing to the quarter finals of the Tournament of Champions in Chicago, where he was stopped by a single body shot from hard-hitting Australian **Tony Madigan**. The loss was no disaster for the young fighter. He was still developing physically and becoming sharper, his talent taking him past more experienced opponents. In 1959, in the midst of a 36-bout winning streak, he defeated Madigan for his first **National Golden Gloves** title, and then outpointed **Johnny Powell** for the **Amateur Athletic Union** [AAU] light heavyweight championship.

His run came to an end in the May of 1959, when he lost a split decision to the southpaw **Amos Johnson**. It was to be his last defeat as an amateur boxer.

By 1960, Cassius was far stronger, almost a man, and it showed in a stellar run of results. He won, consecutively, the Kentucky Golden Gloves, the Tournament of Champions and then the big one, the **National Golden Gloves** title at **Madison Square Garden**, this time fighting as a heavyweight. He gave away some 40lbs to his final opponent, **Gary Jawish**, but won the title with a third round KO.

All of his boxing success left Clay ambivalent towards his high-school career,

PROFILE **Ali's parents** CASSIUS AND ODESSA CLAY

Cassius Clay Snr, otherwise and often known as Cash, and his wife Odessa were proof of the maxim that opposites attract. Odessa Clay, whose grandfather Abe Grady came from Ireland, raised their children Cassius Jr and Rudolph as Baptists, and made sure they had a strong and settled home life. "Their mother taught them right," said

Cassius Snr. "She taught them to be spiritual and be good to everybody."

Cassius Snr was, as Ali later told Jose Torres, "a hep cat, a hep fella, 57 years old, crazy about the girls... My daddy is a playboy. He is always wearing white shoes and pink pants and blue shirts and says he'll never get old."

Indeed, Cash's penchant for women led to many of the arguments in the Clay household – arguments that, if he was drunk, would sometimes turn violent. Odessa called the police on three occasions seeking protection. The couple lived separately from the early 1970s, although they still appeared together in public. Cassius Snr died in 1990, and Odessa Clay in 1997.

which was drawing to a less than climactic close. Although the gym channelled his energy and he was rarely involved in school-yard fights or classroom disruption, he spent a lot of his time day-dreaming. His principal at **Central High**, **Atwood Wilson**, proved a forward-thinking man, assigning Clay to classes that were aimed at helping him in his future boxing career. He took instruction in book-keeping and income tax, in the hope that he wouldn't be exploited once he started making money in the pro game.

Before any such opportunity came, Clay prepared for the climax to his amateur career. A successful defence of his AAU light heavyweight title put him through to the **US Olympic Trials** for the Rome games of 1960.

The trials were held in **San Francisco**. Clay had already attracted his first bout of adverse publicity: his **constant bragging** about his skills led to sections of the press objecting to his participation in a "decent amateur tournament".

Clay backed up his boasts with his fists until he reached the final eliminator, when the Army champion **Allen Hudson** decked him in the first round of their contest. Cassius clawed his way back into the fight, but the result was in doubt until he clipped Hudson with a fast right and followed up for a late stoppage. Cassius was going to Rome.

Yet before he could board the plane – a source of apprehension for Cassius, as his fear of flying had already taken hold – he had to graduate from Central High. He was ranked 367 out of 391 pupils, an indication that, despite his quick mind and remarkable personality, he had struggled with the basic tenets of education.

Joe Martin understood that the ring presented **Cassius Clay** with his great opportunity in life, and a successful **Olympics** would be his passport to a bankroll in the pro ranks. He lectured his protégé on the need to represent his country well, and to seize his chance when it came.

"I told him this was his one chance of money and fame, and he better take it," Martin remembered. It wasn't just Martin who thought so. **Sports Illustrated** named Clay as "the best American prospect for a gold medal" in Rome.

The Olympic Village might have been constructed especially for Cassius, proto-citizen of the world. He met athletes from every nation, taking hundreds of pictures with his ancient box camera. He traded lapel pins, put on impromptu displays of shadow boxing and fancy footwork in the streets, managed to befriend **Bing Crosby** and gave the visiting world heavyweight champion **Floyd Patterson** a tour of the village – and a warning that he'd soon be out for his title. **Nat Fleischer** of **Ring** magazine found him playing his harmonica for a delighted crowd. For every person who thought him brash, Clay won 10 admirers, disarming everyone with his enthusiasm for **Rome** and for the games.

For all of his clowning, Clay trained hard, and the US boxing team became

Joe Martin, cop and gym owner, inspects his proud protégé's first prize, a Golden Glove

a tight-knit unit, rooming together and urging each other along. Cassius began well in his quest for glory, stopping the Belgian **Yvon Becaus** inside two rounds with the slick combination punching that had become his trademark. His second bout went the three-round distance, but Clay emerged a unanimous points winner over the more experienced Russian, **Gennadiy Shatkov**.

The semi-final threw him a tougher challenge. Staring at him from the opposing corner was **Tony Madigan**, the rugged Australian who had defeated him in the 1958 Tournament of Champions. Clay had avenged that loss a year later, and now he took a narrow but deserved decision in this crucial bout. Madigan was a come-forward brawler, but Cassius, bigger and stronger, had the physical tools to defy him. Rasping jabs and lightning speed took him to victory.

The Olympic schedule meant that Cassius then had to wait almost two weeks for the gold medal bout. He was to fight the Polish representative **Ziggy Pietrzykowski**, something of a veteran with 230 fights on his record. Ziggy was the holder of a bronze medal from the 1956 Games, won with a fearsome southpaw style that seemed designed to give Clay trouble. When the first bell rang, it did. Clay had twice lost to southpaws in America, and it looked like he would again in **Italy**. Pietrzykowski won the first round easily and hurt Clay with some strong punches.

But, showing the kind of instinctive feel for fighting that would characterise his career, Clay switched styles in round two and stood up to the Pole, winning the close exchanges with some hard right-hand shots. Cassius was now on top and he would not cede his advantage. In the final round he produced some brilliance right on cue. Perfectly timed combinations fired into Pietrzykowski's head and body. Only the bell saved the battered Pole from a knock-out, as he finished the fight slumped against the ropes, blood running from his nose and from a cut above his eye. Cassius Clay was the **Olympic Light Heavyweight Champion** of 1960.

The black boy from Louisville, Kentucky was now the hottest prospect in American boxing. Joe Martin met him at Idlewild (later JFK) airport with the news that he had sponsors in place to launch Clay's professional career. Cassius enjoyed four days of VIP treatment in New York during which he met his hero, **Sugar Ray Robinson**. When he got back to **Louisville**, he was met like a conquering king.

A parade took him right back to Central High, from where he had graduated just a few months previously. Now, there was a banner raised above the entrance in his honour. For once even Cassius Clay was lost for words.

PROFILE **Ali's brother** RAHAMAN ALI (FORMERLY RUDOLPH CLAY)

Two years younger than Cassius, Rudolph Arnette arrived in 1944 and completed the Clay family. "Muhammad and I had a few fights between us," Rahaman said of their childhood. "All brothers do, but it was nothing serious. He always had to be the leader and we let him because he was very intelligent and quick."

The brothers began boxing together, with Rudolph displaying enough talent to make it to the professional ranks himself. He made his pro debut with a win over Chip Johnson on the undercard of Cassius's first fight with Sonny Liston.

"That night was ecstasy, the epitome of joy," he told Thomas Hauser. "I've always shared my brother's joy. So when he became heavyweight champion of the world, I became champion, too."

Like Ali, Rahaman converted to Islam. He ended his boxing career in 1972 with a 14-3-1 record – he lost a supporting fight on the bill of the first Ali-Frazier fight. He was part of Ali's entourage for much of Muhammad's career: "I give him $50,000 a year for drivin' and jivin' and that ain't bad," the champ said.

The Louisville Lip

The deal that took **Cassius Clay** into the ranks of American professional boxers was reflective of its times. He was backed by the newly assembled **Louisville Sponsoring Group**, consisting of 11 wealthy white Louisville businessmen, headed by a distillery owner named **Bill Faversham**. The contract that Cassius Clay accepted seemed a good one: a $10,000 signing on fee and a guaranteed $4,800 per year for two years, plus an advance of $6,000 against earnings from the following four years. The sponsors would also cover all training expenses, Faversham would act as a manager, and 15 per cent of Clay's earnings would automatically be paid into a pension fund to be accessed upon his retirement from boxing.

The funding came from the businessmen's pockets. They agreed to pay $2,800 each in return for receiving 50 per cent of Clay's earnings for the first four years of the contract and 40 per cent thereafter. The deal was co-signed by **Cassius Clay Snr** and **Odessa Clay**, along with Cassius, who was too young to sign alone.

A hero's welcome: Yet gold medallist Clay was still bound by Jim Crow laws in his home town

It had not been the only offer for Cassius's services. **Archie Moore**, the veteran World Light Heavyweight Champion, and **Sugar Ray Robinson**, his hero, had both made tentative approaches. **Joe Martin** had his deal together at the airport, but Cassius, guided by his father, refused them all. Sugar Ray was Ali's idol but when the two met, when Ali was a young man, it was something of a disappointment for the up and coming boxer. "I asked for his **autograph**," he recalled later. "He didn't give it to me, He said he was in a hurry. So he didn't. It means so much to get a signature and he was in a hurry." Years later, when the two met, Ali reminded Robinson and gave him his own autograph. "I said, 'I'm bigger than you'. He said, 'Give me your signature.' So I wrote, 'Be a good boy.'"

Three days after signing his contract with the **Louisville Sponsoring Group**, Cassius was stepping into the ring as a professional boxer for the very first time (for full details of all of Ali's professional bouts, see The Fights, page 85).

> "I DON'T WANT TO FIGHT LIKE ARCHIE MOORE. I WANNA FIGHT LIKE SUGAR RAY... I'M THE HEAVYWEIGHT SUGAR RAY"
>
> **Cassius Clay**

His opponent brought Clay back into contact with the law just days after leaving Joe Martin behind: **Tunney Hunsaker** was the police chief of **Fayetteville, West Virgina**. Hunsaker had a 17-8 win-loss record and was regarded as a tough challenge for the new **Olympic champion** first time out. Indeed, Sponsoring Group leader **Bill Faversham** wasn't particularly happy with the match, but it had been arranged prior to Clay's signature drying on the group's contract. The fight was promoted by **Bill King**, who had guaranteed Clay $2,000 – a very decent cheque for what was essentially still a local, non-televised event. Interest in Louisville was high and 6,000 people filled the **Freedom Hall** for the fight.

When he entered the ring, resplendent in his USA Olympic Team shorts, it was obvious that Clay, just 18, was not yet the fully fledged heavy; he was barely bigger than a light heavyweight fighter. He still had some growing to do, but his fine condition contrasted graphically with that of the slightly flabby Hunsaker.

Cassius's failure to knock out the battling cop over six pretty uneventful rounds led to some criticism from the newspapers. True, he had won comfortably enough, but had not really exploded onto the scene in the grand manner of a future world champion.

The Sponsoring Group decided that Clay needed a little seasoning before his next fight, and he also needed to leave behind **Fred Stoner**, with whom he had prepared for the Hunsaker fight. His amateur days had been glorious, but they were over. The professional game was far more demanding, and no one knew that better than **Archie Moore**, the 47-year-old World Light Heavyweight Champion known as **The Mongoose**.

Moore was still fighting at his advanced age, and he was also training fighters at his camp in **San Diego, California**. It was a rudimentary place where Moore's charges were expected to run up and down the wooded hillsides in heavy boots, chop firewood for the cabins and take frequent dips in the cold swimming pools. Archie, with wry humour, had dubbed the establishment **The Salt Mine**.

Moore had offered to represent Cassius Clay after Clay's Olympic gold, but had been rejected. Yet he was still more than happy to agree to Bill Faversham's request that Clay relocate to **California** for some schooling by "The Professor" as Moore had decided to style himself.

The Sponsoring Group did not choose Moore and the Salt Mine entirely for sporting reasons. With Clay still legally a minor until he reached the age of 21, he would be in a strong position to challenge the contract he had signed with the Group should he want to – most American states, including **Kentucky**, did not recognise contracts made with minors. California, because of its entertainment industry, did. Many a child star had put pen to paper in **Hollywood** and been bound to the deal they had made.

Flanked by his parents and members of the Louisville Sponsoring Group, Clay signs his contract

Clay hit the Salt Mine like a dervish. Moore was astounded by his ability to train: Clay ran up and down the steep hills tirelessly, and he loved to spar, engaging in several hard sessions with Moore himself.

Clay's mouth was in top gear, too. Clay stubbornly insisted that he didn't need Moore's instruction on techniques such as infighting (where boxers are engaged in eyeball-to-eyeball exchanges) arguing that he was so fast he'd never need to. "I don't want to fight like Archie Moore," he complained. "I wanna fight like Sugar Ray… I'm the heavyweight Sugar Ray Robinson."

Moore quickly became exasperated with his charge. "I saw an utterly astounding potential in that young man," he recalled. "I wanted to make an all-round fighter out of him. He was green… It was useless arguing with him – though he'd listen hard enough if I taught him something that was useful to his style of fighting."

Moore's wife and children, and Archie himself, loved the young man, despite everything. On one occasion, **Dick Sadler**, a trainer who worked with Moore and who would go on to manage **George Foreman**, had to accompany the irrepressible Clay on a cross-country train ride from **San Diego** to **Dallas**, where they were to watch Moore fight **Buddy Thurman**. Throughout the journey, Cassius kept jumping up and yelling, "I am the greatest… I am the greatest!" at the passing towns and stations, interspersing this with endless repetitions of the chorus of his current favourite song, **Chubby Checker**'s The Twist. "Seven hundred miles of twisting and 'I am the greatest'," Sadler said. "It drove me crazy."

Moore eventually telephoned Bill Faversham and asked him to take the rambunctious Cassius back to **Louisville**. Faversham exclaimed, "What that boy needs is a good spanking."

"He sure does," Moore replied. "But I don't know who's going to give it to him – including me."

> "WHAT THAT BOY NEEDS IS A GOOD SPANKING!"
> "HE SURE DOES, BUT I DON'T KNOW WHO'S GONNA GIVE IT TO HIM!"
> **Bill Faversham and Archie Moore**

Moore was saddened to see Cassius leave the Salt Mine, but he remained philosophical. Their paths would cross again.

Faversham began the search for a new trainer. **Ernie Braca**, who worked with **Sugar Ray Robinson**, was an obvious choice, but he was unavailable. **Fred Stoner** was again briefly considered, but his lack of experience in professional boxing weighed too heavily against him. Eventually, at the suggestion of **Harry**

Markson, who ran boxing at **Madison Square Garden** in **New York**, Faversham contacted **Angelo Dundee**, a trainer who was based at the **Fifth Street Gym** in **Miami**, which he co-owned with his brother Chris. Dundee appeared perfect; he was an experienced trainer, but still young at 37. He was a corner man, but more importantly, Dundee was something of an amateur psychologist. He had an innate understanding of fighters and what made them tick. If anyone could make sense of Cassius Clay, Angelo could.

When Faversham's call came, Dundee was able to tell him that he had already encountered the boy twice during trips to **Louisville**. In 1957, Clay had rung Dundee and asked if he could visit him and his fighter **Willie Pastrano** at their hotel. Clay and his brother **Rudolph** had stayed for two or three hours, shooting the breeze. Then, when Dundee and Pastrano returned to Louisville in 1959 for a fight with **Alonzo Johnson**, Clay asked Dundee if he could spar a round with Pastrano. Dundee usually spurned such practice – amateurs and pros didn't mix well and Pastrano was some fighter, a future light-heavyweight world champion. But Clay sparred a round and impressed Dundee, who felt he might even have bested Pastrano over the three minutes.

Faversham and a couple of other Group members visited Angelo at the Fifth Street Gym and a deal was struck – Dundee would receive $125 per week, a fee that wasn't renegotiated until after Clay had become world champion. On 19 December 1960, Cassius arrived in **Miami**.

Dundee laid out a clear career path for Clay – one that involved fights with a series of opponents designed to show the young man different styles and techniques whilst also building his confidence with, hopefully, a nice run of wins.

Dundee and Clay gelled almost immediately. Unlike **Moore** and **Sadler**, Dundee understood Cassius. He realised that the great trick in handling him was to encourage his exuberance and free thinking, to cajole him with praise and to allow him to assume that he had resolved any problems himself.

Dundee described how he would watch Clay spar and then launch into an outrageously flattering recap of his efforts – "Hey, that's a beautiful uppercut: you're throwing it off your left foot and bending the knee just fine…" – none of which Clay had actually done, but which he would execute perfectly when he went out for the next round.

Dundee's other great contribution to Clay's early development was his decision to leave Clay's unorthodox technique well alone. His natural gifts far outweighed any slight deficiencies that conventional wisdom might identify. In short, Dundee took a rough diamond and polished it.

The early fights came and went in a blur. **Herb Siler** was knocked out in four rounds, **Tony Esperti** in three, **Jim Robinson** in one, **Donnie Fleeman** in seven

Cassius Cay, like Elvis Presley, celebrated his fame by buying a pink Cadillac

and **Lamar Clark** in two, all in the space of six months. "The fun I had during those early years was second to none because it was just me and Muhammad," Angelo told **Thomas Hauser**, Ali's biographer, 30 years later. "It was absolute joy. And that's the key to Muhammad. When you have fun, you can excel."

Cassius Clay, never shy about extolling his own virtues, began to sound off for real, making a public prediction of the round in which he would defeat Lamar Clark. Dundee realised that this was a great motivational tool for his man and encouraged him to keep doing it. the **Louisville Lip** was starting to emerge.

His next two fights, against **Duke Sabedong** in **Las Vegas** and **Alonzo Johnson** in **Louisville**, were tough points wins, but useful primers. In Las Vegas, Clay met the wrestler **Gorgeous George** at a radio station and gleefully adopted the flamboyant mat man's technique of boasting outrageously about his own ability whilst decrying his opponent. Back in Louisville, he fought on national television for the first time against Johnson, and learned that the heat of the television lights could affect his performance. On a stultifying southern night, he laboured to produce his best and was booed by his hometown crowd.

Neither Dundee or Clay were seriously perturbed. Clay was still an apprentice to his trade. His devotion to training was paying dividends. He now stood over 6ft 2in tall and had added a stone of muscle to his lanky frame. When **Ingemar Johansson**, the former heavyweight champion, visited **Florida** to train for a rematch with the new champ **Floyd Patterson**, Clay volunteered himself as a sparring partner. The novice made the challenger look foolish, dancing around the lumbering Johansson and lacing him with vicious jabs as **Dundee** looked on. Not only did Cassius outbox Johannson, he taunted him as he did so: "I should be fighting Patterson, not you. Come on sucker, hit me…" Johansson lost his cool, throwing wild punches and exhausting himself. The session was halted after a mere two lopsided rounds.

As the wins kept coming and the boxing world's attention began to turn to him, Cassius became even more vocal. Having adopted Gorgeous George's methods of selling a fight, he stirred in his mix of poems and predictions. He was becoming a compelling figure: tall, handsome and charming. He was funny and cheeky, making most of his pronouncements with a smile on his face.

Sports Illustrated magazine, then a young publication just finding its feet, adopted him as something of a mascot. At least until he became politicised, Cassius Clay's brash statements were treated as fun, and made easy copy for newspapers and magazines.

To the delight of the ever-growing media entourage that surrounded his fights, Clay rounded out 1961 with two more stoppage wins, both in rounds that he had called beforehand. First **Alex Miteff** was knocked out in six, and then

Willi Besmanoff was dispatched in seven. Dundee became annoyed with his charge during the Besmanoff fight. Clay had his man beaten by round five, but proceeded to carry him for two more rounds simply so that he could knock him out in the round that he had predicted he would.

"When he wasn't playing around," Angelo reported to **Bill Faversham** afterwards, "he looked like a champion."

Outside of the ring, Cassius was enjoying himself, too. He'd used some of his $10,000 signing-on fee from the Louisville Sponsoring Group to buy his first car, a pink Cadillac. However, he was still an innocent in many ways, shy with women and devoted to his sport, not touching alcohol or tobacco.

On his first trip to **New York City** as a professional fighter, made in February 1962, he cut a delightful figure. He wore a suit and a bow tie at all times, and he entranced the New York writers and fight fraternity. **John Condon**, the director of publicity at **Madison Square Garden**, New York's famous home of boxing, said: "Everything was brand new to him, and he was full of life. A pleasure to talk to and a pleasure to be with. He used to say to me, 'Let's go watch the foxes, John.' The foxes were girls and we'd stand out front of **Jack Dempsey's** restaurant on 49th Street and watch the girls go by… He just ate everybody up and had everybody falling in love with him."

His natural gift for self-promotion even extended to walking the streets and travelling on the subways, introducing himself to passing strangers and inviting them to come and see him box.

The man that Cassius had come to New York to fight was **Sonny Banks**. Clay and Dundee had accepted the bout at five days' notice because it offered Cassius some valuable exposure on national television. Come fight day, buoyed by headlines about the newly christened **Louisville Lip**, the Garden was almost full to see if Clay could back up his prediction of a fourth-round knockout.

Perhaps a little carried away by all the hype, Clay was uncharacteristically lax, leaving himself open to a long left hand from Banks which put him on his backside for a mandatory eight count. The crowd came alive as Clay fought to regain his skittered senses. He survived comfortably enough before stopping Banks right on cue after 26 seconds of round four.

The events in New York had opened plenty of eyes to **Cassius Clay**, but in the view of **Angelo Dundee**, it had all been a little too much, too soon. He told the **Louisville Sponsoring Group** that he was rejecting an offer from Madison Square Garden for Clay to return, instead keeping him down in **Miami** for a fourth-round knockout of **Don Warner**, and then visiting the West Coast for his first bout in **Los Angeles**, a fourth-round stoppage of **George Logan** in a fight promoted by the former World Heavyweight champion **Joe Louis**.

PROFILE **Ali's assistant trainer** DREW 'BUNDINI' BROWN

Bundini Brown's official role might have been as an assistant trainer, but his contribution to Ali's remarkable career at various times incorporated cheerleader, poet, joker, talisman, navigator and foil.

Brown was born in Sandford, Florida in 1929 and worked as a shoe-shiner until he joined the US Navy aged just 13 (he claimed to have been discharged for chasing an officer with a meat cleaver). He spent 12 more years in the merchant navy, travelling the world and picking up the mysterious nickname Bundini from a girl in the Lebanon.

Brown met Cassius Clay when the pair were introduced by Bobby Nelson, Sugar Ray Robinson's brother-in-law, a day before Clay fought Doug Jones. Characteristically, the pair were bickering immediately over Clay's ability to call the round on his opponent. Soon Bundini was a key member of Ali's ever-growing entourage, a man who George Plimpton described in his book *Shadow Box* as "strangely gentle in the midst of all that violence".

It was Bundini, too, who came up with the immortal rhyme, "Float like a butterfly/Sting like a bee/His hand can't hit/What his eye can't see." Bundini had several spells of exile from the Ali camp, most seriously when he wouldn't convert to Islam, but the pair always made up. He was often Ali's whipping boy, and yet was accused of exploiting Ali, too. Ultimately, he was, in Ralph Thornton's words, "a magnificent, uncontrollable force". His death in 1988 brought Ali some sadness.

In Los Angeles Clay first made the acquaintance of **Howard Bingham**, a young Mississippi-born, Compton-raised photographer on assignment from a paper called **The Sentinel**. The friendship was to become one of the most significant of **Ali**'s life. As well as taking hundreds of thousands of images of Ali throughout his epic career, Bingham was to become a sort of unofficial curator of Ali's legacy, as well as the butt of much of his teasing.

Clay dotted between New York and Los Angeles, filling up his record. By the time he had TKO'd **Billy Daniels** at the Garden and stopped **Alejandro Lavorante** at the **Los Angeles Sports Arena**, his record stood at 15-0 with 12 wins inside the distance. Clay was quite clearly closing in on a title shot.

Wins over the veteran **Archie Moore** (now nearing 50 years of age) and the dogged **Doug Jones** took Clay towards his goal. Moore, who was on the end of Clay's powerful shots for four long rounds, told reporters that Clay was probably ready to fight the champion, the fearsome **Charles 'Sonny' Liston**. "I would hesitate to say he'll win," Moore said, "but he would furnish Liston with an exceedingly interesting evening…"

In New York for the Doug Jones fight, Ali made another significant friend, a former merchant marine named **Drew Brown**, whose mysterious nickname "Bundini" was given to him, he claimed, by a Lebanese girlfriend. Bundini was to become a talismanic figure in Ali's life. Officially an assistant cornerman to

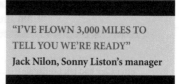

"I'VE FLOWN 3,000 MILES TO TELL YOU WE'RE READY"

Jack Nilon, Sonny Liston's manager

Angelo, he was unofficially a cheerleader, psych-up man, clown and concoctor of the oft-repeated phrase "Float like a butterfly, sting like a bee." Just days after meeting Cassius Clay in New York, where they had been introduced by **Bobby Nelson**, **Sugar Ray Robinson**'s brother-in-law, Bundini was travelling in the limo with him to **Madison Square Garden** for the scrap with Jones.

Bill Faversham now faced the task of keeping Clay active but out of harm's way until the chance to challenge Liston came. After rejecting the possibility of fighting **Floyd Patterson** – whom Liston had just slaughtered twice in quick succession – and **Ingemar Johansson**, Faversham signed up for a trip to England to take on the evergreen British champion **Henry Cooper**.

The fight took place at **Wembley Stadium** in north London on 18 June 1963. The date was the anniversary of the **Battle of Waterloo**, and Cooper vs Clay became almost as famous a scrap. Cooper provided Clay and **Angelo Dundee** with the biggest scare of their careers, dumping Clay on the canvas with his huge left hook at the end of the fourth round. Cassius got up, but he was out on his feet, saved only by the bell that ended the round. Cooper said later: "We nearly had him. I knew when I hit him that he was in trouble, but unfortunately it was too late in the round."

In search of valuable seconds, Angelo slipped his thumb into a small tear that he'd spotted in the seam of Ali's glove, widening it enough to allow some of the horsehair to poke out. Dundee's gamesmanship bought Clay an extra 60 seconds or so while an unsuccessful search for a replacement glove went on. Dundee admitted the stunt years later to Cooper but the British boxer wasn't angry: "If something like that had happened to me, my trainer would have done the same."

With a newly cleared head, Clay butchered Cooper, "almost tearing his head from his shoulders" in the words of one reporter. Blinded by the blood from some awful cuts, Cooper was stopped in the fifth after a noble challenge.

Sonny Liston's manager **Jack Nilon** approached Clay afterwards in the Wembley dressing rooms. "I've flown 3,000 miles to tell you we're ready," he said.

"I am the greatest!"

assius Clay met **Sam Saxon** on a Miami street in 1961, just a few months after Clay had left Louisville to join **Angelo Dundee** at his Fifth Street Gym. Saxon was a former hustler, a drifter who had changed his life after hearing a speech by **Elijah Muhammad**, the leader of a religious group called the **Nation of Islam**. (For more background on the Nation of Islam and Ali's role in the American Civil Rights struggle, see Social History, page 173.)

Saxon had reinvented himself as "**Captain Sam**" and spent his free time spreading the word on behalf of the Nation's representative in Miami, **Ishmael Sabakhan**. Captain Sam and Cassius Clay hit it off. Clay took Saxon home to see his scrapbook. He told Saxon – as he told almost everyone – that he was going to become the heavyweight champion of the world.

The young fighter also impressed Saxon with his knowledge of the Nation of Islam. He had first encountered the group in 1959 during a trip to Chicago for a **Golden Gloves** tournament. In his book on the emergence of Ali, *King of the World*, the writer **David Remnick** reports that an aunt of Cassius remembered him bringing a recording of Elijah Muhammad's speeches home with him.

Elijah Muhammad's rhetoric appealed to Cassius – he preached a message of racial pride and of discipline, of clean living and self-respect – and Cassius attended some meetings of the Nation of Islam in Louisville.

Captain Sam stimulated this interest. He took Clay to his local mosque, where they listened to the preacher, Brother John. Many years later, Ali would say that this visit "was the first time in my life that I felt truly spiritual".

Cassius began to spend time with Nation of Islam members, reading each week from the Nation's newspaper *Muhammad Speaks*. The texts had some provocative titles like "A White Man's Heaven Is A Black Man's Hell." The Nation realised that the young fighter might become a valuable voice, as well as being a high-profile recruit.

They called the Nation's regional minister **Jeremiah Shabazz**, who travelled from Atlanta to Miami to speak with Cassius about the Nation. What Shabazz had to say resounded within Cassius. His philosophy took many of the disparate strands of ideology that had appealed to a young man growing up in a segregated society and tied them together. Shabazz told Clay that, according to the Nation's teaching, God was black. He explained that the Nation did not subscribe to **Martin Luther King's** policy of peaceful protest – they should stand up and take what was theirs by right.

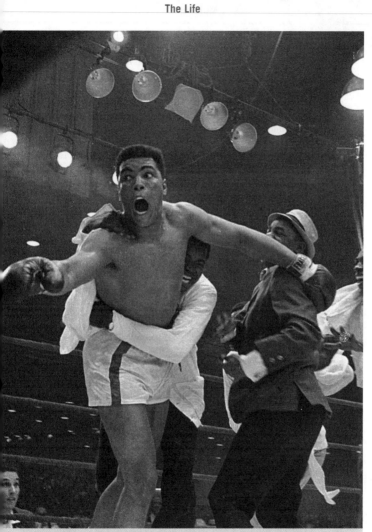

Cassius Clay causes the boxing shock of the 1960s by stopping the indestructible Sonny Liston in 1964

Shabazz also explained that the Nation considered the white race to be evil. "This was 1961," Shabazz told Ali's biographer, **Thomas Hauser**. "There was a lot of outright injustice going on…. And the thing that really got Cassius was when we began to explain that for someone to do this to another human being, they can't be what he thought they were. You can't be God's people and mistreat other people the way white folks were doing."

Cassius said that he would think hard about joining the Nation of Islam. His brother **Rudolph,** who had joined Cassius in Miami, became even more enthused than the fighter.

In 1962, Cassius heard **Elijah Muhammad** speak for the first time. He also met a charismatic Nation of Islam orator called **Malcolm X**. Malcolm held Cassius spellbound as he spoke about the Nation. The fighter was undergoing a political and social awakening. Malcolm X arranged for a man named **Archie Robinson** (later Osman Karriem) to assist Cassius and Angelo Dundee in running their training camp. Malcolm began to appear more regularly in Clay's entourage as the fight with Sonny Liston came closer.

If Cassius Clay was coming to terms with the American Black experience of the first half on the 20th century, then **Sonny Liston** had been living it. It seemed that even the barest details of his life were not worthy of proper record. He did not know where or when he had been born. Sonny's mother Helen told journalists that he had arrived on 18 January 1932 and the occasion recorded in the family Bible. A birth certificate, most likely forged by his boxing managers to gain him a licence, gave a date of 8 May 1932. Sonny's arrest records make it more likely that he was born some years earlier, probably in 1927 or 1928. His place of birth was variously given as Little Rock, Pine Bluff or Forrest City, all small towns in eastern **Arkansas**.

What was certain was that Liston's childhood was one of the most deprived his country could offer. His father Tobe was a sharecropper who'd already had 12 children before taking up with Sonny's mother Helen. Tobe and Helen had a further 11. Sonny grew up in a shack with cardboard walls and claimed not to have owned shoes until he was 10. Tobe put him to work in the fields at the age of eight. Sonny was beaten so often he bore the scars on his back into adulthood.

> "WHEN SONNY GAVE YOU THE EVIL EYE, I DON'T CARE WHO YOU WERE – YOU SHRANK TO TWO FEET TALL" **Harold Conrad**

When Sonny was 13, Helen left the family to go and work in a shoe factory in St Louis. Tired of the beatings from Tobe, Sonny stole some pecan nuts from his brother-in-law's tree and sold them to buy a ticket to **St Louis**. Once there, he barely went to school, instead working in menial jobs and only eating on days when he had the money to do so. Inevitably, Sonny began to put his size and strength to more productive use. He embarked on a series of hold-ups, wearing the same yellow and black shirt so often he became known as the **Yellow Shirt Bandit**.

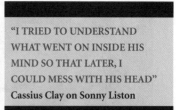

"I TRIED TO UNDERSTAND WHAT WENT ON INSIDE HIS MIND SO THAT LATER, I COULD MESS WITH HIS HEAD"
Cassius Clay on Sonny Liston

He was first arrested in 1949, and by 1950 had been sentenced to five years in the Missouri State Penitentiary for two counts of robbery and another two of larceny. It was in prison that he learned to box. His natural gifts were fearsome: an iron pole of a left jab, a big punch in each of his huge hands and a sullen demeanour that hinted at the violence within.

When Sonny got out of jail on parole in 1952, he began to plough through the pro ranks. Despite an early loss to **Marty Marshall**, who broke Liston's jaw ("Only because I was laughing…" Sonny would retort), he was soon considered a genuine prospect. He was also filling in time working as an enforcer for his new manager **Frank Mitchell** and Mitchell's friend **John Vitale**, a Sicilian mobster who ran half of the organised crime in St Louis.

"Sonny Liston was a mean fucker," the fight promoter Harold Conrad told Ali's biographer **Thomas Hauser**. "When Sonny gave you the evil eye, I don't care who you were, you shrank to two feet tall. And one thing more: he could fight like hell."

Sonny's ascent continued. Despite a further stint in the workhouse in 1956 – this time for beating up a cop – and sinking further into the control of other mobsters – men like **Frankie Carbo** and **Blinky Palermo**, who ran most of the action in pro boxing – he became World Heavyweight Champion, defeating **Floyd Patterson** in two minutes and six seconds on 25 September 1962.

For white America, Liston had become the living embodiment of the "bad negro", an illiterate, inarticulate thug. For Sonny, there was no respite from his own, either. The National Association for the Advancement of Coloured People (**NAACP**) had urged Floyd Patterson not to fight Liston, saying that Sonny "offers little in the way of an example to the youth of America".

To Sonny, denounced by white and black alike, this lack of support came as absolutely no surprise. His whole life had seen him fight against bad odds. "The NAACP never helped me," he said. "Nobody ever helped me. Nobody gave a damn if I lived or died."

This was the man, then, that Cassius Clay was to fight for the heavyweight

Clay goes berserk at the now legendary weigh-in for the first Liston fight

championship of the world. In the eyes of the press, the result was simply not in doubt: Sonny Liston would win. The only doubt centered on the outcome of the bout. Would Clay live, or might Sonny kill him? One newspaper dispatched a journalist to plot the route from the **Convention Hall** in **Miami Beach**, where the fight would take place, to the nearest hospital.

Even the **Louisville Lip** himself expressed his fear of Sonny, when one of the many pranks he embarked upon to hype up the fight backfired. Confronting Liston in a Las Vegas casino, when the champion was already annoyed enough because of a losing run at the craps table, Clay got his face slapped "for being too fucking fresh," as Sonny put it. "That's the first time since I known Sonny Liston that he scared me," Clay admitted.

If Liston represented something America did not wish to confront, then Cassius Clay was, now, it seemed, barely a more acceptable alternative. While the press had been perfectly willing to portray The Louisville Lip as an exuberant and brash young man, this view began to cloud as Clay became more closely associated with the **Nation of Islam**.

America had grown used to its black champions being respectful and almost subservient, accepting of their place in society. Both **Joe Louis** and **Floyd Patterson** had fulfilled this role. Neither Liston nor Clay would.

Once Clay's campaign to fight Liston had won the champion's signature on a contract, he began to analyse his man. **Angelo Dundee** was already convinced that Clay had the physical tools to do the job. He had the speed to work around Liston's jab, the punch the champ relied upon to break his opponents down.

But more than that, Clay had what it took mentally. He embarked on a programme of study: "I watched Liston outside the ring," he told **Thomas Hauser**. "I tried to understand what went on inside his mind so that later, I could mess with his head."

It was an audacious plan, one designed to make **Liston** so angry with Clay that he would forget about boxing and just try to button the Lip permanently, leaving Clay free to exploit his opponent's lack of control. But the seasoned observers in the press still felt that Cassius was too lightweight to handle a brute like Sonny.

Yet Clay's campaign began to have an impact on Liston's psyche. As the fight grew closer and closer, and Clay's stunts becameever more brazen – he took a bus load of cheerleaders to Liston's gym to wave signs at him; he drove to Liston's house in the middle of the night and challenged him to a fight – Liston began to believe that he was stepping into the ring with a nut, a flake, a man who might do anything.

This unpredictability got to Liston. On the morning of the fight, at the weigh-in, Clay again began to scream and shout, convincing the doctor that he was on the verge of hysteria. It was an act, but Liston, already suffering from a shoulder injury, was rattled. After the weigh-in, Clay was calm. "I was scared," he would say later, "but I knew I had no choice other than to go out and fight."

Once Clay had survived the first couple of rounds, his confidence grew. Sonny's diminished exponentially. He couldn't nail Clay, who buzzed around him, firing quicksilver jabs into his puffing face. In the third, Clay opened a cut on Liston's face. For the first time since **Marty Marshall** had broken his jaw, Sonny had been visibly damaged in the ring. He wasn't laughing this time. The fight was slipping away from him. He was becoming drained by the effort.

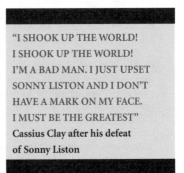

"I SHOOK UP THE WORLD!
I SHOOK UP THE WORLD!
I'M A BAD MAN. I JUST UPSET
SONNY LISTON AND I DON'T
HAVE A MARK ON MY FACE.
I MUST BE THE GREATEST"
**Cassius Clay after his defeat
of Sonny Liston**

The story of the pivotal event in the fight has been told many times, but it contains a mystery that has never been solved. Towards the end of the fourth round, another session he was winning comfortably, Cassius noticed that his eyes had begun to sting. At the bell, he could no longer see, and he began to panic, yelling at **Angelo Dundee** to cut off his gloves. What Angelo did next became key to the destiny of **Muhammad Ali**, and probably of **Sonny Liston**, too, though Sonny's course might have seemed set from childhood. With Nation of Islam members yelling at Angelo that he was trying to lose Clay the fight, the trainer kept calm and spoke sternly to Cassius as he washed out his eyes.

"Get out there and run," he told him, and Cassius responded. Somehow he avoided Sonny for a minute or so until his eyes stopped streaming and his vision returned. When it did, the fight was as good as over. Clay was the better man and he proved it, breaking down Sonny Liston until, at the end of the sixth round, Sonny quit on his stool. It was one of the most remarkable results in the history of boxing. Clay went crazy, screaming at the ringside press: "I'm the king of the world…" He wasn't, but he was close enough: World Heavyweight Champion at the age of 22. He celebrated by grabbing his friend **Sam Cooke**, the black singer, and declaring that Cooke was "the world's greatest rock and roll singer". (Cooke, like Malcom X, would soon be shot to death in mysterious circumstances.)

Clay was a worthy champion: he had overcome a brute of a fighter – a man people had said was unbeatable. More than that, he had done so against formidable odds, fighting against **Liston** while half-blinded by the mysterious substance that had got into his eyes – something that would have tested any man.

The precise nature of that substance has never been established. During the fateful break between the fourth and fifth rounds, Angelo Dundee had dabbed a finger into Clay's eye and then put it in his own. He felt the same stinging sensation Clay was complaining of, and presumed that it was caused by some kind of liniment that had been rubbed into Liston's sore shoulder and had then been transferred into Clay's eyes by the fighter's gloves.

Another, darker explanation for the incident was offered to the writer **David Remnick** by some of Liston's associates, who said that Sonny's corner man, **Joe Pollino**, had "juiced" his man's gloves, an illegal tactic they had used before to enable Sonny to KO difficult opponents.

The evidence remains inconclusive. What is clear is that Dundee's quick thinking kept **Cassius Clay** in the fight. Had Cassius lost, he might have faced some years on the outside – Liston would almost certainly not have offered a rematch. Clay's subsequent announcement of his conversion to Islam would never have had such a massive impact on world opinion, and his prominence as a public figure – though it would surely have happened anyway – could have turned out differently.

As it was, Cassius Clay was young, handsome, rich and the heavyweight champ. He now had a platform that would enable him to present his political, social and personal agenda to the world, and he was just about to do so.

"I ain't got no quarrel with them Vietcong"

The new World Champion was on the verge of a public conversion to the **Nation of Islam**. He was also at the centre of a power struggle within the organisation itself. On one side stood the Nation's leader, **Elijah Muhammad**. On the other stood **Malcolm X**. The pair had become divided, at first by comments made by Malcolm after the assassination of John F. Kennedy in 1963, for which he was suspended from the Nation for 90 days, and then by more serious divisions over the future direction of the Nation.

The split was a damaging one. Elijah Muhammad was the spiritual leader of the Nation, but Malcolm had become its driving force. Since his own conversion while in prison serving a 10-year sentence for burglary, Malcolm had preached Elijah's message with flair and fervour, winning many thousands of converts and thrusting a small organisation on to the national stage. His personal style – adopting the X in place of his "slave name" of Little; popularising the sharp gray suit, bow tie and fedora hats that became a kind of uniform – gave an identity to the Nation and a feeling of both separateness and belonging for its members.

Clay knew and liked both men. Malcolm had entranced him when he spoke, and the pair had become friends. Elijah Muhammad, "The Messenger", remained

---

PROFILE **Elijah Muhammad's** NATION OF ISLAM

The Nation of Islam that Cassius Clay joined officially on 26 February 1964 had its roots in Detroit, with a door-to-door salesman called WD Fard. Fard met Elijah Poole in 1931 and found a willing disciple for a brand of Islam that married a variety of different influences. It adopted the Koran as a Holy Book, but added an entirely new cosmology too (for fuller details on the genesis of the Nation of Islam, see the Social History section). When Fard disappeared in 1934, Elijah Poole, who had been renamed Elijah Muhammad by Fard, became the leader of the Nation, the 'Messenger' who would

spread Fard's word. The Nation took its support from poor black communities, where Elijah's message of racial pride, self-sufficiency and discipline offered inspiration and hope.

The Nation began to expand more rapidly when Malcolm X (formerly Malcolm Little) became leader of a mosque in Harlem. Malcolm's charisma and fire, allied to Elijah's message attracted thousands more. The subsequent split between Elijah and Malcolm left Ali choosing sides. He picked Elijah, who remained the Nation's leader until his death in 1975.

Cassius's inspiration. **Elijah Muhammad** had held back from publicly endorsing Cassius before the fight with Sonny Liston, however, fearful that a crushing defeat would reflect badly upon the Nation.

Now that Clay had won, Malcolm saw that if he could deliver the fighter to the Nation as his latest convert just hours after he had become champion of the world, Malcolm might rehabilitate himself with Elijah Muhammad and reinforce his power base within the Nation. Clay's victory over Liston had been so unexpected, the **Louisville Sponsoring Group** had been caught out like everyone else. There was no victory party prepared, no valedictory offering for the new champ. By the time they had thrown something together, Cassius was at Malcolm's hotel, eating a large bowl of ice cream and chatting to **Jim Brown**, a famous gridiron player with the **Cleveland Browns**.

At a press conference the next morning, a journalist asked if Clay was now "a card-carrying member of the '**Black Muslims**'."

"Card-carrying? What does that mean?" Clay replied. "I believe in **Allah** and in peace. I don't try to move into white neighbourhoods. I don't want to marry a white woman. I'm not a Christian any more… I'm free to be what I want."

This was taken by the press as confirmation of Cassius Clay's conversion to Islam. Clay also tried to educate reporters, who knew next to nothing about the Nation or his new beliefs.

"'Black Muslims' is a press word," he told them. "The real name is '**Islam**'. That means peace. Islam is a religion and there are 750 million people all over the world who believe in it and I'm one of them. People brand us a hate group. They say we want to take over the country. That's not true. Followers of Allah are the sweetest people in the world. They don't tote weapons, they pray five times a day. The women wear dresses that come all the way to the floor and they don't commit adultery. All they want to do is live in peace."

Cassius Clay immediately adopted his "waiting name" of "Cassius X" before Elijah gave him the name Muhammad Ali, which means "The Praiseworthy One". His brother Rudolph became **Rahaman Ali**, "The One Who Loves".

Malcolm X's proximity to Ali as he made his public declaration of allegiance to Islam did not, however, mean that he had won his power struggle with Elijah Muhammad. Back in Chicago, the Messenger himself was welcoming the champion's announcement, too. Ali quickly made it clear that he would never turn against the Messenger ("He's such a small man physically, but he's so great") and Malcolm's relationship with **Elijah Muhammad** and the Nation then began to deteriorate beyond repair. After making a pilgrimage to Mecca, Malcolm formed his own "non-religious, non-sectarian" group called the **Organisation of Afro-American Unity**.

A couple of months after the fight with Sonny Liston, Ali went to Africa for a month with **Rahaman**, his friend **Osman Karreim**, **Howard Bingham** and **Herbert Muhammad**, one of Elijah Muhammad's eight children. The trip proved an awakening for him. His faith deepened and he felt a deep attachment to the people he met.

Osman Karreim said: "It was in Africa that he became something he hadn't been before… I saw Cassius Clay become Muhammad Ali."

There was one other pivotal moment during the trip. During his visit to Ghana, Ali once again encountered **Malcolm X**, who had travelled separately to Africa for a visit of his own. The pair saw each other in the lobby of the Hotel Ambassador. But Ali snubbed Malcolm, a gesture that would hurt Malcolm deeply.

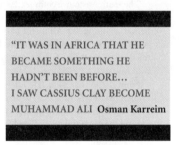

"IT WAS IN AFRICA THAT HE BECAME SOMETHING HE HADN'T BEEN BEFORE… I SAW CASSIUS CLAY BECOME MUHAMMAD ALI **Osman Karreim**

Ali would never have the chance to make amends. Malcolm X was assassinated in February 1965 in Washington Heights, Manhattan. One gunman, **Talmadge X Hayer**, was arrested and two others escaped. A few hours after the shooting, there was a fire in Ali's apartment in Chicago, although Ali was in Miami at the time. Malcolm's former ministry, Harlem Mosque No.7, was also destroyed by fire.

One of the men eventually tried for Malcolm's murder, **Thomas 15X Johnson**, was a member of the Nation of Islam, and had once acted as a bodyguard for Cassius Clay. Talmadge X Hayer had been seen at several Nation meetings. Both refused to reveal who had ordered the execution, although rumours swirled that Malcolm had become the victim of the feud.

Soon after the killing, Elijah Muhammad told a gathering in Chicago that: "Malcolm died according to his preachings. He preached violence, and violence took him away."

Nineteen sixty-four had been a climactic year for **Muhammad Ali**. Everything in his life had changed: his name, his religion, his finances and his sporting status. In the midst of this maelstrom, he had fallen in love and got married. Ali met **Sonji Roi** through **Herbert Muhammad**, son of the Messenger. Sonji was employed by Herbert to make phonecalls for funds on behalf of the Nation, and yet she was far from the kind of girl that would "wear dresses that come all the way to the floor". She was beautiful and fun to be around; she enjoyed spending time in nightclubs and bars. Sonji had endured a fractured childhood, raised by her godparents after her father was murdered when she was two and her mother died when she was eight. She had given birth to a son when she was still a teenager.

Sonji and **Ali** first went out in July 1964, and Ali was entranced enough to ask her to marry him during their first date. Sonji didn't know if he was joking or not, but they continued to spend lots of time together. By 14 August, they were married, even though Herbert Muhammad had opposed the union.

Conventional wisdom has always held that Sonji introduced Ali to the wonders of love and sex, and that during their brief time together, he was torn between the strict tenets of his faith and Sonji's beauty and sensuality.

The truth was more complex. As a younger man, Ali had been so shy around women that some of the press pack had thought that he might be gay. In reality, he was anything but. Ali might have been a late starter, but once he started, he couldn't stop. His doctor, **Ferdie Pacheco**, famously called him a "pelvic missionary", and Ali would admit to **Thomas Hauser** that the biggest conflicts with his faith came through his many affairs.

Sonji herself has said: "He knew what to do when I met him. It's just that I might have made him want to do it."

Along with his marriage licence, Ali inked another significant contract at around the same time: he offered **Sonny Liston** the chance to regain his title in a rematch set for November 1964.

The fight, like the marriage, was dogged by trouble from the start. If Sonny Liston had been a champion unpopular with both black and white society, then **Muhammad Ali** was about to give him a run for his money. His conversion to the

---

PROFILE MALCOLM X

Malcom Litle was serving a ten-year sentence for burglary in Charlestown State prison when he was introduced to the Nation during visits from his brother Reginald. The message chimed with Malcolm who, as a child, had seen white supremacists apparently murder his father and burn down his parents' house. He was an excellent student and had hoped to become a lawyer until a teacher told him that such a career was unrealistic "for a nigger". Disillusioned, the downward slide to prison began. On his release in 1953, Malcolm joined up, dropping his 'slave name' and replacing it with a symbolic X.

With his quick intellect and innate charisma, he rose rapidly. In Malcolm's hands, Elijah's message came alive. His split with the Nation in 1964, which really began when he discovered evidence of Elijah's numerous affairs, proved fatal. He started up his own organisation, but was assassinated by three men with affiliations to the Nation in New York in February 1965.

Muhammad Ali, the praiseworthy one

Nation saw him denounced by individuals and groups as varied as former champ **Joe Louis**, **Dr Martin Luther King** (who opposed racial segregation of any kind), several members of the **US Senate** and even Ali's father, **Cassius Clay Snr**, who maintained that his son had been "brainwashed". **The World Boxing Association** (WBA) threatened to strip Ali of his title, only pulling back when the **New York Athletic Commission** announced that they would continue to recognise Ali as the champion, whatever the WBA decided.

All around Ali, chaos reigned. America was being dragged towards its future through a violent era tagged the **Days Of Rage**. On each coast, in New York and in Los Angeles, civil disturbances led to riots in **Harlem** and **Watts**. Throughout the South, disorder took hold. **John F. Kennedy** had been assassinated. **Martin Luther King** – as **Malcolm X** had done – understood that he might face a similar fate. Muhammad Ali also realised that his high profile put him at risk.

The fight with Liston was dragged down in the undertow. Upon signature of the contracts, Ali, Liston and everyone else associated with the bout were suspended by the WBA. Neither camp cared, particularly.

Everyone understood that this was the fight that matched the world's best two heavyweights, and one that the public most wanted to see. Revenues from the closed-circuit television broadcasts across the country would more than compensate for the lack of the WBA's shiny belt.

Then, four days before the bout, **Ali** collapsed with a hernia and required immediate emergency surgery to correct the problem. It would take him six months to regain the fitness he needed to face Sonny.

Liston was at his sanguine best when his wife Geraldine called him to the television to hear the news of Ali's illness.

"Shit, could have been worse," he said. "Could have been me…"

Yet the delay was to affect Sonny far more than it would Ali. Nearer to 40 than 30, Liston had made a terrific effort to get in shape for the fight. He had trained harder than ever before, and he had rediscovered the "old" Sonny, the brute who had laid Patterson out twice and who was once more taking pleasure in smearing the noses of sparring partners all over their luckless faces.

Liston was again made favourite for the bout on its rearranged date of 25 May, 1965. His loss in Miami had become regarded as a fluke by most seasoned observers, a one-off aberration that would be put right in a rematch.

The mayhem surrounding Ali continued as his hernia healed and the fight grew closer. Malcolm X had been assassinated on 21 February. Now Ali's marriage to Sonji was coming under increasing pressure from influential members of the Nation, including **Herbert Muhammad**.

Yet Ali's spirits remained high. He was training well, and he had got even bigger and stronger. He was no longer the lean, light heavy of his early pro days: he had added power and bulk to his speed and footwork.

Angelo Dundee was in absolutely no doubt that his man would best Sonny once more. "Liston buys everything," Angelo said. "He's a one-way fighter. He can't lick a two-way, let alone a four-way fighter, a guy that can go back and forward, side-to-side."

The negative energy that surrounded Liston and Ali seemed to jinx the fight. The venue kept being moved as a series of states found convenient reasons to avoid having the boxers within their boundaries. The whiff of violence and murder surrounding the **Nation of Islam** and Liston's presumed connections to organised crime meant plenty of objections were being voiced. The papers were full of stories suggesting that **Muhammad Ali** might be assassinated in retaliation for Malcolm X's murder. Finally, the **Maine** town of **Lewiston** agreed to house the fight at a hockey stadium called St Dominic's. Lewiston's remote location, a population of under 50,000 and limited seating at the venue would all contribute to the smallest attendance at a modern heavyweight title fight.

When the fighters blew into town, the Nation mounted a large security operation around their man, and the local police chief, **Joseph Ferrand**, put every cop he could find on duty.

Sonny Liston seemed fit and ready for anything that the night might throw at him. After his medical, the Maine Athletic Commission doctor said that he was "the fittest man I've ever examined".

It was an illusion. In reality, the postponement caused by the discovery of Ali's hernia and the subsequent operation had ruined Sonny. As soon as he had heard about his opponent's misfortune, Sonny had poured himself a large drink and he hadn't stopped since. His body was getting tired and old, his temper had grown even worse and his spirits had sunk. The intimidating aura that had surrounded Liston for so long and which had won him so many fights was dissipating. Ali, by contrast, was relatively sombre, yet confident.

The crowd that entered the **St Dominic's arena** – all 4,280 of them – braved a heavy police cordon and an atmosphere thick with violence. Liston stepped through the ropes outweighing Ali by 216lbs to 206lbs, but the extra pounds would prove to be no advantage to Sonny.

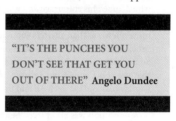

"IT'S THE PUNCHES YOU DON'T SEE THAT GET YOU OUT OF THERE" **Angelo Dundee**

The ensuing fight, all one-and-a-bit minutes of it, has become one of the most mythic and mysterious ring encounters of the past century. For the first 20 seconds or so, Ali danced and Liston moved slowly after him. He threw a few lefts, which Ali took on the gloves and arms without returning fire.

Then Ali jerked backwards from another of Sonny's straight lefts before rolling forwards and upwards, clipping Liston's jaw with a right hand of such speed and beauty some swore that the punch never landed. Liston fell to the canvas, quite literally before he knew what had hit him.

"It's the punches that you don't see that get you out of there," **Angelo Dundee** said later, "and Sonny didn't see it coming. Not many people did." Ali now stood over the prone Liston, yelling at him to get up and fight.

The fight referee was the former heavyweight champion "**Jersey" Joe Walcott**, a great boxer but an inexperienced official who, for some seconds, failed to get the excited champion to a neutral corner.

Liston got to his feet before Walcott could begin a count, and Walcott failed to consult the timekeeper, **Francis McDonough**, before wiping Liston's gloves and telling him to fight on (McDonough later estimated that Liston had been on the floor for "at least 20 seconds").

As Ali stepped towards Liston, **Nat Fleischer**, the editor of **The Ring** magazine, yelled at Walcott to stop the fight. Walcott looked at McDonough, who confirmed that he had indeed counted Liston out. Walcott waved the fight off, and the crowd, already confused by the speed of the knockdown punch, began yelling and booing. In the midst of the pandemonium, Liston was led to his dressing room, where he asked for some smelling salts. He was in no doubt that **Ali** had hit him – hard.

Immediately after the bout, the media and the fight crowd were divided about such extraordinary events. Many felt that there had been a fix, many others thought that Sonny, realising that he couldn't win, had simply taken the quickest route to his $500,000 cheque.

Ali, rapidly recovering his equilibrium, watched replays of the finish and declared that he'd terminated Sonny's challenge with "**my secret anchor punch**". He said the shot had been devised by the first black heavyweight champion **Jack Johnson** and had been passed on to Ali by the veteran comedian **Stepin Fetchit**, who'd joined his entourage and was soon to join the **Nation of Islam**.

The champion may have been in light-hearted mood, but the fight brought more questions than answers about his reign. The *Ring* magazine ran a piece that proclaimed, "Boxing wants no more of Liston," so convinced were they that Sonny had taken a dive. The former heavyweight champion **Jack Dempsey** said that the sport would not recover from the mess in **Lewiston**. A bitter war of words broke out between Ali and the former champion **Joe Louis**, who said that Ali wasn't fit to hold the title.

A resolution was also placed before the governor of California calling for an investigation to discover whether a fraud had been perpetrated on those who'd paid to watch the closed-circuit broadcasts. **New York State** even considered a draft bill to ban boxing. Once more, controversy surrounded Muhammad Ali.

Viewed again at a distance of four decades, the slow-motion footage of Ali's "anchor punch" (or "phantom punch" as it also became known) is conclusive enough. The fight film clearly shows Ali hitting Sonny Liston, using a fast, downward punch that shakes his opponent to his boots and knocks him down. It was a legitimate shot, and it seemed that its percussive power, and the force of Ali's personality, took full effect.

"Ali knocked me down with a sharp punch," Liston confessed in 1967, some two years after the fight. "I was down but not hurt, but I looked up and saw Ali standing over me. Now there is no way to get up from the canvas that you are not exposed to a great shot. Ali is waiting to hit me, **the ref can't control him**… You know Ali is a nut. You can tell what a normal man is going to do, but you can't tell what a nut is going to do, and Ali is a nut."

Ali, seen as little more than a callow youth before his first bout with Liston, had slain a monster: he'd beaten the unbeatable ogre and ended an era in heavyweight boxing. Liston slipped into a slow decline that would end with his mysterious death in Las Vegas in December of 1970.

Yet America seemed as dissatisfied with the new champ as they had been with the old. Ali's conversion to Islam, his affiliation with the Nation and his change of name unsettled people. The so-called "fix" with Liston brought more disapproval. Neither did the public especially like the fact that just 29 days after beating Sonny, he petitioned the Florida courts to annul his marriage to **Sonji Roi** on the grounds that she had failed to live up to a promise to follow the tenets of **Islam**; subsequent documents alleged many specific instances of her refusal, and the divorce was made final six months later.

Yet one problem would loom above all the others, one that would irrevocably alter the course of Muhammad Ali's life. On 9 March 1962 **Cassius Clay** had been classified 1-A by the US Draft board. That meant he was fit and available to be inducted into the **US Army**.

In January 1964, a month before the first fight with Sonny Liston, Clay had been ordered to attend the **Armed Forces Induction Centre** in Coral Gables, Florida to take military qualifying examination. He had taken a physical, which he passed easily, and the standard army intelligence test. Cassius had been unable to answer many of the questions, so he had left much of his paper blank. The Army insisted on retesting him and Clay scored just 16 per cent. The pass mark was 30. He was immediately reclassified "1-Y" – not qualified for US Army service under acceptable standards.

There had been a hostile public and political reaction to this news, not unpredictable given Ali's obvious mental agility and his dazzling verbal skills.

Angelo Dundee first trained Cassius Clay for his second professional fight, against Herb Siler in December 1960, and he remained in The Greatest's corner for the rest of an epic career. Recruited by Bill Faversham after Archie Moore didn't work out, Dundee took Ali into the Fifth Street Gym in Miami that he ran with his brother Chris. Like most of the best boxing trainers, Dundee was part coach and part psychologist. He understood Clay immediately and gave the young man his head. Two pieces of sharp thinking also kept Clay's career alive. The first was in the Cooper fight after Clay had been decked, and the second in the championship bout with Liston, when his man was temporarily blinded. Happy to admit that many of Ali's tactics were as much of a surprise to him as they were to anyone else, Dundee remained at the top long after Ali's retirement. He took Sugar Ray Leonard to his world titles and was in George Foreman's corner when he knocked out Michael Moorer to win back the heavyweight crown aged 45.

Yet these gifts did not necessarily translate into the ability to solve the maths problems and logic puzzles that appeared in the Army's exam. Cassius Clay had barely graduated from high school, and it was widely known that he had problems with basic reading and writing skills.

"When I looked at a lot of the questions," he explained, "I just didn't know the answers. The fact is, I was never too bright in school. I had a D-minus average. I ain't ashamed of it, though. I mean, how much do school principals make a month? I said I was The Greatest. I never said I was the smartest!"

The Army were satisfied with the results of Clay's test. Their psychologists had been convinced that he had not been faking. A Republican senator announced that the test outcome was in line with the fighter's high-school achievements.

The argument became moot when, in January 1966, with the war in Vietnam showing no sign of ending, the mental aptitude requirement for induction into the US forces was lowered from 30 percent to 15. Ali was duly reclassified 1-A and now became eligible for the **draft** and looked likely to serve – along with a disproportionate number of other black Americans – in **Vietnam**.

Ali was at home in **Miami** when the news emerged. Immediately, he was called and questioned by a series of reporters. After stonewalling for a while, he could keep quiet no longer.

"Man," he said. "I ain't got no quarrel with them Vietcong…"

With those eight words, **Muhammad Ali** had just talked his way into history. Opinions across the world would be polarised. He would be decried as a traitor and hailed as a hero. In London, mass protests were organised against his draft, while in America, the **Central Intelligence Agency** would feel obliged to monitor an Ali rally (although its report, in the excised version released for public consumption, would hardly make titillating reading) and, as the controversy deepened, the **FBI** would interview 35 of his family and friends.

"WHEN I LOOKED AT A LOT OF THOSE QUESTIONS, I JUST DIDN'T KNOW THE ANSWERS. I DIDN'T EVEN KNOW HOW TO START ABOUT FINDING THE ANSWERS" **Muhammad Ali**

Looking back, it's hard to recapture just how much of a risk Ali took making that statement in the political, social and sporting climate of the day. Yet it's also clear, that with a couple of sentences, Muhammad Ali had set out on a course which would make him far more than the greatest boxer in the world – he would become one of the essential icons of the second half of the 20th century, in the select company of figures like Elvis, Marilyn, JFK, Dylan and the Beatles.

IF YOU'RE
GOOD ENOUGH

JOIN
THE NEW
Action
U S
ARMY
OFFICE

Muhammad Ali sets out on a course that changed his life

A champion in exile

li's knack for a quote, his ability to condense complex issues into a single, headline-making sentence, was never better illustrated than by "I ain't got no quarrel with them Vietcong." The next day, the comment led newspapers across the nation. It was an inflammatory statement in conservative times: opinion in America was yet to turn against the war in Vietnam. Hard-hitting, old-school columnists like **Red Smith** and **Jimmy Cannon**, never big fans, were quick to turn their guns on Ali – who they and almost everyone else still referred to as "Cassius Clay".

Smith compared him to "those unwashed punks" who demonstrated against the war, while Cannon raged against Clay and "the whole pampered, style-making cult of the bored young".

Ali had plenty of anger in him too, but his had been focused on one man: **Floyd Patterson**. The former champion had aligned himself with the establishment, speaking out against Ali and the Nation of Islam. As soon as Ali beat Sonny Liston for the first time, he was vowing to develop "a brutal killer instinct" to deal with Floyd, who had said, "no Muslim deserved to be champion" and that he was planning to win the title back "for America".

As with Ali's scraps with Liston (and his later fights with Frazier and Foreman), the bout with Patterson became emblematic of a wider issue. As **David Remnick** wrote in *King of the World*: "To Ali, who had learned from Malcolm X, Patterson represented the toadying posture of old-style Negro politics. Patterson was the integrationist, the accommodationist, the symbol of sit-ins…" Even as Ali prepared to fight Liston for a second time, he was taunting Patterson, getting him ready. "You're nothing but an Uncle Tom negro, a white man's negro, a yellow negro… Get in the ring and I'll lick you now…" Underneath his usual good humour, Ali nursed a grudge.

Patterson was quick to seize the high ground, ready to exploit white America's fear of Ali, the champion they could not control. The war of words escalated; Patterson's lines might have been tooled by Jimmy Cannon: "I have the right to say the Black Muslims stink," Patterson told **Sports Illustrated** in October 1965. "Cassius Clay is disgracing himself and the negro race. No decent person can look up to a champion whose credo is, 'hate whites'. I have nothing but contempt for the Black Muslims and that for which they stand." Ali responded with his usual display of verve, claiming he would point to the exact spot on the canvas he would knock Patterson to: "That would be something, wouldn't it?"

As soon as the fight began, on the evening of 22 November 1965 – the second anniversary of John F. Kennedy's assassination – it was apparent that Patterson could not back up his boasts with actions. He was a curious and strangely fragile character, no match physically or mentally for Ali, especially an Ali fuelled by burning indignation. Initially Ali embarrassed Patterson by not throwing a punch in the first round, instead just shaping up to unload and enjoying the sight of Patterson flinching away from him. Things grew worse for Floyd after he was affected by a muscle spasm in his back early in the second round.

By the middle rounds of the fight, it was apparent Ali could finish Patterson whenever he wanted. He just didn't want to. He punished his opponent, taunting him as he did so. The referee, **Harry Krause**, wanted to stop the contest after 11 rounds, but Patterson pleaded to be allowed to continue. "I wanted to go down with something that would be worthy of a knockout," Patterson later told the writer **Gay Talese**. "Then in the twelfth, Clay became a punching maniac… A happiness came over me. I knew the end was near…"

Krause finally stepped in. Ali had produced a performance of rare skill, yet it had been a cruel showing, too. Floyd, privately a sensitive man, would often pack what he called a "loser's suitcase" for his fights, which included a false beard and glasses so he could disguise himself if he was defeated. Now his humiliation was compounded by his pre-fight comments. **Frank Sinatra**, who had called Patterson to his hotel suite before the fight to wish him luck, shunned him afterwards.

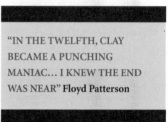

"IN THE TWELFTH, CLAY BECAME A PUNCHING MANIAC… I KNEW THE END WAS NEAR" **Floyd Patterson**

(Patterson recalled: "I was talking to him in his suite and then he did a strange thing: he got up and walked all the way over to the other room, so far away that I could hardly talk to him.") It was left to Ali himself to cheer Floyd with some kind words.

The reaction of the press was less forgiving. Ali's performance was represented as being deliberately devised to hurt and humble Floyd Patterson by keeping him on his feet. Ali denied it, ("I hit him with my best punches," he claimed), but the fight had displayed a darker side of his character, one that would emerge again as the pressure upon him grew.

In 1966, Ali's confrontation with the US Army grew, a contest with much broader implications than any boxing match. His divorce from Sonji was made final on January 7. On 17 February he received the call from the US Army telling him he had been reclassified 1-A. It became increasingly obvious that Ali's

> "WHAM! I'LL JUST KEEP DOING THAT UNTIL HE CALLS ME MUHAMMAD ALI. I WANT TO TORTURE HIM" **Muhammad Ali**

most dangerous opponent was outside the ring. In sporting terms, after beating Sonny and Floyd, there were no particular challenges out there for him. Ali had only got his shot against Liston because Sonny had beaten up everyone else, and now Ali was working his way through that same list.

During the calendar year, he fought five times, taking out tough Canadian **George Chuvalo** on points in Toronto, stopping **Henry Cooper** in London on another bloody cut and then winning two virtual exhibitions against overmatched opponents, a knock out of **Brian London** in three rounds and the stoppage of Karl Mildenberger in 12.

It was only with the year's final encounter, an extraordinary fight with **Cleveland 'Big Cat' Williams** in Houston, that Ali's genius was given full vent. The three rounds the pair fought out are still spoken of as among Ali's best; it was certainly here that his talent ran at its purest. The fight hangs like a ghost over the years of exile that followed soon afterwards, years that would almost certainly have been his prime days as an athlete.

Williams was known as a fearsome puncher and his height and power made him a dangerous man, but his skills had been compromised by events outside boxing. In 1964, he was shot by a Texas highway patrolman following an argument over a speeding ticket. The bullet passed through his right kidney and damaged his hip bone, and Williams required four operations before he could resume his boxing career. When he did, it was minus the rip and zip that the bullet had taken out of him. By the time he came to fight Ali, Williams was a shot fighter, in all senses of the term.

The day before the fight, the journalist **Jerry Izenberg** had told Ali of his fears for Williams's health if he incurred a bad beating. Izenberg told the champ that he would be doing Williams a service by knocking him out quickly.

Ali must have been paying attention. In front of a record crowd for an indoor boxing match – more than **35,000** filled the Houston Astrodome – the champion approached a kind of perfection. In three rounds, he hit Cleveland Williams over 100 times, while being hit just three times himself. He unveiled the dance steps he soon christened **The Ali Shuffle**. He knocked poor Cleveland down twice before a five-punch combination split Big Cat's nose and left him spread-eagled on his back, unconscious but not badly hurt. The bell only delayed the inevitable.

This time, even the press had to acknowledge the quality of Ali's performance.

He was by now the complete package, the heavyweight version of Sugar Ray Robinson that he had dreamed of becoming. Liston had been thought of as invincible because of his brute strength, his dark aura. Ali, on the other hand, was considered unbeatable by virtue of his brilliance.

Ernie Terrell, his next opponent and holder of the discredited WBA belt stripped from Ali after his conversion to the Nation of Islam, made the same mistake as Floyd Patterson. In the fractious build-up to a bout that had been planned for more than a year, Terrell consistently referred to his opponent as Cassius Clay, a tactic that continued to enrage and motivate Ali.

"I'll keep on hitting him and I'll keep on talking," Ali said. "Here's what I'll say. 'Don't you fall, Ernie.' Wham! 'What's my name?' Wham! I'll just keep doing that until he calls me Muhammad Ali… I want to torture him. A clean knockout is too good for him."

Unlike Patterson and Cleveland Williams, though, Ernie Terrell was approaching his peak as a boxer. He was tall and lean with an awkward style, and he'd beaten many of the same opponents as Ali during a 15-fight unbeaten streak. He had first encountered the young Clay in 1962, when the pair had sparred in preparation for fights they had on the same bill, Terrell against Herb Siler and Clay versus Don Warner. Plenty of pundits still either unable or unwilling to acknowledge Ali's quality had been lobbying for a Terrell fight, sure that Terrell's awkward style might bring trouble the champ's way.

Once again, a record crowd filled the **Houston Astrodome** for the bout. Ali's knack for galvanising opinion one way or another had undoubtedly added to his box-office appeal. And in the ring, Ali once again revealed his cruel streak. Terrell began the fight well enough, utilising a peek-a-boo defence that kept Ali from him for a while. But soon, Ali's buzzing punches took effect. Terrell sustained a small fracture under his left eye. His face began to swell badly, and as his physical pain grew more intense, Ali piled on the mental anguish.

"What's my name?" he asked Terrell after each assault. "Tell me my name…"

As he had done with Floyd Patterson, Ali ignored Dundee's pleas to finish his man. By the 14th round, Terrell was flinching every time Ali shaped up to unload. The bout went the full distance, and then Ernie Terrell went straight to the hospital for an operation on his eye.

Here were the opposing halves of Ali's personality, on display in consecutive bouts in the same venue. Cleveland Williams was dispatched to spare him hurt, Ernie Terrell was kept upright to add to his. Much of the ground that Ali had gained with the media following his performance against Williams was surrendered again after the Ernie Terrell battering. Jimmy Cannon complained that it was "a kind of lynching".

The Terrell affair would also have an impact outside the ring. Throughout 1966 and 1967, Ali's confrontation with the **United States Army** had been drawing towards a climactic confrontation. After being recategorised as 1-A, fit for service, Ali had lodged an appeal requesting exemption from the draft. In March 1966, he appeared before Local Board 47, where he claimed exemption as a conscientious objector. The request was denied by the board and denied again on appeal. The case then moved to a special hearing in front of a retired judge. Ali's appeal was predicated on fulfilling three criteria as a conscientious objector: he sincerely objected to military service; his objection was based on religious training and he was opposed to war of any kind.

He swore on oath this was the case. He pointed out he had in fact jeopardised his life within America by declaring his objection, when it would have been easy for him to accept a soft commission into the army, entertaining the troops with boxing exhibition matches.

The judge ruled that Ali was "sincere in his objection" and recommended his conscientious objector status be recognised.

The **Department of Justice** immediately wrote to the appeal board and refuted this ruling, counter-claiming that Ali's objection was motivated by "political and racial" grounds rather than religious ones. It was an argument that struck at the heart of American opinion of the time. In effect, the Nation of Islam was being categorised as a political group rather than a religious one.

The appeal board decided to ignore the judge's recommendation and continued to deny Ali conscientious-objector status. That meant he would face induction at a date to be determined.

As the case moved forward, Ali further alienated the white establishment by allowing his contract with the Louisville Sponsoring Group to expire and signing up **Herbert Muhammad** as his new manager. He was now fully aligned with the Nation of Islam. Against such a background, Ali's treatment of Terrell had not reflected well on him. He had declared himself a conscientious objector, yet he had, deliberately it seemed, set out to hurt a man as badly as possible in the boxing ring. A month after the Terrell fight, the **Presidential Appeal Board** upheld Ali's 1-A status and he was ordered to report for induction into the US Army. The date was set for 28 April 1967 in Houston, Texas.

Before his life changed irrevocably, Ali fitted in one more fight, a title defence against the respected veteran **Zora Folley**. The bout took place at Madison Square Garden. It was another sublime performance, with Folley dropped to the canvas in the fourth and finished off in the sixth with a right cross thrown, like the famous phantom punch, at such speed it seemed not to have landed at all.

Folley had no doubt he had just faced the finest boxer in the world. "He could write the book on boxing," he said afterwards, "and anyone that fights him should be made to read it."

Angelo Dundee claimed the performance surpassed everything that had come before: "Cleveland Williams, that was a great fight, but against Folley, he was fantastic… the greatest he ever looked was against Folley."

The win left Ali with nothing more to do than wrestle with the implications of his forthcoming induction day. The potential penalties were severe and extended far beyond the loss of his boxing titles. The maximum penalty for refusing to serve was five years' imprisonment, plus a fine of up to **$10,000**. Right up until 28 April, rumours persisted that Ali would yield and agree to join up, even though he continued to maintain he was prepared to face jail rather than bear arms for a cause he believed to be wrong. On 25 April, his lawyers had one last throw of the dice, claiming Ali should be regarded as a Nation of Islam minister, as he had spent much of his time preaching their cause in public.

The claim was thrown out, and so, in a moment of poignant theatre, Muhammad Ali took his place in a line of US Army inductees at 8am on 28 April at the Entrance Station in Houston. There were 25 other men waiting with him. Outside, a few protesters cheered for Ali.

The induction began with each man taking one step forwards as their name

In Ali's last fight before exile, he stands over Zora Folley, prone on the canvas

was read out. When the name "**Cassius Marcellus Clay**" was called, Ali remained in line. He was warned as to the consequences of refusing induction and again his name was called. Once more, Ali refused to step forward. He then presented the officials with a written statement which refused induction on the grounds that he was "a minister of the religion of Islam."

Sports broadcaster **Howard Cosell** read out a statement from Ali which said: "Muhammad Ali is aware of the possible implications and consequences [of his actions]. He says he hopes to immediately resume his boxing career, that he won his title fairly within the four corners of the ring and that this is the only way he can be deprived of it. He is also aware that certain authorities in the world of boxing will seek to strip him of his title."

Within an hour, the **New York State Athletic Commission** had suspended Ali's licence to box and stripped him of his title; the rest of the country quickly followed the commission's lead. On 8 May a grand jury in Houston indicted Ali. He was freed on **$5,000 bail**, and his prosecution was set in motion. Ali's wilderness years had begun. Cosell was disgusted: "It was an outrage. Due process of law hadn't even begun, yet they took away his livelihood because he failed the test of political and social conformity. Nobody said a damn word about the professional football players who dodged the draft but Ali was different: he was black and he was boastful."

The legal battle would be long and fraught, but it was played out against two more significant conflicts; the war in Vietnam in which, in 1966 alone, around 6,000 American servicemen had been killed; and the war for the hearts and minds of the American people.

As Ali's exile began, his opposition to the war was a minority view and he suffered for it. **Sports Illustrated** recalled this period, saying: "The noise became a din, the drumbeats of holy war. TV and radio commentators, little old ladies… bookmakers and parish priests, armchair strategists at the Pentagon

Unable to box or leave the country, Ali hit the lecture circuit to spread his word

and politicians all over the place joined in a crescendo of get-Cassius clamour."
But as the loss of life in Vietnam mounted and the dreadful pointlessness of the
conflict became more steadily apparent, the burgeoning peace movement began
to hold sway. As the peace protests grew, Ali came to be seen by these disparate
groups of hippies, activists and ex-servicemen as something he had not set out to
be – a symbol of the free-thinking man victimised by the establishment.

Ali was just grateful for the support. He needed it, even though the Nation's
own struggle was more important to him and to most of the Nation as a whole
than the fight against the war. Indeed, soon after Ali's refusal to be inducted,
Herbert Muhammad had organised a meeting of 10 prominent black athletes,
including American footballer **Jim Brown** and basketball star **Kareem Abdul-
Jabbar**, who discussed with Ali the possibility of him joining up. Jim Brown told
Thomas Hauser, Ali's official biographer: "We wanted Ali to understand all of the
implications of his acts and to make sure he was given a choice."

Ali's trial began in July 1967, as America began to sustain heavy casualties in
Vietnam. It lasted just two days, the first of which was devoted to selecting a jury.
Ali was found guilty and **Judge Joe Ingraham** handed down the maximum
penalty of a five-year jail term and a $10,000 fine. Although Ali was immediately
freed on bail pending appeal, his passport was confiscated and his means of
earning a living denied him.

With his life in a strange kind of limbo and his future deeply uncertain, he
began to travel to Nation of Islam meetings, addressing audiences around the
country. The meetings raised his spirits and at one of the earliest, in Chicago, he
met a tall, handsome young woman named **Belinda Boyd**, who had first seen Ali
when he'd spoken at her school in 1961. They quickly fell for each other: Ali
loved her humour, sense of fun and her devotion to Islam. They were married on
17 August 1967, and 10 months later Ali was a proud father for the first time, to
a girl named **Maryum**. The couple went on to have twin girls, **Rasheeda** and
Jamillah, and a son, **Muhammad Jnr**.

Ali began to pick his way through his new life, a life now bound by principle.
There would be no concession from him, even with the threat of five years in jail
hanging over him and his family. Although he had earned well in the ring, Ali
now had no income. His divorce settlement with Sonji Roi had been generous
(which is why Ali would often say his first wife was a tougher opponent than any
he had fought in the ring) and money had never been a priority for him.
Suddenly, he had to face up to the prospect of not having any.

Yet Ali's true support quickly began to show itself. After **Jeremiah Shabazz**
found him a couple of speaking engagements on college campuses, Ali took on
a booking agent and found that students across America wanted to hear him

speak. He undertook a tour of around 200 colleges and relished having an audience once more. Ali's speeches were funny and true and he spoke with the voice of a man whose actions had matched his words. He told audiences why he thought it was wrong to fight in Vietnam while his people in America were being mistreated, how he was being excluded from boxing and how he didn't need money or titles to be fulfilled in his life. He'd sometimes end by asking the crowd "Who's the heavyweight champion of the world?" and would stand back and smile as they yelled back, "You are!"

The withdrawal of Ali's boxing licence extended even to exhibition bouts, denying him the right to enter a ring anywhere in America. And yet fight people and the sporting public understood: he was still king, even without his crown. Boxing's governing bodies attempted to cover for Ali's absence by organising elimination tournaments to find men who could fight for the vacant title. Most of them were fighters Ali had already beaten.

"Let them have their elimination bouts," Ali said. "Let the man that wins go to the backwoods of Georgia and Alabama, or to Sweden or Africa. Let him stick his head in an elementary school, let him walk down a back alley at night. Let him stop under a street lamp where some small boys are playing and let him say, 'What's my name?' and see what they really say. Everybody knows me and knows I am the champion. You see, they know who the real champion is and all the rest is sparring partners…"

At many of the WBA elimination bouts, strains of "Ali, Ali" echoed down from the stands. Boxing fans weren't fooled. Yet from the elimination competition came a champion. **Joe Frazier**, a compact and explosive fighter with the most devastating left hook on the planet, rose up from a background far humbler than Muhammad Ali's, to defeat **Buster Mathis** and take the title.

When Muhammad Ali finally returned to the ring, his rivalry with Frazier would become one of the most famous in the history of professional sports. To Frazier, Ali would become a totemic figure of hate and long before the pair ever fought, Ali's name chased Frazier across the ring as fans shouted his name. Even when he took to the stage in Las Vegas to sing with his pick-up band **The Knock Outs**, as he loved to do, Joe Frazier would hear people in the crowd yelling that Muhammad Ali was coming back to "whup his ass".

Ali was never sure when, or even if, that day would ever come. His appeal against his draft conviction and sentence continued through the courts. The **FBI** put him under surveillance, where his conversations with Elijah and Herbert Muhammad, and Martin Luther King, were monitored. In May 1968, the Fifth Circuit court of appeal upheld the conviction. In December 1968, Ali actually went to jail for a week as a result of a driving indiscretion, and the experience was a sobering one. Conditions were bad and the loss of his freedom impacted upon him hard, yet he remained resolute in his determination to resist the draft. "A man's got to be real serious about what he believes to say he'll do that for five years," Ali told Thomas Hauser, "but I was ready if I had to go."

> "A MAN'S GOT TO BE REAL SERIOUS ABOUT WHAT HE BELIEVES TO SAY HE'LL DO THAT FOR FIVE YEARS" **Muhammad Ali**

Elijah Muhammad, leader of the Nation of Islam, was ambivalent at best towards Ali's return to boxing. He regarded it as a sport that often pitted black men against one another for the entertainment of white men. He told Ali that the Nation would take care of him if the return never came.

It was this attitude that led to a brief split between Ali and the Nation early in 1969. Ali gave a television interview in which he claimed that he would come back to boxing "if the money was right". Elijah Muhammad interpreted this as Ali placing money above principle and suspended him from the Nation for one year. The dispute was eventually resolved by **Herbert Muhammad**, who negotiated the peace with his father, allowing Ali to return to the fold.

The circumstances that would bring an end to his exile were complex. The separate issues of the Vietnam war and the Civil Rights struggle in America began to blur in the overall atmosphere of protest. Disparate groups like white middle-class hippies and hardline organisations such as the Nation of Islam were loosely uniting against a common establishment foe. Ali continued to speak mostly on behalf of black people in America, although he did address anti-war rallies too and became a lightning rod for the entire protest movement. **Esquire** magazine took up his cause, running a famous cover which featured Ali in his boxing gear punctured with "The arrows of outrageous fortune." (see page 282) They also organised for more than 100 notable people to demand his reinstatement in the pages of the magazine.

As the political climate began to shift, Ali became involved in some other ventures designed to cash in on his celebrity and pay his bills. He appeared on television quiz shows, starred in a **Broadway musical** called **Buck White** and got involved in an unsuccessful fast food venture called **Champburger**, an enterprise that looked doomed the moment they settled on the name. He took up an offer to become a sparring partner for British heavyweight **Joe Bugner** as Bugner prepared for a fight in the US; and he became involved in the making of the documentary feature, **AKA Cassius Clay** released in 1970.

It was at this time that Ali also participated in the strangest fight of his career, against the legendary former champion **Rocky Marciano**. Marciano, who had gone undefeated throughout his professional career of 49 fights, was named by **The Ring** magazine as the best heavyweight ever after winning a fictitious computer tournament organised by the magazine's journalists. The computer concept was then extended to a bout with Ali.

Marciano, who had been retired for 13 years, got back into training, and he and Ali fooled around in front of the cameras, fighting 75 one-minute rounds, which followed a variety of possible outcomes of a fight, between them. The resulting "statistics" were then fed into a computer, and the footage edited to reflect the computer's opinion of who would win. Three weeks before the broadcast of the completed film, Marciano died in a plane crash. The film was shown on closed-circuit television, with the outcome only revealed at the end, when Marciano won by a knockout in round 13 (in Britain, where Marciano was less iconic, the **BBC** broadcast a version in which Ali won by stoppage). Ali received $10,000, plus a percentage of the film's earnings.

Throughout 1968 and 1969, attempts were made to have Ali re-licenced for real, all of which failed, as did an effort to have his passport returned so he might travel overseas to box. And yet, as Thomas Hauser wrote, "Ali… had correctly anticipated history's bend." As a new decade began and after three years in the wilderness, an end to his torment was in sight.

As the **Vietnam** war continued its nightmarish course, many Americans saw in Muhammad Ali a man who had remained sincere and told the truth as he saw it. Among the black community, he was increasingly regarded as a warrior who

---

PROFILE **Ali's best friend** HOWARD BINGHAM

After Ali retired and the millions stopped rolling in, almost all of his vast entourage melted away. Howard Bingham did not. The friendship that began when they met on a street corner in Los Angeles in 1962 when Bingham was a young photographer assigned to cover Cassius Clay's fight with George Logan is stronger today than ever. "Everybody says I love people," Ali told his biographer Thomas Hauser, "so it's only fair that I have the best friend in the world, and that's Howard Bingham."

As a photographer, Bingham has taken more than half-a-million pictures of Ali for almost every major publication, and has recently helped to create and curate GOAT, the monumental Taschen book on Ali (see page 198). In addition to his work with Ali, Bingham covered "virtually every urban uprising" of the 1960s for *Life* magazine, and became one of the first African-American stills photographers in the movie business. He remains Ali's personal chronicler, and his closest friend.

fought for his people. He was now a far more significant figure than any other sportsman in America. In exile, he had become a force for change. It became increasingly apparent that Ali would not go to jail. In November 1968, **Richard Nixon** was elected as president of the United States, promising the electorate that he would find a way of withdrawing from Vietnam. In June 1970, the **Supreme**

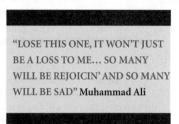

"LOSE THIS ONE, IT WON'T JUST BE A LOSS TO ME... SO MANY WILL BE REJOICIN' AND SO MANY WILL BE SAD" **Muhammad Ali**

Court ruled that conscientious-objector status could be offered to those motivated by religious beliefs. Ali's own appeal against conviction was working its way towards the Supreme Court, too.

Harold Conrad, who had steadfastly supported Ali and was behind many of the attempts to re-licence him, sensed that the mood had changed while he was promoting Joe Frazier's bout with **Jimmy Ellis** early in 1970, when the authorities in Atlanta, Georgia (a state which had no state boxing commission) indicated they would have no objections to licensing Ali to fight again.

Conrad began to plan a "superfight" between Ali and Joe Frazier. The plan ultimately fell through, floundering when the inevitable negotiations over money led to Frazier pulling out, but nonetheless, Conrad knew it would be a simple matter to find another opponent for Ali. He duly turned up the durable **Jerry Quarry**, a white Californian who had acquitted himself well in a loss to Frazier and was heavyweight boxing's main "White Hope" in this era.

Quarry was more than happy to fight and so in September 1970, Muhammad Ali re-entered Angelo Dundee's Fifth Street Gym, fairly certain he would be able to resume his boxing career. After some rounds of sparring, Angelo estimated that Ali was "around 75 per cent" of what he had been when his exile had begun.

Ali, careful to avoid any inflammatory statements, and mindful of the fact that he had no really accurate idea of how good he might still be, kept a far lower profile than he had been used to in the build-up to his fights. He felt the weight of expectation upon him, too. "Lose this one," he admitted to **Sports Illustrated**, "and it won't just be a loss to me. So many people will be rejoicin' and hollerin' and jumpin' up and down, and so many million faces will be sad, so sad they'll feel like they been defeated."

Later in September, Ali boxed an eight-round exhibition in Atlanta, primarily to ensure that any remaining political opposition to his comeback would be unsuccessful. The event was a success, and the bout with Quarry was confirmed for 26 October 1970.

The greatest comeback

While the effect of his absence on his boxing skills was unknown, it had certainly increased Ali's box-office appeal. For a 10-round fight with no title at stake, he was paid $300,000. Ali now transcended boxing, his return more than just a boxing match. People wanted to attend in order to show solidarity with him. The resultant crowd was studded with stars like **Bill Cosby** and **Sidney Poitier** and political figureheads such as **Jesse Jackson** and the wife of Martin Luther King. *Sports Illustrated* reported that the crowd represented "the most startling display of **black power and black money** ever seen."

This remarkable gathering saw a Muhammad Ali marked by the years of exile. He appeared to have altered little; slightly heavier and more fully muscled maybe, but then he was no longer a raw-boned kid. Ali was now 28 years old, and his situation was unique in the annals of professional sport. At the height of his powers, as king of his world, he had stopped fighting for three-and-a-half years. Not even Ali knew exactly what would happen when the bell sounded and he and **Jerry Quarry** went to work.

That uncertainty added to the frenzied atmosphere at ringside. The fight began and Ali made a blazing start, landing punches at will and forcing Quarry to miss with the speed of his footwork. He looked like the same Ali, yet he wasn't, not quite. Quarry was a pressure fighter, skilled at taking punishment and still moving forwards to bring some hurt of his own. He was also younger than Ali, a new experience for the former champ.

Through rounds two and three Ali slowed and then almost stopped altogether. The legs that had carried him through his early career were now a bit less steady. Quarry forced him to the ropes and unloaded his punches unscientifically. Ali made little effort to escape, instead using the give in the ropes to sway away from the harder shots and absorbing others on his gloves and arms. Observers were confounded by the tactic. The ropes usually spelled nothing but trouble for a fighter, yet it was a technique that would come to characterise the second half of Ali's career.

He had little further need of it once he had opened a horrid cut above Quarry's left eye with a solid right hand in round three. Split almost to the bone, Quarry was unable to continue, despite his strong protests to the referee Tony Perez. **Bundini Brown**, back in Ali's corner, had to jump between Quarry and Ali as Quarry chased Ali across the ring, unable to contain his disappointment.

Critical reaction to the fight was favourable towards Ali, but the fighter himself was not fooled. He admitted that he might have had to fight the full 10 rounds had Quarry not been cut.

Ferdie Pacheco, Ali's doctor, and later a shrewd boxing analyst for American fight broadcasters HBO, gave an honest assessment of the returning Ali to Thomas Hauser. "He discovered something that was very good and very bad," Pacheco said. "Very bad in that it led to the physical damage he suffered later in his career; very good in that it eventually got him back to the championship. He discovered he could take a punch."

Ali was back. **Julian Bond**, a Civil Rights campaigner who had worked closely with Martin Luther King, said "it was like nothing I'd ever seen, it was a coronation; the King regaining his throne." A month after Ali stopped Jerry Quarry, **Joe Frazier** knocked out Bob Foster to retain the title that had been stripped from Ali. The pair seemed on course to meet in an historic fight. Next, Ali took on **Oscar Bonavena**, a rugged bull from the pampas of Argentina. The bout took place at Madison Square Garden, a return to New York made possible by legal action on behalf of Ali by the NAACP, who contested the State Athletic Commission's decision not to licence him and won.

Again Ali was unable to call on the incendiary brilliance of his youth. He and Bonavena fought out 14 uneven rounds, with Ali good for the first four, Bonavena for the next four. They exchanged fiercely in the ninth, with each man temporarily shaken up. First Ali landed hard on Bonavena, then the Argentinian responded with a heavy shot of his own. Ali admitted after the fight he had been shaken by Bonavena's power, but he retained enough of his wits to circle out of trouble, waiting for the bell to bring him respite.

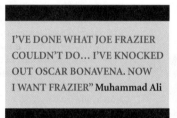

I'VE DONE WHAT JOE FRAZIER COULDN'T DO… I'VE KNOCKED OUT OSCAR BONAVENA. NOW I WANT FRAZIER" **Muhammad Ali**

The bout slumped towards a messy end until, in the 15th and last round, Bonavena went in search of the knockout and walked on to a left hook of Ali's that dropped him for a technical knockout. With a tearful Bundini kissing his cheek, Ali grabbed a microphone and called from the centre of the ring: "I've done what Joe Frazier couldn't do… I've knocked out Oscar Bonavena. Now where is he? I want **Joe Frazier**!"

Frazier was sitting at ringside with his manager, Yank Durham.

"Go up and shake his hand," Durham said to Frazier.

"I ain't got nothin' to say to that clown," Joe replied.

Ali's reasons for chasing Frazier hard weren't entirely sporting. Although public opinion had shifted far enough to permit his return to the ring, the threat of imprisonment was still hanging over him as he awaited a date in the Supreme Court for the final verdict on his appeal over his draft conviction. Time was of the essence: in six months, he might be in jail rather than in the gymnasium.

So, instead of allowing his body to recuperate after two bouts within six weeks of one another, and with public anticipation of their meeting resulting in the unprecedented purse offer of $2.5m each, Ali signed to meet **Joe Frazier** on 8 March 1971 at **Madison Square Garden**.

The encounter was immediately (and for ever after) billed as **The Fight of the Century**. Ali's unique circumstances meant that two undefeated champions would face one another across the ring for the title. Better still, if the old maxim that styles make fights held true, Ali-Frazier was bound to be a classic: it offered the classic match-up of **boxer versus slugger**. Both fighters had enjoyed stellar amateur careers, too. Frazier had matched Ali's Rome gold medal with an Olympic gold of his own, won four years later in 1964 in Tokyo.

And yet the greatness of their rivalry, the epic nature of their trilogy of fights, could not simply be explained by sporting reasons alone. Ali's feelings about Joe Frazier might have been ambiguous – except for Terrell and Patterson, he rarely bore anyone genuine ill-will – but Frazier's emotions were simple. Ali inspired a rare and implacable rage within him; put simply, Joe Frazier wanted nothing less than to destroy Muhammad Ali.

The bad blood that led to their feud had not existed for long. Early in Ali's exile, Frazier had offered his support, appearing in public with him and helping Ali to stay in the boxing public's eye. Ali in turn joked that he could envision himself and Frazier as old men, sitting on the porch and swapping stories. The pair had homes in Philadelphia, and would often speak on the phone about a possible fight should Ali return to the ring.

And yet, as soon as the bout was announced, Ali's pre-fight hype began to run out of control. At its heart were the differences between the men. Frazier was a true believer, too, but a Baptist, one of 13 children raised up the hard way. Just like Sonny Liston's, Joe Frazier's father had another huge family, a further 13 children, born out of wedlock down in rural South Carolina. At 15, already married, Joe had gone to New York and then to Philadelphia, where he worked in a slaughterhouse. When he found he could box, his life changed for the better. After winning his Olympic gold in Tokyo he turned professional under the guidance of **Yank Durham**.

Soon Frazier was burning it up in the pros, earning the nickname **Smokin' Joe** for his rough style and iron left hook. Ali's journey into exile offered Joe his chance, which he accepted by busting up Buster Mathis to take the vacant New

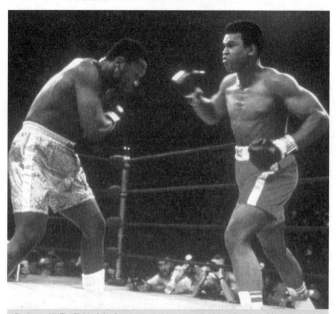

Frazier vs Ali: The Fight of the Century, a classic contest between slugger and boxer

York State world title. He defended six times before unifying the belts with a fifth-round TKO of Jimmy Ellis to take the WBA crown.

Both Frazier and Ali were undefeated, perfectly matched in the ring. The disparity came outside of the ropes, and it was here that the roots of their feud lay. Where Ali was a politicised figure, a symbol, Frazier was the opposite: a boxing man who burned only to prove himself within the ring. For Joe, pride was everything, respect the currency he valued most. He was a proud, powerful black man, entirely self-made from a background that reeked of the authentic black experience in the first half of the American century. Frazier's father was a sharecropper, his childhood grindingly poor. Without his fists, Joe Frazier might have disappeared into Philadelphia and never come out. Yet it was at this background, at these emotions, that Ali struck. His campaign to sell the fight mocked Frazier as an Uncle Tom, a white-man's stooge.

"Anybody black who thinks Frazier can whup me is an Uncle Tom," Ali said.

He cast Frazier in the same role he had cast Floyd Patterson, that of an old-style black man, an establishment figure whom he needed to knock out for his people. Yet when Ali yelled out, "I'm fighting for the little man in the ghetto," he demeaned Joe Frazier far more than he needed to in order to sell tickets. In the words of Frazier's friend **Dave Wolf**, "Joe, due to his background and upbringing, was almost the stereotypical black person Ali claimed to be fighting for." Frazier was enraged by Ali's posturing, but lacked the media-savvy skills to hit back in kind. The media bought into Ali's vision. When Frazier pointed out, "a lot of guys around him [Ali] are white," no one was listening.

Ali's reasons for beginning such a vicious war of words were complex, and probably known only to him. They were designed to sell tickets, though the fight was already the hottest ticket around, a **$5m** superbout to be broadcast live on closed-circuit television across America and in 35 other countries. They probably served a psychological purpose, aimed at giving Ali some kind of edge in the fight. Perhaps Ali needed to speak them to summon the necessary intensity to take Frazier on. Maybe his anger at the loss of his titles, at the dramatic change in his life, simply found its focus in his opponent. Also, on a deeper level, Ali fought best when he felt he was representing his people.

Whatever his motives, aside from selling the fight, Ali's words became counter-productive. Having stoked up Joe Frazier, he would reap the whirlwind at **Madison Square Garden**. Frazier was fuelled not just by his considerable pride and that relentless desire to prove himself to the world, but by his hatred of Ali.

The arena was almost unbearably tense before the fighters walked to the ring. Every seat was full, and could have been sold 10 times over. **Frank Sinatra**, admitted on a working press pass, took the shot *Life* magazine used on its cover.

Ali and Frazier took to the ring almost simultaneously. Ali walked to Frazier's corner and patted him on the head.

"Chump," he said.

Frazier's reply was succinct enough.

"I'm going to kill you," he said.

Ali enjoyed a nine-inch advantage in reach over Frazier, 80 inches to 71, and even when Frazier bulled himself into range, Ali swayed away from his most dangerous shots. Yet for rounds three and four, Frazier battered Ali on the ropes. Ali fought his way into the lead, staying on the ropes but firing back at Frazier, but Frazier simply didn't care. He wanted a knock-out win and he was slugging his way towards one. Yet Ali almost ended the fight in round nine, producing the finest boxing of his comeback as he wobbled Frazier with some hard combinations. Having worked an opening, Ali attempted to close out the fight in the next round, messing up Frazier's face and stinging him time and again.

When Howard Cosell died at the age of 77 in 1995, the *Washington Post* called him, "arguably the best-known and most controversial sports broadcaster in the history of the medium." Cosell's mission was to "tell it like it is" and he became one of Ali's staunchest defenders during his refusal to take the draft, for which Cosell received death threats. Ali was not his only cause, he spoke up against racism of all kinds, corruption in sports and its growing commercialism.

"Howard Cosell was a good man and he lived a good life," Ali said on his death. "I have been interviewed by many people but I enjoyed my interviews with Howard the best. I can hear him now saying, 'you're not the man you used to be...'"

That particular comment had come before Ali took on George Foreman, and Ali took great delight in Cosell being proved wrong. "Howard Cosell, you said I ain't the man I was five years ago," Ali said. "Well Howard, I talked to your wife and she says you ain't the man you were two years ago..."

Frazier survived, and in the 11th, he prospered. Ali, perhaps overconfident, slipped over. Once he was back on his feet, Frazier charged at him as if he'd scored a knockdown. Ali cockily waved him in, and immediately regretted it as Frazier landed a big left that caused Ali's legs to betray him.

What kept Ali on his feet during the ensuing onslaught, only he may know, as he staggered around on drunken legs. Joe landed hook after hook until it seemed Ali must go down. But Ali forced his body to lie and exaggerated his distress to the point where Frazier, convinced that his opponent was about to go down, delayed going in for the kill. Bundini Brown was so concerned that he hurled water at Ali, an **illegal act that got him suspended** from Ali's corner at a later fight. Ali survived the round.

Frazier had turned the fight his way with one shot. Ali clung on before, in round 15, Frazier hit Ali with one of the most famous left hooks in boxing history. Ali fell to the canvas, left leg stretched outward. To the astonishment of everyone, including the referee **Arthur Mercante**, who didn't have time to take up a count, Ali was up almost as soon as he'd touched the ground.

As the final bell rang, the crowd screamed for a draw, but the result was clear enough. Mercante scored the bout eight rounds to six for Frazier with one even. Ali was beaten for the first time and Joe Frazier could truly call himself Champion of the World. The price was high. Several weeks later, Frazier spent three weeks in hospital in Philadelphia, physically and mentally exhausted.

Down, not out

A li faced defeat with dignity. If his exile had taught him anything, it was that a boxing match was not the most important thing in the world. "Probably be a better man for it," he told the writer **Robert Lipsyte** the day after his loss, and with his cheek still bearing the swelling induced by Frazier's brutal left hook. "News don't last long. Plane crash, 90 people die, it's not news a day after. My losing's not so important as 90 people dying. The world goes on. You'll all be writing about something else soon. I had my day. You lose, don't shoot yourself."

Joe Frazier was presenting his own battered mug to the world, too. "What can you say about me now?" he challenged the press men who had favoured Ali. "I always felt like the champ. I fought everyone they put in front of me, God knows… He takes one good punch. That shot I hit him with in the 15th round, I went back to the country to throw. God he can take it!"

Ali was already rationalising the fight. "I've lost one out of 32," he told journalist **George Plimpton**. "And that was a decision that could have gone the other way. If I was beat real bad, really whupped, and the other fighter was superior, then I'd look at myself and say I was washed up."

Within days, he seemed to have fully recovered his equilibrium. If anything, defeat was more of a watershed in the public perception of **Muhammad Ali** than his comeback had been. Whilst sections of the press and other denizens of the old order crowed, the wider view had softened. Ali became now something of an underdog, and the sporting public love an underdog. As an image makeover, the defeat to Smokin' Joe was a triumph. Diarist and critic **Kenneth Tynan**, a big fan of Ali's, was one of many for whom the fight had an iconic significance that went way beyond boxing, calling it "a belated epitaph for the 1960s: flair, audacity, imagination, outrageous aplomb, cut down by stubborn, obdurate, 'hard-hat' persistence". The comparison was a tad harsh on Frazier but Tynan went on: "In Clay's towering vulnerability, his apparent unconcern about exposing himself to punishment, there is breath-taking hubris, as well as death wish remarked on by more than one commentator." For Tynan, Frazier's triumph was like having **Nixon**, not Kennedy, in the White House: "Cavaliers had better beware. The Roundheads are back in force."

The loss of his title stung Ali the most. He told Thomas Hauser that he saw himself as the **champion during his exile** because his belt had not been taken from him in the ring. Now that idea was gone. For the first time ever, Ali realised how much the title meant to him. He vowed to do all he could to regain it.

Ali rested his body for a couple of months before he began training again. Soon after, he received the news for which he had waited almost four years. On 28 June, the US Supreme Court **quashed his conviction** for draft evasion, voting unanimously in his favour after some complex legal argument. His longest fight was over, the weight of prison finally lifted from his shoulders. Ali described his feelings as "numb" to *Sports Illustrated* magazine immediately after the verdict: "It's like a man's been in chains all his life and suddenly the chains are taken off. He don't realise he's free until he gets all the circulation back in his arms and legs and starts to feel his fingers."

Now the narrative of Ali's extraordinary story had a clear arc. He was free to pursue his real goal, the reclaiming of his title. It almost had the most bizarre of starts, with plans sketched out for a fight with **Wilt 'The Stilt' Chamberlain**, a legendary basketball player who was 7ft 2in tall and weighed almost 300lbs, but who had never laced on a pair of gloves. The scheme foundered, in part because of Ali's habit of laughing and shouting "Timber!" every time he saw Chamberlain. The serious business began with a bout against **Jimmy Ellis**,

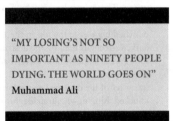

"MY LOSING'S NOT SO IMPORTANT AS NINETY PEOPLE DYING. THE WORLD GOES ON"
Muhammad Ali

a former sparring partner of Ali's and another of Angelo Dundee's charges. Ali won with a TKO in the 12th, coasting to the win after a fourth round right hand effectively took Ellis out of the fight.

He was back again, but the road to a title bout would be far longer than anyone imagined. He took a series of fights that did little to bring another shot at Joe Frazier any closer. During the next 12 months, Ali beat **Buster Mathis**, **Jurgen Blin** and **Mac Foster**, won rematches with **George Chuvalo** and **Jerry Quarry** and travelled to Dublin to beat **Al 'Blue' Lewis**, one of his more unlikely fights.

At the end of 1972, he fought **Floyd Patterson** for the second time. Floyd had become, in boxing terms, an old man at 37 with loads of miles on the clock. He represented no threat at all to Ali, but the match caught on with boxing fans, and over 17,000 people turned up at Madison Square Garden to see it.

Ali was far more engaged by the pre-fight appearance of Joe Frazier than he was by Floyd. As Frazier stepped into the ring to accept the cheers of the crowd, Ali made a rush for him, launching into a long tirade at his nemesis. Frazier laughed and settled back to watch the fight, which Ali won after Patterson failed to answer the bell for the eighth, cut over one eye and exhausted from the effort of snatching a couple of rounds from his younger, bigger opponent.

Frazier too had been knocking over uncompetitive opponents and a rematch with Ali was a logical fight for both men. The sums being thrown around by promoters would not disgrace a heavyweight title bout today – $5m dollars each was mooted, an enormous prize for 1972. Frazier was the reluctant party. After all, the first fight had hospitalised him for three weeks. But Frazier skipped Ali and signed to fight another lesser-known man, the big-punching **George Foreman** in Kingston, Jamaica, for a purse of less than $1m. Ali became frustrated, winning a fight with Bob Foster to fill in time, and even discussing a film project with Warner Bros.

Frazier had made a huge mistake that would cost both him and Ali. Foreman, another Olympic gold medallist like Ali and Joe, was 25 and approaching his prime. The avuncular, chubby Foreman who, today, sells low-fat grills on infomercials across the world bears little relation with the Foreman who punched his way to the top in the 1970s. The young Foreman was moody and dark, a street guy bent on the destruction of whoever stood in front of him. He took Frazier apart without mercy, battering him to the floor six times in less than a round and a half. One blow lifted Frazier off his feet. Yet Foreman admitted he was wary of the damage he was doing: "If you hit Joe Frazier, he liked it. If you knocked him down, it made him mad." Not as mad as the result made Muhammad Ali. "They woke me up to tell me," Ali said. "And I thought, there goes my five million…"

With Frazier at least temporarily in the strange limbo of the deposed champ, Ali began to train still harder. He defeated the Hungarian-born British heavyweight **Joe Bugner** over 12 slow rounds in Las Vegas, and signed up to fight the little-known **Ken Norton** a month later just to keep in trim and maintain his momentum. It was as big a mistake as Frazier had made in fighting Foreman. Norton may have been a nobody, but he'd slid up in the heavyweight ratings to number seven under the sharp eye of **Eddie Futch**, who had trained Frazier for his win over Ali. He was raw, a former US marine with a soldier's physique, wide shoulders and a narrow midsection that had Angelo Dundee joking he might "snap in half". But he was also hungry enough to realise that a fight with Muhammad Ali represented a rare chance to break into the big time, and he had a punch hard enough to mask some of his shortcomings as a strategic boxer.

Luck was on Ken Norton's side when he hit Ali with an insignificant punch at some point during round two which, thanks to the fact that Ali's jaw was open and it landed straight on the bone, **split the jawbone** apart. Dark blood ran from the corner of Ali's mouth. Angelo, realising the bone was broken, wanted to stop the fight. Ali refused and in an act of remarkable bravery, fought nine more rounds with the injury. He knew he could not afford another loss and he dug deep. By the 12th he was exhausted, drained by the effort and a dominant last three minutes won Norton a narrow decision.

Ali left the ring with his face grossly misshapen. Bundini stepped from it in inconsolable tears. Ali immediately underwent 90 minutes of surgery to wire the fracture back in place. "Funny," Ali said afterwards, "the jaw didn't hurt too much during the fight… only on the way to the hospital." He went on to blame a light training schedule for the defeat and a special robe given to him by his celebrity pal **Elvis Presley** and then promised to rededicate himself.

He planned a rematch with Norton before fights with Frazier and then Foreman. This scheme was considered fanciful by a boxing press who were writing Ali off, beaten twice since his comeback. "He has a big name, and not much to defend it with," said Jimmy Cannon. Even the American television commentator Howard Cosell, with whom Ali enjoyed a magnificent on-screen rapport, thought the great man had reached the end of the line.

Ali worked hard to attract interest in the Norton rematch, scheduled for September 1973. He trained even harder, retreating to the Pennsylvanian camp he'd bought 12 months before. The training camp was an idea he'd had since pitching up at Archie Moore's 'Salt Mine' in the Californian hills all of those years ago. The site was at **Deer Lake**, a remote and pretty hillside on which Ali constructed a series of log cabins for himself, his entourage and pretty much anyone else who wanted to show up. For decoration, he painted the names of legendary boxers on the giant boulders that lay scattered around the property.

At Deer Lake, which he named **Fighters' Heaven**, he could rise early and run, he could spar in the gym, and he could fool around with his friends and his kids. For the first time since the Frazier fight, Ali got himself into top condition. He understood that his career would not survive another defeat by Norton, and he worked everyone so hard that even Angelo Dundee claimed to have dropped 10 pounds in weight.

Ignoring the pundits' cynicism, the public took to the idea of Ali's redemption. Interest in the Norton fight overshadowed George Foreman's first title defence, and Ali's huge following in Europe added more emphasis to it.

Ali predicted a quick win, but got no such thing. The truth was, Ken Norton's style was always likely to give a boxer like Ali problems. He was tall and he threw punches from a strange position, almost leaning backwards. Norton was vulnerable

"THE JAW DIDN'T HURT TOO MUCH DURING THE FIGHT… ONLY ON THE WAY TO HOSPITAL." **Muhammad Ali**

to big punchers, but not particularly to boxers like Ali, who relied on cumulative effect to gain a victory.

Ali began well, but then Norton caught him up over the middle rounds, his youth lending strong advantage. Again, the fighters were to be separated by who boxed the best last round, but this time it was Ali who dug deepest, forcing Norton back with flashing combinations and benefiting from his work at Deer Lake. Ali took a narrow decision. Norton, predictably, didn't agree with the verdict, saying later: "Ali was boxing and boxing went as Ali went. So every time anyone had a close fight with Ali, he won."

The first part of Ali's three-part objective was complete, and the second would not have to wait too long. Ali flew to Indonesia for a regulation 12-rounder with **Rudi Lubbers**, before finally getting Joe Frazier's signature on a rematch contract. The decision to wait for such a bout had cost each man a defeat, and around $2.5m. They signed to fight for $850,000 each, plus a percentage of the gross take that would push their individual earnings over $2m. The money, though, was not an issue for either man. Ali vs Frazier II, just like Ali vs Frazier I, was all about pride. Once more they would fight at **Madison Square Garden**. The first time they had met there, each man had a claim to the title. This time, neither did, but the lack of a belt did not detract from the intensity of emotion that they carried into the ring.

The build-up to the contest was once more bitter and bad-natured. The pair traded insults, with both reading from much the same script as they had before. Five days before the fight, **Howard Cosell** interviewed them together for the ABC

TV network. The film of their first bout was shown, and both were invited to comment on it at the end of each round. Things were civil, until Frazier remarked that he had put Ali in hospital after the fight. Ali, enraged, fired back, "Why'd you say that about the hospital? I went to the hospital for 10 minutes. You were in the hospital for three weeks."

"Just for a rest," Frazier countered.

"That shows how dumb you are," Ali said, and as he did so Frazier rose from his seat and pulled Ali out of his. The pair wrestled on the floor, fell off of the dais and into the studio audience before they were separated.

Ali was playing, but Joe Frazier wasn't fooling around. Howard Cosell could see it and he was genuinely scared by the fight. Ali, too, became alarmed when he realised Frazier was serious. The pair were each fined $5,000, but Frazier felt he had gained an advantage.

In truth, Joe had never let the enmity from their first fight slide. In his Philadelphia gym, he had the picture of his 15th-round knockdown of Ali blown up to fill one wall and he stared at it as he trained. To the Madison Square Garden ring, he brought only bad intentions.

This time though, they were not enough. Ali had figured Frazier out, and in front of 20,000 people, he coldly dismantled him. Frazier was a pressure fighter, never happier than when he was boring in on his opponent's chest, getting close enough to feel his breath. Ali countered with an exhibition of fine movement and combination punching, never allowing Frazier to force him backwards to the ropes or the corners. In the second round, he juddered Frazier with a right hand and might have done further damage, had referee **Tony Perez** not stepped in between the fighters in the mistaken belief that the bell had sounded.

Every time Frazier did get to Ali, Ali grabbed him in a powerful clinch, tugging Frazier's head down to stop him punching. Ali's serene progress was barely interrupted: in the ninth the pair briefly stood toe to toe and exchanged heavily, then Ali cruised away again to a comfortable points win.

Frazier mumbled and grumbled but he could have few complaints. Ali had bested him with lessons learned, and in doing so had put himself firmly back on centre stage. Frazier demanded a third scrap, a decider. Ali was happy to accept ("Joe can have all the chances he wants") but first he would fight once more for the title he coveted. And once more, circumstances would combine to make the event one of the most memorable and remarkable in the history not just of boxing, but of professional sport.

The Rumble in the Jungle

Ge_eorge Foreman was another Sonny Liston, a fearsome puncher who everyone said Ali could never beat. George could be as surly as Sonny, too, but was less damaged. He had come from a hard place, the back streets of Houston, but he was not doomed as the late Sonny so obviously had been.

When Foreman fought Ali, he was in his physical prime, an awesome specimen. His record was every bit as as imposing as his physique and his presence: 40 fights, 40 wins, 37 by knockout. Just like Liston, he destroyed men for the hell of it and because he could. In his previous eight fights before the bout with Ali, he had not been required to go beyond round two. Nor was he beating up bums and stiffs. He had annihilated **Frazier**; he had terrified **Ken Norton** – and these were the men who had defeated Ali.

Foreman had another link to Liston in his trainer, a former song and dance man named **Dick Sadler**, who had worked with Sonny for some years. They made a comical pair, George and Dick, because Sadler was as tiny as Foreman was huge, and the little man had a nice line in wry humour to offset Foreman's monolithic silences.

The drama that would become the Rumble in the Jungle, the fight heard around the world, needed a third player, an Iago figure, and he duly arrived in the electrifying form of **Don King**, an ex-con and numbers racketeer from Cleveland, Ohio, fresh out of jail for the manslaughter of Sam Garrett. King had kicked Garrett to death on the street. Garrett's last words had been, "I'll pay you the money, Don…"

King's ascent from the ghetto was remarkable in its own way. He possessed a formidable intellect to go along with his cunning, and he had an iron nerve, too. Allied to those qualities, he had a limitless supply of what he liked to call "wit, grit and bullshit," and he spent more time talking and hyping than Muhammad Ali did – which was saying something. In jail he had read every book that he could ("I made time serve me") and as a result was able to quote great reams of classic literature from memory.

The speed of his rise from prisoner to promoter of the biggest fight the world had ever seen was best illustrated by the fact that he had listened to the first Ali-Frazier fight in March 1971 on prison radio. Less than three years later, he was taking Ali and Foreman to Zaire to fight for $5m each in a title bout anticipated across five continents.

King pulled this off by bringing street thinking to big business. He began small, persuading Ali to take part in an exhibition bout in Cleveland to benefit a local hospital. King was taken with boxing straight away, and he figured out that a black promoter might do well, given that most fighters were black and most promoters white.

Through the matchmaker and manager Don Elbaum, King got a half share in the contract of a powerful heavyweight named **Earnie Shavers**. Soon, he had the whole thing and he never looked back. He worked with a closed circuit television company for the Foreman-Norton fight, and when he heard Ali would take on Foreman for $5m, a fee other promoters regarded as ludicrous, he seized his chance. He teased his way into the deal, guaranteeing Herbert Muhammad the five million, and then raised it by the most extraordinary means. Some of the cash came via the close circuit company he worked with, Video Techniques, some of it was television money from Europe, but the majority came from the most sinister player of all, **Joseph Mobutu Sese Seko**, the ruler of Zaire.

Mobutu, a ruthless dictator who liked to be referred to as "The Great Leopard," wanted the world to know his name. He had taken power in a bloodless coup at the end of a brutal civil war that had broken out when the country, formerly the Belgian Congo, had become independent in 1960. His programme of eradicating all traces of colonialism from the country, known as **Authenticité**, united many disparate groups within Zaire. The fight was to be the ultimate demonstration of

Ali's superior hand speed begins to tell against Foreman as the Rumble unfolds

Mobutu's success and power. Don King persuaded Mobutu to pay a cool **$10m** to put himself and his country in front of the watching world.

With both men's signatures on an option, King had the fight in place. In addition to the bout, he planned a grand spectacle of black power and culture called From The Slave Ship To The Championship, a two-day music event that would showcase musicians like **James Brown**, **B.B. King** and **Bill Withers** (the festival did eventually go ahead, although the title was withdrawn after the Zairian people objected). Ironically, given this stellar talent on display, the musical souvenir of the event most people remember is the exploitation single **Black Superman**, by British singer/songwriter **Johnny Wakelin**, a UK smash and No.21 in the US charts. The follow up, a UK hit, was chiefly famous for its key line: "See the rumble in the jungle there... in Zaire."

Ali was delighted to compete in Africa. In a way he felt as though he was coming home, at least spiritually. He would forge a strong connection with the people of Zaire, and he would use it for inspiration much as he had done in America with his own people. When he arrived in Zaire he said, "It don't seem possible, but 28 million people run this country and not one white man is involved. I used to think Africans were savages. But now that I'm here, I've learned that many Africans are wiser than we are. They speak English and two or three more languages. Ain't that something?"

As was his wont, Ali had soon painted Foreman as the outsider in Africa. George wasn't press friendly; indeed, George wasn't friendly at all.

The bout was arranged for 25 September 1974, at 3am to serve US broadcasting interests ("I don't mind," Foreman said archly, "I've had most of my fights at three in the morning...") Three weeks beforehand, the fighters, their entourages, the promoters, the world's press and television, and then the musicians arrived in Zaire.

The bout had attracted some of the world's best writers. **Norman Mailer** (who would write a famous book, *The Fight,* about Zaire – see page 192), **George Plimpton** and **Budd Schulberg** were among those having their notebooks filled each day with Ali's pre-fight wit.

> "I DON'T MIND... I'VE HAD MOST OF MY FIGHTS AT THREE IN THE MORNING" **Foreman on the timing of the Rumble**

"George Foreman is nothing but a big mummy," was one of his favourites. "I've officially named him 'The Mummy'. He moves like a slow mummy and there ain't no mummy gonna whup the great Muhammad Ali." The truth, though, was that few among the press or the boxing community expected Ali to beat Big George. Foreman was an overwhelming favourite; for Ali to regain the title at the age of 32 would be a feat unprecedented in boxing. Just as when he had fought Liston, there was some speculation as to whether Ali would leave the ring alive.

Foreman went about his work methodically. The fighters trained near the presidential compound in N'Sele, where they resided in luxury. The press grumbled and groaned about being stationed in Kinshasa, which was far less luxurious; the real Africa. Yet they travelled each day to watch Foreman hammer the heavy bag and knock his sparring partners around. In Foreman's mind was one thought: "I was going to knock his [Ali's] block off, and the thought of doing it didn't bother me at all," he told Thomas Hauser.

Ali's clowning kept spirits in his camp high. He and Bundini would shout "Rumble, young man, rumble" at each other, and Ali had seized on a local phrase, "Ali boma ye," which meant "Ali kill him" as his own private mantra. He would greet crowds of locals and have them chant "Ali boma ye," over and over. But as the fight drew nearer, tension grew. Ali understood more than anybody the size of the challenge he faced, and he decided a strategy. He told anyone who'd listen that he was going to dance away from Foreman and become impossible to hit.

And then eight days before the bout, Foreman caught an elbow in the eye from one his sparring partners, **Bill McMurray**, and a cut opened up. To Ali's despair, the fight was postponed to give the cut time to heal. At first he wanted to fly home, but then good sense prevailed and everyone stayed in Zaire and waited a month for Big George.

The press grew bored and began filing stories about conditions in Zaire, exactly the sort of publicity Mobutu had sought to avoid. Foreman became bad tempered, moving to the Hotel Continental and brooding on his problems, which included a recent divorce and some serious financial difficulties. The fight could not come quickly enough. Even the weather grew impatient; the rainy season was about to break.

The ring was constructed in the middle of a field in the **20th of May Stadium** in Kinshasa. One corner was sinking into the mud. The ropes, which were new, became slack in the heat, even though Angelo Dundee himself shortened them using a knife and the corner turnbuckles.

Ali slept until 2am and then was driven from N'Sele to the stadium. The atmosphere in his camp was low. It was Ali who was trying to lift Bundini and co, rather than the other way around. In the dressing rooms underneath the stadium, where Mobutu was rumoured to have held 400 petty criminals, 40 of whom he executed as a warning to Zaire's people, **Herbert Muhammad** visited Ali. He told Ali that he was fighting not just for him, but for his people, and that if he did his best, Allah would be with him.

Foreman went to the ring with Dick Sadler and another face familiar to Ali, Archie Moore. Ali was seconded by Angelo and Bundini. As the fight began, Ali seized the initiative, running across the ring and hitting Foreman with a hard right hand – a trick Archie would immediately have recognised, as it was he who had taught it to Ali. For the rest of the round, Ali stuck and moved, peppering Foreman with right-hand leads and disturbing his equilibrium.

"**Ali boma ye!**" yelled the crowd.

Foreman's strategy was predicated on driving Ali to the ropes. In round two, Ali went there of his own accord. Even Angelo Dundee had no idea what was about to unfold. In a move of counter-intuitive brilliance, Ali had found that the way to beat George Foreman was to give him exactly what he wanted.

For five rounds, Foreman blazed away at Ali, who rolled on the heat-slackened ropes like a ship on heavy seas. At first, Dundee and Bundini and Wali Muhammad yelled at him to stick and move, but slowly, his "Rope-a-dope" tactic became apparent. Foreman's storm blow itself out, his great strength spent on Ali's arms and gloves. "Is that all you got, George?" Ali taunted him. "They told me you could punch…"

In round eight, Ali's moment of redemption came, a moment he had anticipated for more than seven years. Rebounding from the ropes, he struck Foreman with two rights, a left and then a final, shocking right hand, and Foreman spun to the ground with his arms flailing, a slain giant.

Ali was engulfed, Foreman shattered, the world shocked.

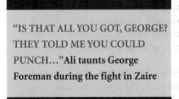

"IS THAT ALL YOU GOT, GEORGE? THEY TOLD YOU COULD PUNCH…"Ali taunts George Foreman during the fight in Zaire

As the new champion was driven back to N'Sele, the route was lined by hundreds of cheering people. Within an hour, the rains came and the stadium dressing rooms were flooded.

When Ali got back to N'Sele he stayed up all night. He showed his magic tricks to some children he found on the doorstep of his cottage. He spoke to reporters, talking not about the fight, but about how he would like to spend his life after boxing, helping people and acting as a minister for Allah. He noted, too, both the burdens and the joy of his fame. He knew that, at that moment, people across the world were united in their pleasure at his win. "Never again say that I will be defeated," Ali declared, "until I'm about 50 years old – then you might catch me."

The Thrilla in Manila

After Zaire, Ali's life changed. The man who had challenged the government was invited to the White House to meet the new President, **Gerald Ford**. He had transcended his sport; he was the closest thing to a folk hero his country had. He delighted in having his championship back, and he joked that he wanted to fight both Frazier and Foreman on the same night. As his body recovered from the bout in Zaire, he began to plan more fights, the first of them against Chuck Wepner, a colourful liquor salesman so prone to cuts he was known as "**The Bayonne Bleeder**."

As Ali prepared at Deer Lake, he heard that Elijah Muhammad had died. Elijah's elder son Wallace became leader of the Nation of Islam and the movement began to change. Ali saw Elijah as a fighter for his people, and Wallace as the man who taught that colour didn't matter.

"He [Wallace] taught us that we're responsible for our own lives and it's not good to blame our problems on other people. And that sounded right to me, and I followed Wallace," Ali told Thomas Hauser.

Others, like Jeremiah Shabazz and **Louis Farrakhan**, did not agree, and the Nation reached a turning point from which it would ultimately divide in two. Ali's perception changed, too. The radical young man of the 1960s now no longer saw the world exclusively along racial lines. His views became those of orthodox Islam, of acceptance and peace. "We Muslims hate injustice and evil," Ali said, "but we don't have time to hate people."

Ali fought three times in three months, easier bouts designed to allow his fans to see him in action rather than in peril. Barely bothering to train seriously, he knocked Chuck Wepner out in fifteen rounds, the Bleeder characteristically covered in blood. Wepner had scored a knockdown of his own, albeit when he trod on Ali's foot as he punched him in the chest. His courage inspired **Sylvester Stallone**, then a young actor who had watched the fight on closed-circuit TV, to write the screenplay for *Rocky*.

Next was **Ron Lyle**, who was stopped in the eleventh, and then stolid Joe Bugner, bent on survival again, who was overcome on points.

And then Joe Frazier stepped into Ali's sightlines once more.

Ali didn't really need the fight. He was 33 years old. Already, the first whispers of retirement had been heard. There was not even that much interest in a third Ali-Frazier match-up. Frazier had been hammered by Foreman, comfortably defeated by Ali and had recently struggled to beat **Jimmy Ellis**. Their ferocious first encounter lay four years in the past. And yet Ali loved to fight, and he would go on long after fighting Joe Frazier again. Perhaps he thought he and Joe had unfinished business. He might even (mistakenly) have foreseen an easy payday.

Enter Don King, and another cravenly ambitious despot, this time **Ferdinand Marcos** of the Philippines. Ali was offered a guarantee of $4m against 43 per cent of gross income (which would result in Ali ultimately earning $6m), Frazier expecting around $3m.

Ali took 50 people to Manila for the fight he'd dubbed "The Thrilla." Taking the rhyme a step further, he began to enrage Joe Frazier with: "It will be a killer/and a chiller/and a thrilla/when I get the gorilla/in Manila." For a third time, the bad blood began to rise. Ali took to carrying around a gorilla toy, which he'd take out and punch for the benefit of the press. Frazier tried to focus his anger on the fight. "I guess he's gonna talk," he told **Sports Illustrated**. "But there will come a moment when he's gonna hear that knock on the door, gonna hear it's time to go to the ring, and then he's gonna remember what it's like to be in there with me, how hard and long that night's gonna be."

Ali continued to mock Frazier, and soon Ali was tearing his man apart, calling him ignorant, ugly and worse. "I want to take his heart out," Joe said darkly.

While Frazier boiled, Ali had other problems. Always a womaniser, he had

"Joe Frazier is the greatest of all times, next to me," Ali admits after the hardest fight of his life

taken his mistress, **Veronica Porsche,** to Manila with him, where he'd introduced her to Ferdinand Marcos as his wife. The story broke in the press, and **Belinda Ali** flew to Manila to confront him. Showing some dignity, she travelled to Ali's hotel, passed on her views and flew straight back home on the same plane that had brought her.

Having survived the ire of his wife, at least temporarily, Ali had to face the cold fury of Joe Frazier. While the setting this time round couldn't quite match the grandeur and symbolism of Zaire, the fight itself exceeded all that had gone before. It was an exhibition of sporting excellence and pure human courage, a contest that demanded everything of both men. In Manila, Ali and Frazier each fought the bout of their lives, and although Ali won and Frazier lost, each became greater that day.

> **"(IT WAS) THE CLOSEST THING TO DEATH THAT I COULD FEEL"**
> **Muhammad Ali on the cumulative effect of Joe Frazier's punches**

They met at 10.45am for the benefit of the closed circuit broadcasts in the US. Ali entered the ring as the betting favourite. Joe Frazier didn't care about that. He bulled into Ali from the start, and the fight assumed the same shape as their second bout as Ali took the early rounds. This time, though, Frazier's sheer ferocity brought him back on terms. In his own memorable phrase, Frazier hit Ali "with punches that would bring cities down."

In the late rounds, the men dropped all pretence at strategy and just threw leather at one another. Ali stood on the edge of exhaustion. Each of Frazier's eyes were swollen almost shut. Meanwhile, Ali described the 10th as: "The closest thing to death that I could feel."

In the 12th, Ali took the initiative, damaging Frazier's face even more. After the 13th, when Ali had almost given everything in trying to stop his man, Frazier's trainer Eddie Futch considered stopping the fight, but thought that Frazier might have one last chance, as Ali looked as close to collapse as Joe did.

The 14th was the final round Muhammad Ali and Joe Frazier would ever fight with one another, and it stands as one of the great rounds of boxing. Frazier could barely see, and Ali threw upwards of 30 hard punches into his ruined face. Still Frazier came forwards. Neither man was willing to yield.

At the bell, Ali could face no more, and called for Angelo to cut his gloves off, but before Angelo could even start to talk him out of it, Eddie Futch pulled his man Joe Frazier out of the fight. Futch told Frazier he was going to stop it but Frazier replied: "I want him boss." Futch ignored him. "I didn't want Joe's brains

Ferdie Pacheco was a young doctor with an interest in boxing whose friendship with Angelo Dundee saw him working in the corner gratis for many of Dundee's fighters. When Dundee hooked up with Cassius Clay, Pacheco encountered the man he would call "The most perfect physical specimen I've ever seen" for the first time. He remained Ali's doctor until his concerns about Ali's declining health caused him to resign after Ali fought Earnie Shavers in 1977. But Pacheco continued his involvement in boxing; working in the corners of 11 other world champions before becoming an Emmy-winning television analyst, covering major bouts for both NBC and Showtime.

Something of a Renaissance man, the Tampa-born Pacheco also published 14 books, wrote a script for the little-known 1996 movie *Virtually Yours* and appeared on television as a cultural critic. He now works as an artist, and a documentary on his life has just been made by the HBO network.

scrambled," he told Thomas Hauser. "He had a nice life and a wonderful family to live for." It was over. Ali collapsed in his corner. Frazier was led away, almost blind and still protesting.

Ali was bruised all over his upper body, from his hips to the top of his head. Ferdie Pacheco estimated that it took him 24 hours to start thinking properly again. Frazier was too badly battered to attend Ferdinand Marcos's after-fight party, where Ali sat, according to Ed Schuyler, "like a man afraid that if he let his breath out, his stomach would fall out with it."

Ali conceded that Joe was "the roughest and toughest" man he'd ever fought. "He brought out the best in me," he went on, "and the best we ever fought was in Manila. I could feel something different happening to me, something different from what I'd felt in fights before."

It was the last truly great fight that either man ever contested. Writer **David Halberstam** has made the point that Ali's greatness wouldn't shine as brightly without "Frazier's equivalent greatness, these fights ennobled him as much as they did Ali." But Frazier never forgot – or forgave – Ali, even admitting, when Ali carried the flame at the 1996 Olympics, he would have liked to push him over. Ali's fourth wife, **Lonnie**, says "It seemed kind of strange for him [Frazier] to say those things. I thought it was to promote his book. Joe has said some vicious things about Muhammad, very inhumane things, and he lost sight of what he was doing. That's not to say what Muhammad did was justified either. I can understand him being angry."

The Greatest of all Times

Muhammad Ali should have retired after Manila. That became the firmly held view of many close to him. He had taken part in some of the greatest, hardest and most dramatic fights of all time. He was champion again. He had nothing else to prove.

And yet Ali fought on throughout 1976, taking daft fights like the one against **Jean-Pierre Coopman**, easy ones like the **Richard Dunn** bout (the last fighter he would ever stop inside the distance), dull ones like the fight with **Jimmy Young**, and risky ones, such as his narrow second rematch with **Ken Norton**. All the while, he flirted with the end, without ever taking the step. In 1977, he fought and won twice, against **Alfredo Evangelista** and the dangerous **Earnie Shavers**, who almost knocked him out.

Ali was tired. Training was becoming much harder. He had divorced Belinda and married Veronica Porsche, and they had two daughters, Hana and Laila, to add to Ali's growing brood. After the Shavers fight, Ferdie Pacheco wrote to Ali with a medical report that detailed noticeable kidney damage; Pacheco also included his resignation as Ali's doctor.

The response of Ali's camp was, "We're only taking easy fights." And so Ali took another easy fight, against a rookie pro named **Leon Spinks**. Spinks offered Ali an angle – he'd won an Olympic gold medal, just like Floyd Patterson, Joe Frazier and George Foreman. Ali boasted that he wanted a full set of scalps and began talking up the bout. The public didn't bite, for once. Spinks had fought only seven times as a professional and offered little threat. Ali barely bothered to prepare in the gym.

Leon Spinks beat Muhammad Ali on points on **Valentine's Day** 1978 in Las Vegas. For the first and only time, Ali had lost his title in the ring. He was deeply hurt. "Losing to Leon Spinks hurt the most," he told Thomas Hauser. "That's because it was my own fault. Leon did the best he could, but it was embarrassing that someone with so little fighting skills could beat me." The next day, he rose at 2am to go running, determined to win the title back.

The rematch, was fraught with problems. Ali was almost frozen out when the WBC threatened to strip Spinks if he failed to defend against the number one challenger Ken Norton, but the public demanded Spinks-Ali II and the match was made. Leon didn't take too well to the title, absconding from training camp and becoming even more of a party animal, even hiring a young **Mr T**, the most conspicuous member of **The A-Team** TV show, as his security.

After a goodwill trip to Moscow, Ali returned to the US and trained harder than he had for some years. While Spinks slacked off, Ali sparred more than 200 rounds, pushing through the pain barrier for what he said would be his last fight, and the crowning achievement for "The Greatest of all Times": the first man in history to win the Heavyweight Championship on three separate occasions.

On 15 September 1978, Muhammad Ali defied the gods and the odds one last time, outpointing Spinks in a fight given its only tension by the unprecedented achievement at hand. By all objective measures it was as bad a fight as the Rumble and the Thrilla had been great ones, and yet a worldwide audience shuffled towards the edge of their seats as a great warrior won one last battle. Ali was three times champion. Who could say now that he was not The Greatest?

Other fights were mooted, but Ali had already hinted broadly that it was the end when he told reporters soon after the Spinks fight, "None of the black athletes before me ever got out while they were on top. My people need one black man to come out on top."

On 27 June 1979, Ali made it official when he declined a mandatory title defence and stepped aside.

Thomas Hauser's *Life And Times Of Muhammad Ali* unearthed a remarkable statistic about Ali's ring career. His gross purses, some $50m-plus dollars, exceeded those of every other heavyweight champion added together. He should have eased into a comfortable afterlife as a wealthy man. At the time he announced his retirement, he was appearing in *Freedom Road*, a TV mini-series in which he starred with Kris Kristofferson, and he and Veronica had moved to Los Angeles, into a mansion in Hancock Park. Yet he carried on fighting.

Muhammad Ali fought twice more as a professional boxer, and both bouts

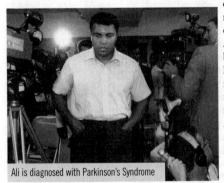

Ali is diagnosed with Parkinson's Syndrome

damaged him. Neither reflected well on the sport or on anyone concerned. Ali's health had already been compromised by his long career. For every round he had fought in the ring, he had probably fought 10 in the gym, and Ali often allowed his sparring partners to hit him hard in order to condition his body to the rigours of fight night.

Ferdie Pacheco had already pointed out the damage to his kidneys. Also, Ali's speech was beginning to slur, and the early states of his present condition, Parkinson's Syndrome (the symptoms without the disease) brought on by boxing, were already apparent.

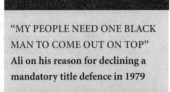

"MY PEOPLE NEED ONE BLACK MAN TO COME OUT ON TOP"
Ali on his reason for declining a mandatory title defence in 1979

The series of events that took Ali back to the ring were complex. Some lay in his character. As **George Plimpton**, one of the writers closest to Ali, observed, "He loved to fight." There was also certainly an element of his personality that needed the spotlight to be on him. There were financial considerations, too. Ali had never cared much for money. He was an incredibly generous man. Aside from the huge entourages that he took around the world at his own expense, giving away money made him happy. He often stopped his drivers so that he might put some cash into the pockets of homeless people. He was taken for a ride by many con-men who realised he was an easy touch. He had been divorced twice and he had a large family to support. Herbert Muhammad also made a lot of money from Muhammad Ali, but as Ferdie Pacheco told Thomas Hauser, "If Herbert had worked for free… Ali would have given it all away… Money just wasn't Ali's main concern."

For a while, Ali's affairs were managed by the powerful agency **IMG** and the First Bank of Chicago, and they attempted to straighten out the myriad deals, but ultimately his finances remained a labyrinthine affair.

There was also the question of how Ali would fill his time. He fancied himself as something of a diplomat ("The **black Henry Kissinger**" he half-joked). Exactly how much – or little – his fame was worth, though, became apparent in 1980, when US President **Jimmy Carter** supported the American Olympic team's boycott of the Moscow games after the Soviet invasion of Afghanistan. He asked Ali to raise support for the boycott during a trip Ali made to several African nations. It was a mission that met with only limited success.

All of these factors may have had a bearing on Ali's decision to fight again, but in the end, as Angelo Dundee pointed out, he came back because he wanted to.

The promoter **Bob Arum** signed Ali to fight the WBA champion **John Tate**, but Tate got beaten and Ali accepted a bout with a far tougher opponent, **Larry Holmes**, who had begun his career as a sparring partner for Ali in 1973.

Holmes was a terrific fighter and an underrated champion. He didn't want to fight Ali, not because he feared an unlikely defeat but because he knew that Ali's pride was such that he would not quit; Holmes would be obliged to deliver a beating in order to stop him. It was Ali versus Cleveland Williams, but the boot was on the other foot this time.

Pacheco publicly opposed the bout. But despite a medical examination by the **Mayo Clinic** that cited evidence of deteriorating co-ordination and slight difficulties with speech and memory, the Nevada State Athletic Commission licensed him to fight. And aside from the medical evidence, boxing people knew Ali was shot. He had not stopped a fighter since 1976.

Ali talked the fight up, but his words were hollow. He occasionally looked good in the gym, but it was a false impression. He suffered terribly over the 11 rounds he fought out with Holmes in Las Vegas on 2 October 1980. It was an awful night for everyone involved. Ali took a terrible beating that ended only when Herbert Muhammad gestured that the fight should be stopped after 11 rounds. Even then, Bundini the dreamer pleaded for one more. Holmes visited Ali afterwards and said "I know something's wrong. I really didn't want to hit you." Ali, Holmes recalled, was just lying on the bed in his room, tired.

After the fight, Ali checked into the **UCLA medical centre**, where tests revealed that his fatigued condition was due in part to the incorrect prescription of medication. Ali acknowledged that he had fought like he was "washed up." Even the money didn't stretch far, especially when Don King persuaded Ali to accept $50,000 in cash in lieu of the final million dollars of his $8m cheque.

Life continued to spiral downwards. In 1981, it was discovered that a man called Ross Fields, under the assumed identity of Harold Smith, had misused Ali's name in order to embezzle **$21m** from the **Wells Fargo Bank** in what became known as the **MAPS scandal**. It was the biggest embezzlement in American history ("Ain't many names can steal that much," Ali remarked dryly).

Whilst the muddle was unravelled, Ali agreed to fight once more. His opponent was **Trevor Berbick**, another troubled man who would later surrender his title to the youngest ever heavyweight champion, **Mike Tyson**. Almost no-one wanted the fight. Eventually it was sited in Nassau and christened **The Drama In Bahama**. Ali made some empty noises about shaking up the world. **Don King** suffered a rare setback when he tried to muscle in on the deal, which was in the hands of a **Nation of Islam** member and ex-con named **James Cornelius**. King claimed promotional rights to Berbick's next three fights after a defeat to Larry Holmes, who King controlled. Cornelius disagreed and following an argument in a hotel room, King was said to have been beaten up.

The fight took place on 11 December 1981. The only mercy was that Berbick lacked the skill to administer too savage a beating. In these sad circumstances, a career that had brought such drama and joy to the world came to a close.

PROFILE Ali's first marriage SONJI CLAY

Herbert Muhammad introduced Ali to Sonji Roi on 3 July 1964. Sonji was 23, a year older than Ali, but had led a different life. Her father had been murdered when she was two; her mother died six years later. In her early teens Sonji had a son. She was an independent woman, and Ali fell for her immediately. They were married a month later. The union was annulled in January 1966, with Ali claiming that Sonji had "failed to live up to a promise" to follow Muslim tenets.

PROFILE Ali's second marriage BELINDA ALI (NOW KHALILAH ALI)

Belinda Boyd first saw Cassius Clay in 1961 when she was 11 years old and he came to speak at her school in Chicago. They met again when Belinda was 16 and working in a bakery owned by the Nation of Islam. Tall and handsome, she was a match for Ali, and they married a year later. They had four children together, Maryum, twins Rasheeda and Jamillah and Muhammad Jnr. Their divorce came after Belinda travelled to Manila to confront Ali about his affair with Veronica Porsche.

PROFILE Ali's third marriage VERONICA PORSCHE

"I used to chase women all the time," Ali admitted to Thomas Hauser for Hauser's official biography. By the time he met Veronica Porsche after she won a contest to become a poster girl for his fight with George Foreman, he had fathered two children out of wedlock. He and Veronica carried on an increasingly public affair before Ali's split with Belinda. They had their first daughter, Hana, before they married in 1977, and they then had another, Laila. The marriage failed soon after Ali's retirement from boxing and they divorced in 1986.

PROFILE Ali's fourth marriage LONNIE ALI

Lonnie Williams was just seven years old when Ali defeated Sonny Liston, but she remembers seeing his bus pull up outside his mother's house in Louisville. The Williams family had moved in opposite, and Lonnie got to see Ali often as she grew up. Ali's mother Odessa and Lonnie's mother Marguerite became close friends.

By 1982, Lonnie was working towards an MBA when Ali called and invited her to lunch. Shocked by Ali's physical decline, Lonnie moved to Los Angeles to care for him. After his divorce from Veronica Porsche they married, and live happily together in Berrien Springs, Michigan with their son Assad.

Ali's friends and family are united in the view expressed by Jeremiah Shabazz that "Lonnie is the best thing that ever happened to Ali. Anyone who cares about Muhammad has to be grateful for Lonnie."

A hero rises

Today, Muhammad Ali lives a life he loves. He resides on a pretty farm in **Berrien Springs, Michigan**, with his fourth wife, **Lonnie**, and their son **Assad**. Ali's Parkinson's Syndrome has robbed him of his quicksilver tongue, and yet his fame means he can touch any crowd without words. For millions, he remains an inspirational figure. In his home town of Louisville, Kentucky, the **Muhammad Ali Center**, a lasting tribute to his greatness, will open in 2005. He remains a devout man, praying five times a day, and working to spread the word of Islam with the autographed pamphlets he sends out to his fans. He travels for much of the year, overcoming his fear of flying and thunderstorms to do so. He's usually accompanied by Lonnie, and his oldest friend, Howard Bingham.

Ali's journey from the deep lows of his fights with Holmes and Berbick to the present day involved some moments dramatic enough to match those of his ring career. He and Veronica were divorced in 1986. His health began to deteriorate, and his finances were in their customary state of flux. The entourage slowly melted away. **Bundini** died in 1988, following a stroke, and two years later **Lana Shabazz**, the cook at Deer Lake, died of cancer.

Ali had first met **Lonnie Williams** in 1962, when she was a little girl and her family moved into the same street as Cassius Snr and Odessa Clay. They remained in touch and a friendship grew. After his divorce from Veronica, Ali asked Lonnie to marry him, and she accepted. The ceremony took place on 19 November 1986. Ali's life began to improve from that date onwards.

His re-entry into public life was gradual, but there were two key moments in which he has again imprinted himself on the world's consciousness. The first came in 1990, when he travelled to Iraq to meet **Saddam Hussein**, returning home with 15 of the 300 Americans held hostage there. The second came at the **Atlanta Olympics** of 1996, when he lit the flame that opened the Games. Three billion people watched on television as Ali raised a shaking hand and ignited the flame's cauldron. As Thomas Hauser, Ali's biographer wrote: "All of them were united, however briefly, in the love of one man." Such has been Ali's impact, first as a sportsman, then as a social figure and a catalyst for change.

As the Millennium spun around, magazines and broadcasters across the world ran polls and votes for the Sportsman of the Century. Muhammad Ali won almost all of them. He'd always said he was **The Greatest**. It seems that the world believed him at last.

Muhammad
Ali
The fights

Floating like a butterfly, stinging like a bee,
There has never been a fighter like Muhammad Ali

"I STARTED BOXING BECAUSE
I THOUGHT IT WAS THE FASTEST
WAY FOR BLACK PEOPLE TO
MAKE IT" **Muhammad Ali**

Cassius Clay VS Tunney Hunsaker | 29.10.60

Venue **Freedom Hall, Louisville, Kentucky**
Outcome **Won, decision, round six**
Record **Fought 1 Won 1 Lost 0 Drawn 0**
Trivia **Joe Louis, Rocky Marciano and Floyd Patterson all began
their pro careers with KOs. Clay's debut proved lower key**

Cassius had conquered **Rome**, but his professional debut was not designed to provide the **Olympic** champ with a knock-over first time out. **Tunney Hunsaker** was police chief of Fayetteville, West Virginia, and a seasoned pro boxer on the side. "I heard he won the Olympics, so I knew I was fighting a tough bird," Hunsaker said, "but I don't think there was ever a fighter, not a good one anyway, who went in the ring thinking he was gonna get beat. I know I never did."

Clay had begun his pro training with **Fred Stoner**, who had coached him and his brother **Rudolph** on and off since they had cycled to the **Grace Community Centre gym** in Louisville as boys. The main aim for Clay was to ensure he was fit enough to box six rounds, as opposed to the three of amateur competition, and that he should begin to appreciate the demands of the pro game.

His fitness was no problem, of course. Clay was already an almost perfect specimen. He had been training like a pro since his early teens. His boxing technique had never been an orthodox one. It was based around his natural gifts; his speed and intuition, his hand/eye co-ordination and his sublime footwork. While this style had worked brilliantly in amateur bouts where the emphasis was on scoring punches, the pro game would be very different. Veteran fighters like Hunsaker would not be discouraged at the first setback. They would not wilt and would probably mess with young Cassius when they could, introducing him to a world of clinching, crafty elbows, boot-on-toe and the other dubious tricks of the hardest game.

> "I TRIED JUST ABOUT EVERY TRICK I KNEW TO THROW HIM OFF BALANCE BUT HE WAS JUST TOO GOOD" **Tunney Hunsaker**

On the afternoon of the fight, **Cassius Clay** and Tunney Hunsaker met in downtown Louisville in a sports store to promote the bout. Hunsaker remembered that Clay had bounced a basketball around nervously, his demeanour betraying his growing apprehension. But come fight-time, Clay shed his skittishness and showed far too much for Hunsaker. He hammered out a six-round decision, sticking and moving but without the verve he had shown in his ascent to the summit of the amateur ranks. Hunsaker however, wearying as the rounds rolled on, was unable to disturb Clay's equilibrium and left the ring in no doubt of the young man's promise.

"He was fast as lightning... I tried just about every trick I knew to throw him off balance but he was just too good," Hunsaker said. Afterwards, Hunsaker told a friend that he was sure that Cassius Clay would become the **heavyweight champion of the world**.

Hunsaker returned to his day job, in which he served for another three decades. Cassius Clay's next three decades would prove slightly more eventful.

Clay VS Herb Siler | 27.12.60

Venue **The Auditorium, Miami Beach, Florida**
Outcome **Won, TKO, round four**
Record **Fought 2 Won 2 Lost 0 Drawn 0**
Trivia **Angelo Dundee's first fight as Ali's trainer. The bout was promoted by Angelo's brother Chris**

Tunney Hunsaker had been more impressed with Clay's performance than the **Louisville Sponsoring Group**. They weren't investing their tax-deductible **$2,800** each to see their man outpoint boxers with day jobs. The group felt Clay needed more seasoning, so he was sent to spar with the great **Archie Moore** in California. The Group were keen to see him resident in California, where the contract he had signed with them as a minor was binding (in many states, including Kentucky, contracts with minors could be ignored). Moore was 47-years-old and still fighting. At his training camp near **San Diego**, which he named the **Salt Mine**, he would hold forth like an ancient sage, offering a masterclass in angles and deception, the tricks of a fighter robbed of power and youth by time. Moore loved Clay's enthusiasm – he marvelled as he ran up and down the steep hills around camp until Moore instructed him to stop. But Clay, headstrong, wouldn't take Moore's instruction. "I don't want to fight like Archie Moore, I want to be the heavyweight **Sugar Ray (Robinson)**," he complained.

In fact, Moore admired Clay's low-slung style and understood he was something special. But within a few weeks, he rang **Bill Faversham** of the Sponsoring Group and told him he was wasting his money. Moore said: "My wife is crazy about him, my kids are crazy about him and I'm crazy about him, but he won't do what I tell him to do."

When Faversham suggested what Clay needed was a spanking, Moore replied: "He sure does. But I don't know who's going to give him one, including me…"

Herb Siler, another journeyman, certainly couldn't offer Clay the required correction. By fight night, the Sponsoring Group had persuaded **Angelo Dundee** to train Clay out of the **Fifth Street Gym** in **Miami** run by Dundee with his brother Chris. When Clay proclaimed before the fight, "I'm gonna beat **Floyd Patterson**,

> "MY WIFE AND KIDS ARE CRAZY ABOUT HIM, I'M CRAZY ABOUT HIM, BUT HE WON'T DO WHAT I TELL HIM TO DO" **Archie Moore**

I'm gonna be champion," Dundee laughed and encouraged his man. He felt it would boost the young fighter psychologically to express himself in that way. The scrap with Siler required no such leap of faith and Clay took his man out in four for his first win inside the distance.

Clay VS Tony Esperti | 17.01.61

Venue **The Auditorium, Miami Beach, Florida**
Outcome **Won, TKO, round three**
Record **Fought 3 Won 3 Lost 0 Drawn 0**
Trivia **The fight took place on Clay's 19th birthday**

Angelo Dundee understood instinctively how to handle the headstrong **Clay**. Without ego himself, Dundee had an array of psychological tricks to gee Clay up. He avoided ever telling Cassius what to do; instead he made suggestions. "He never bosses me, tells me when to run, how much to box," Clay said. "I do what I want to do. I'm free."

Dundee realised that he didn't have to encourage Clay to train. The fighter would begin the day at 5am with a run, before running from his digs to Dundee's gym through a rough part of the city later in the day. Dundee applied a maxim given to him by a trainer called **Charlie Goldman:** "If a guy's a short guy, make him shorter. If he's a tall guy, make him taller…" Dundee extended it to allow for Clay's genius. He let the fighter be himself, going against conventional wisdom that a boxer should punch to the body, wear his opponent down. Clay was a headhunter: "Punch a man's head and it mixes his mind," he told Dundee.

> "IF A GUY'S A SHORT GUY, MAKE HIM SHORTER. IF HE'S A TALL GUY, MAKE HIM TALLER"
>
> **Angelo Dundee**

Clay's physical presence was increasing. He used calisthenics, work on the heavy bag, sparring and running to put on more than a stone of muscle in a few months. The youth was becoming a man. His speed hid a growing power.

Back at **Miami Beach** just three weeks after fighting Herb Siler, Clay marked his improvements with a third-round knockout of **Tony Esperti.** Even Dundee was impressed: "No one is faster than Cassius," he said.

Clay VS Jim Robinson | 07.02.61

Venue **Convention Hall, Miami Beach, Florida**
Outcome **Won, TKO, round one**
Record **Fought 4 Won 4 Lost 0 Drawn 0**
Trivia **Third bout in an 11-week blitz, just three weeks after stopping Esperti**

As Clay's professional career began to bloom, it became apparent that he was an exceptional athlete, even at this early stage. **Ferdie Pacheco** was a Miami doctor who loved boxing and who worked the corner of Dundee's fighters as a hobby. He became Cassius Clay's doctor.

"He was the most perfect physical specimen I have ever seen," Pacheco said. "You just couldn't improve on the guy."

The Miami fight crowd were beginning to notice the young man on the undercard, although they had yet to take him to their hearts. Dundee was still matching him carefully, trying to find opponents who could show him something he hadn't yet seen. The match with **Jim Robinson**, another worthy club fighter, only showed Clay how well his confidence was coming along. No longer at all daunted by the pro ring (if he ever had been), Clay took to Robinson from the first bell, hitting him at will. The fight was over within two minutes.

Clay VS Donnie Fleeman | 21.02.61

Venue **The Auditorium, Miami Beach, Florida**
Prediction **"If I can't beat this bum I better change my plans. He ain't even ranked"**
Outcome **Won, TKO, round seven**
Record **Fought 5 Won 5 Lost 0 Drawn 0**
Trivia **Clay sparred with ex-champ Ingemar Johansson in preparation**

Clay was moving with increasing ease through the hoops Angelo Dundee and the **Louisville Sponsoring Group** were holding out. Yet the first real signpost to the size of his talent would come before he stepped through the ropes to dispose of **Donnie Fleeman**. **Ingemar Johansson** had come to Florida to fight **Floyd Patterson** for the heavyweight championship of the world. The bout was a rematch: Johansson had destroyed Patterson in their first scrap.

There are conflicting tales as to how Cassius Clay ended up sparring with, and humiliating, Johansson. Both involve the press man for the Patterson vs

Johansson fight, **Harold Conrad**. Conrad maintained that he asked **Angelo Dundee** if he knew of anyone willing to spar with Johansson. Other commentators thought Conrad had heard about Clay before he approached Dundee. Whatever the truth, Clay was soon yelling, "I'll go dancing, with Johansson" across the **Fifth Street Gym**.

From the second the pair crossed the ring towards each other, the 19-year-old Clay was boss. He jabbed **Johansson** half to death and while he did so he taunted his man: "You shouldn't be fighting **Patterson**, I should…" It was an astonishing display against a boxer just weeks from fighting for the title. Johansson was made to look foolish as he swung at Clay and missed, not just by inches but by feet. **Gil Rogin** of *Sports Illustrated* said: "I've never seen anything like it before or since." After two rounds of sparring, Johansson's trainer **Whitey Bimstein** called the session to a halt.

Angelo Dundee had selected **Fleeman** as Clay's fifth professional opponent because he was a teak-tough Texan who wouldn't take a backward step. But Fleeman, like Ingemar Johansson, couldn't cope with Clay's speed. He plodded forward like a soldier into the guns and Clay picked him off at will. The fight was over in seven rounds, mainly because **Clay** decided that seven was enough.

Clay VS Lamar Clark | 19.04.61

Venue **Freedom Hall, Louisville, Kentucky**
Prediction **"This Clark will fall in two"**
Outcome **Won, KO, round two**
Record **Fought 6 Won 6 Lost 0 Drawn 0**
Trivia **Clay's bragging had many fight fans turning up hoping to see him beaten**

Clay's return to **Louisville** did not appear to be a straightforward one. **Lamar Clark** was a cut above anyone Clay had been in the ring with before, with the exception of the sparring session with **Ingemar Johansson**.

He came to the fight with a quite astonishing record of 45 knockout wins in a row, albeit against opponents of variable quality. Nonetheless, they'd still needed hitting and **Clark** was rough and tough and a handful for anyone. Or at least, he should have been. **Clay** simply destroyed him.

Back in the same ring where he'd outpointed **Tunney Hunsaker** on his debut, Clay raised the stakes for himself: for the very first time, he **predicted** the round in which he would win the fight.

Angelo Dundee had no doubt the trick would work as a psychological tool, and it concentrated Clay's mind wonderfully. Nothing delighted him more than living up to his own hype. **Ferdie Pacheco** told the writer **David Remnick**: "The more confident he became, the more his natural ebullience took over. Everything was such fun to him. Maybe it wouldn't have been as much fun if someone had knocked him lopsided, but no one did."

Shortly into the second round, **Clay** broke Clark's nose with a stiff straight right hand and within a minute or so had put Clark on the floor twice. The referee stepped in to spare Clark as he visited the mat once more and Clay had made his first fight prediction come true.

Clay VS Kolo 'Duke' Sabedong | 26.06.61

Venue **Convention Center, Las Vegas, Nevada**
Opponent's nickname **Duke**
Outcome **Won, decision, round 10**
Record **Fought 7 Won 7 Lost 0 Drawn 0**
Trivia **Clay meets the wrestler Gorgeous George – and learns a new trick**

The fights came thick and fast for Louisville's rising star. Now, for the first time he fought in **Las Vegas**, boxing's new Mecca, against **Sabedong**, a giant Hawaiian who would cause him some concern. Ultimately, Clay would come through easily enough. However, a far more more significant meeting came a couple of days before he would undergo the experience of having Sabedong whack him below the belt in an attempt to provoke an upset.

As part of his promotional duties, Clay appeared on a Las Vegas radio programme. Another guest on the show was a wrestler called **Gorgeous George**. A flamboyant character known as **Liberace in tights**, George was a showman: he wore hair curlers into the ring and would allow a minion to comb them out before the fight began; he instructed another to daub him with aftershave and then to spray insecticide on to the mat. And when talking up a fight, he would work himself into a frenzy over his opponent: "If this bum beats me, I'll crawl down Las Vegas Boulevard on my hands and knees. But it won't happen. I'll tear his arm off. For I am the greatest wrestler in the world!"

Young Clay, no shrinking violet himself, was entranced by George's style, and became even more so when he heard that George's bouts were always sold out. He went to Gorgeous George's show as the wrestler's guest. "I saw 15,000 people coming to see this man get beat," he said, "and his talking did it."

Duke Sabedong was big, strong and unlikely to be fazed by Clay's lip. He started fighting dirty and he used his experience to give **Clay** a tough test. The younger fighter was in no danger of losing; Sabedong lacked the speed and skill truly to trouble him, but it was all useful experience nonetheless.

The **Louisville Lip** learned he wouldn't always have everything his own way, but in his usual fashion shrugged off his difficulty – he blamed his sluggish showing on Dundee's decision to fly them to Las Vegas rather than take the train.

Clay VS Alonzo Johnson | 22.07.61

Venue **Freedom Hall, Louisville, Kentucky**
Outcome **Won, decision, round 10**
Record **Fought 8 Won 8 Lost 0 Drawn 0**
Trivia **On hearing the result, the crowd booed the Olympic champion**

C assius Clay was beginning to attract attention, partly for his outspokenness, but mostly for his irresistible skill in the ring. He was about to become the first fighter just out of the amateur ranks to have his fights shown on national television. **Teddy Brenner**, who was the matchmaker at **Madison Square Garden**, had the responsibility of finding 50 fights per year for the **Gillette Cavalcade of Sports** programme. Most of these bouts took place at the Garden, but others took place around the US. Brenner decided the time was right for the Olympic hero to make his small-screen debut. **Alonzo Johnson** was another seasoned pro, a cute operator minus a destructive punch. He was also the first nationally ranked fighter to step into the ring with Clay.

It was to prove another tough night. It was a sultry southern summer in **Louisville** and the ring grew even hotter under the wash of the TV lights. The fight went the **full 10 rounds** and by their end, Clay was lathered in sweat. When the referee raised his arm, his hometown crowd turned on him. They booed and hissed the decision and for the first time, the golden boy realised that boxing could be a fickle business.

Clay VS Alex Miteff

07.10.61

Venue Freedom Hall, Louisville, Kentucky
Prediction KO, round six
Outcome Won, TKO, round six
Record Fought 9 Won 9 Lost 0 Drawn 0
Trivia Clay shook off a big right hand in round two – he could take a punch, too

Angelo allowed his man some recovery time after the long fight with Alonzo Johnson. When Clay returned to his hometown ring for his seventh bout of the year, it would once more be before the television cameras, and this time against a noted puncher. **Alex Miteff** was Argentinian, and no mug. He possessed a murderous right hand, as Clay was to discover.

Teddy Brenner, who had once more made the match, recalled the unusual build-up for Clay's biographer, **Thomas Hauser**: "We realised that no one had brought boxing gloves. The stores were closed, it was too late to bring gloves in from someplace else. Finally, we found two pairs that were half horsehair and half foam rubber. Most gloves were all horsehair, but these were half and half. They'd been lying around in some gym and they were as hard as rock…"

Brenner felt the gloves would favour Miteff, the big puncher, despite Clay's pre-fight prediction of a sixth-round stoppage.

Brenner was on the point of being proved right when, in the second round, Miteff landed a peach of a right hand on Clay's jaw. Clay took the punch and recovered quickly. It was one of the first

> "NO ONE HAD BROUGHT GLOVES. WE FOUND TWO PAIRS, HALF HORSEHAIR, HALF RUBBER, HARD AS ROCK" **Teddy Brenner**

signs that he possessed a **cast-iron chin**, along with all of his gifts. It was an ability that would have great implications later in Clay's career – and in his life.

Miteff was known as a slow starter, whose powerful body punches brought him more into the fight as the bout progressed. By the start of the sixth round, the fight was even, but Clay quickly turned the night on its head. He caught Miteff with a **single right hand** and the Argentinian was still trying to figure out what had happened to him when he was back in the dressing room. "Did Cassius Clay knock me out?" he asked his trainer. The ebullient Cassius was the darling of his hometown crowd once again.

Clay VS Willi Besmanoff

29.11.61

Venue **Freedom Hall, Louisville, Kentucky**
Prediction **"Besmanoff must fall in seven"**
Outcome **Won, TKO, round seven**
Record **Fought 10 Won 10 Lost 0 Drawn 0**
Trivia **Clay predicts he'll win the heavyweight title before his 21st birthday**

A sked for a prediction as he approached the last bout of his first full year as a professional, Cassius Clay told a television interviewer: "I'm embarrassed to get in the ring with this unrated duck. I'm ready for top contenders like **Floyd Patterson** and **Sonny Liston**. Besmanoff must fall in seven!"

Willi Besmanoff didn't take kindly to the insult. He was a stocky German with a decent enough record and he was a proud man too. Unfortunately for him, he had been inactive for some six months and he was about to face a fighter already filled with belief in his own indestructibility.

Besmanoff leaped at Clay, determined to impose himself on the fight, but he was soon snatching at shadows. The prodigiously gifted Clay simply ghosted away from the stout swinger and hammered him at will. The fight could and would have been over after a couple of rounds, had Clay not been determined to give the ringside reporters a story by making his pre-fight prediction come good.

As the crowd began to get restless and with **Angelo Dundee** urging him loudly to "stop playing around," Clay carried Besmanoff into the seventh. Once there, he jumped from his stool and dropped poor Willi with a quicksilver right. The game German got up again, but was immediately put back down with two cruel lefts and another right. The referee stopped the fight and Clay left the ring to address reporters. "When I lay a man down," he said, "he's supposed to stay down. I should be champ before I'm 21... you write that down in your notebooks!"

> "WHEN I LAY A MAN DOWN, HE'S SUPPOSED TO STAY DOWN. I SHOULD BE CHAMP BEFORE I'M 21... YOU WRITE THAT DOWN IN YOUR NOTEBOOKS!"
>
> **Cassius Clay, the Louisville Lip**

Reporting back to Bill Faversham of the Louisville Sponsoring Group, Angelo Dundee said: "When he wasn't playing around, he **looked like a champion**." Teddy Brenner, meanwhile, decided to take Cassius Clay to Madison Square Garden at the first opportunity.

Clay VS Sonny Banks

10.02.62

Venue **Madison Square Garden,
New York City**
Prediction **"Banks must fall in four"**
Outcome **Won, TKO, round four**
Record **Fought 11 Won 11 Lost 0 Drawn 0**
Trivia **The press begin to refer to Ali as
'the Louisville Lip' and 'Gaseous Cassius'**

Brenner's opportunity came a little more quickly than he'd expected. A heavyweight bout he'd made for the Garden fell through at five days' notice. He rang Angelo Dundee and asked him if Clay would fight **Sonny Banks** in a replacement fight. Dundee was flattered by Brenner's offer: here was a major acknowledgement of Clay's ability and appeal. But he asked Brenner for some time to discuss the opportunity with Bill Faversham.

The pair were confident Cassius could handle Banks, who had only had two more pro fights than **Clay**, but they had to consider the downside, too. Defeat at the **Garden** on national television could severely hamper Clay's progress and could cause considerable damage to his confidence too. After all, he had been a pro boxer for less than a year and a half. Dundee and Faversham decided to back their man. They took the bout, figuring the experience and the exposure offered a fine return on their risk.

In truth, the **New York** boxing scene was staid, shady and still whiffed of the Mob involvement that had blackened the sport throughout the **1950s**. Cassius Clay hit the city hard. He showed up at the monthly lunch of the **New York Boxing Writers' Association** at **Jack Johnson**'s restaurant on Broadway in a rented tuxedo and offered the assembled journalists his manifesto: he was going to be the heavyweight champion, perhaps the youngest ever to hold the belt. He described exactly what he was about to do to Sonny Banks. "The man must fall in the round I call," he rhymed. "In fact Banks must fall in four."

It was manna from heaven, a story that came and slapped itself down right there on the hungry hacks' plates. For the next few days, the papers were full of **Gaseous Cassius**, the **Louisville Lip** and **Mighty Mouth**.

Gorgeous George's crowd-pulling tricks worked for Clay, too. The fans rolled up at the Garden eager to see the Lip get knocked flat on his back. They weren't to be disappointed. Clay allowed himself to be carried away by his own invective.

Banks was overmatched, but he could punch. Clay began round one by mugging and sticking out his chin. Banks hit him on it with a long left hand and Cassius Clay hit the deck for the first time in his life. "On the way down his eyes were closed," remembered **Angelo Dundee**, "but when his butt hit the canvas, he woke up." Clay's cornerman **Gil Clancy** recalled Dundee turning white as his man fell.

But the Lip was more shocked than hurt. He jumped up and began to dance around Banks. Within a couple of rounds he had regained his equilibrium. He waited until the 26th second of round four to drop Banks, whose own powers of recovery couldn't match those of his opponent. Clay wasn't slow to let the reporters know about his correct call: "I told you. The man fell in four!"

Clay VS Don Warner | 28.02.62

Venue **Miami Auditorium, Miami Beach, Florida**
Prediction **KO, round five**
Outcome **Won, KO, round four**
Record **Fought 12 Won 12 Lost 0 Drawn 0**
Trivia **Warner refused to shake hands at the weigh-in and felt Clay's wrath**

Angelo Dundee got Cassius Clay out of **New York** as soon as he could and refused to allow him to go back, despite several offers from the promoters at Madison Square Garden. He had been alarmed by the Banks knockdown and figured that New York had emboldened the over-confident youngster to an unacceptable degree. Instead, he hustled Clay back to **Florida** and the the Fifth Street Gym. His next fight would be against **Don Warner**, a two-handed puncher who had a good record of wins inside the distance. "He was a tough **left-hooker** from Philadelphia," Angelo Dundee recalled.

Yet Clay quickly showed how much he had learned. Having made his now-required prediction – this time that Warner would be disposed of in five – Clay began well. Every time Warner tried to get his big left away, Clay jabbed and feinted, leaving Warner off-balance and unable to land a good punch. The knockout came a round ahead of the prediction; the bloodied Warner was knocked through the ropes during round four.

When a reporter challenged Clay about his failure to predict the correct round, Clay responded that, as Warner had refused to shake hands with him at the weigh-in, he had been docked one round for poor sportsmanship. His **wit was becoming as quick as his fists**.

Clay VS George Logan

23.04.62

Venue **Memorial Sports Arena, Los Angeles, California**
Outcome **Won, TKO, round four**
Record **Fought 13 Won 13 Lost 0 Drawn 0**
Trivia **The bout was promoted by the legendary former champion Joe Louis**

Clay's first professional engagement in Los Angeles proved almost as exciting as his debut in New York, for the press at least as he rolled into town full of fun and good-natured arrogance. One of the reporters dispatched to cover a press conference at the Sports Arena was **Howard Bingham**, a budding photo-journalist who worked for a black newspaper, **The Sentinel**. After the conference, he saw **Clay** and his brother **Rudy** standing on a street corner and offered them a ride. Clay and Bingham formed a lifelong friendship.

The meeting with **George Logan** was less significant. Clay entered the ring as 6-1-on favourite. Logan threw lots of left hooks and found himself hitting nothing more substantial than air. Clay's quicksilver hands cut his fragile brows to ribbons and the referee stepped in with Logan struggling to see the blur of leather flying his way. It was all over in four rounds once more.

Clay VS Billy Daniels

19.05.62

Venue **St Nicholas Arena, New York City**
Outcome **Won, TKO, round seven**
Record **Fought 14 Won 14 Lost 0 Drawn 0**
Trivia **Clay was now eighth-ranked heavyweight in the world**

The bible of boxing, **The Ring** magazine now had Clay as the eighth heavyweight **contender** in the world in their famous rankings. He had won 13 on the trot, 10 by way of knockout or stoppage. **Billy Daniels** was also unbeaten, but less experienced. He'd won seven straight, all by KO, and he was a local boy. Dundee described him as "a cute sucker," and the bout turned out to be closely fought, with Clay a lick or two from his best. Daniels was taller than Clay and he began well, scoring with some neat headshots. Clay struggled to strike up his usual humming rhythm. By the seventh, Daniels was slightly ahead on points, and, as **Angelo Dundee** observed later, "it was a tough fight until

Muhammad busted him up…" Suddenly finding some form, Clay opened up a cut over Daniels' eye and the referee had no option but to step in.

Clay VS Alejandro Lavorante | 20.06.62

Venue **Memorial Sports Arena, Los Angeles, California**
Prediction **KO, round five**
Outcome **Won, KO, round five**
Record **Fought 15 Won 15 Lost 0 Drawn 0**
Trivia **Lavorante would die after suffering brain damage in his next fight**

Clay crossed America for his next fight, a return to LA and a chance to renew acquaintance with his friend **Howard Bingham**. He enjoyed that and relished crossing swords once more with the media. The **Louisville Lip** predicted a fifth-round win over **Alejandro Lavorante**, who had by far the best credentials of any fighter Clay had faced. Indeed, many of the reporters who gleefully noted his prediction felt Lavorante might well be the man to bring Cassius Clay down to earth. He was a big and grizzled Argentinian who had reached as high as the number three heavyweight contender in the rankings. He had lost only narrowly to **Archie Moore** and had defeated **Zora Folley**, both of whom Clay would also face before his exile.

If Clay had battled his biorhythms against **Billy Daniels**, everything about him was in perfect harmony as he stepped through the ropes before a crowd of 12,000 – testament to his drawing power on the West coast. There had been some talk of Lavorante punishing Clay for his habit of keeping his hands low and his head up, but instead the Argentinian went to the body, landing some digging hooks that alerted Clay to his presence.

Lavorante quickly began to wish he'd kept a lower profile. Clay simply battered him in a sublime exhibition of boxing. Lavorante was wobbled in the second and then found he couldn't keep Clay's jab out of his eyes. Soon he was tired and bleeding from the assault before hitting the canvas twice in a fourth round that must have seemed endless to him. Exactly on cue in round five, a right hand left Lavorante unable to continue.

In the crowd, Clay had spotted **Archie Moore**. Buzzing from his win, he taunted the veteran, yelling, "You're next, old man!"

There were to be no happy returns for Alejandro Lavorante, though. His end was an awful one. He sustained terrible head injuries in his next bout against Johnny Riggens and he spent more than a year in a coma before passing away.

Clay VS Archie Moore

15.11.62

Venue Memorial Sports Arena,
Los Angeles, California
Opponent's nickname The Mongoose
Prediction "Moore to fall in four"
Outcome Won, KO, round four
Record Fought 16 Won 16 Lost 0 Drawn 0
Trivia Archie had been the undisputed light
heavyweight champion for eight years and
was still boxing at the age of 47. After his
ill-fated attempts at training Cassius Clay for
his second professional fight, Moore went on
to train 1968 Olympic heavyweight champ
George Foreman

Archie Moore told **Thomas Hauser**, Ali's biographer, that the match with Clay wasn't a fight either man wanted; **Moore** took it because he needed the money, pure and simple, Clay saw the attraction of a marquee name on his record. It was not a fight for the cognoscenti: the up-and-comer versus the faded legend was a storyline they'd seen played out hundreds of times and the outcome was rarely pretty.

Here was the ultimate example. Clay had fought professionally 15 times, Moore over 200. Clay was 20-years-old, still a minor; Moore was 47 and had been a professional boxer for six years longer than Clay had been alive. Clay had of course briefly been under Moore's wing in Moore's capacity as trainer, and adding further zest was the willingness of both to indulge in a battle of words before the fight – they were the two best self-promoters in the sport. It meant at least the pre-fight skirmish was well-matched. Clay opened up with the prediction of a fourth-round win.

"The only way I'll fall in four is by toppling over Clay's prostrate form," Moore retorted. "Even his contemporaries hope I beat the socks off him." Clay was not slow to respond: "I wish people would get together and work out a pension for him or something, or I'm going to have to do it once and for all…"

"Sometimes he sounds humorous," the famously verbose **Archie Moore** retaliated, "but sometimes he sounds like a man who can write beautifully but not punctuate…"

Clay finished up with a rhyme: "Archie's been living off the fat of the land/I'm here to give him his pension plan/When you come to the fight, don't block the aisles or door/ You will all go home after round four…"

This "tournament of words" as Moore described it, worked well. A massive 16,200 tickets were sold for the bout, producing a record indoor gross for California of **$182,600**. Clay was a 3-1 favourite, but even those thin odds seemed generous. In his prime Archie Moore had been a light-heavyweight, but now, his girth was amply padded, his hair was grey, his shorts were pulled up somewhere around his chest to hide a multitude of sins. Archie knew his one chance would come if Clay got careless and he could seize the opportunity to land one of those sneaky right hands that seemed to drop out of a clear blue sky.

The **contrast** between the fighters was extreme. Clay was the perfect human specimen: he gleamed with youth and health, he was loaded with sleek, conditioned muscle. His reflexes were ungodly. Standing next to Archie, he looked almost divine.

The fight began. Clay was initially respectful, on his guard for Moore's cunning but after a couple of minutes he realised that the years had robbed Moore of anything that might seriously trouble him. His jab zipped home again and again. Moore replied just once, in the second round, when he caught Clay with a right coming out of a clinch.

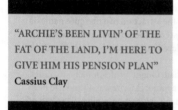

"ARCHIE'S BEEN LIVIN' OF THE FAT OF THE LAND, I'M HERE TO GIVE HIM HIS PENSION PLAN"
Cassius Clay

"He had a style," Moore told Ali biographer **Thomas Hauser** later. "He would hit a man a lot around the top of the head. And if you hit the top of a man's head you disturb his thought patterns. A fighter has to think… He made me dizzy and knocked me out."

The KO came in round four, as Clay had predicted. He dropped Moore with an uppercut and a flurry of follow-ups. The old man beat the count, just, but one more punch was enough. It was over. Moore was generous in defeat, predicting that the pretender might already have the skills to guarantee "an exceedingly interesting evening" should he get to fight **Sonny Liston** for the heavyweight title.

Clay VS Charlie Powell

24.01.63

Venue **Civic Arena, Pittsburgh, Pennsylvania**
Opponent's nickname **Frankenstein**
Prediction **KO, round three**
Outcome **Won, KO, round three**
Record **Fought 17 Won 17 Lost 0 Drawn 0**
Trivia **Shortly after the fight, *Life* magazine published one of Ali's poems**

Clay blew into Pittsburgh with all of his usual bluster, but he didn't get things all his own way. Having just beaten up the aged Archie Moore, he arrived at the weigh-in for his next bout, with **Charlie Powell**, to find himself facing a man bigger and more heavily muscled than he was. Powell was an athlete, a former football player who was not intimidated by the **Louisville Lip**'s schtick in the slightest. Charlie had also brought along his brother **Art**, another footballer, who was more than willing to trade words with Clay.

Cassius was rattled. He put his vest back on the wrong way round and when Powell pointed it out, he stomped for the exit, only to find he'd opened the door to a janitor's closet.

It was a **rare defeat** outside of the ropes, but any thoughts such silliness might undermine Clay's confidence in the boxing ring were quickly banished. Clay ensured the script contained no such ad-libs.

Despite the Pittsburgh winter, 17,000 came to watch Cassius Clay fight. The combination of his bravura skills and his knack for self-promotion had made him one of the biggest draws in boxing.

Powell began the fight well enough, catching Clay with a fine shot to the solar plexus, which Clay swallowed before firing back. Powell based his strategy on the assumption that he was strong enough to take a couple of Clay's punches to land one of his own, but, like Archie Moore, he quickly realised Clay's power was deceptive. "I was getting dizzier and dizzier," Powell said. "He throws punches so easily you don't realise how much they shock…"

The knockout arrived on time once more – coming towards the end of round three, meaning that seven of the last eight fights had ended exactly as Clay predicted they would.

> "I WAS GETTING DIZZIER AND DIZZIER. HE THROWS PUNCHES SO EASILY YOU DON'T REALISE HOW MUCH THEY SHOCK"
> **Charlie Powell**

Clay VS Doug Jones

13.03.63

Venue **Madison Square Garden, New York City**
Prediction **"Jones likes to mix, I'll let it go six"**
Outcome **Won, decision, round 10**
Record **Fought 18 Won 18 Lost 0 Drawn 0**
Trivia **Clay's prediction fails for the first time**

C assius Clay was clearly the biggest attraction among boxing's rising stars, and a return to New York seemed sure to add to his momentum. But the fight with **Doug Jones** was a strange affair in which little went to plan. The build-up was struck by a **newspaper strike** that went on for 113 days. Shorn of his usual audience of hacks, Clay rattled around as many radio and TV networks as he could making his prediction, which was for a win in the sixth round, a choice he rapidly repudiated: "I'm changing the pick I made before," he sang, "instead of six, Jones goes in four…"

He railed against the newspaper strike, too, claiming he was going to see **President Kennedy** to get something done. "People want to see my picture," he moaned. Strike or not, the fight ticket became the hottest in town. The Garden sold out for the first time since **Joe Louis** fought **Rocky Marciano** there in 1951. "They're dusting off the seats where the pigeons used to sit," Clay proclaimed happily.

Come fight night, he produced the worst performance of his career thus far, while Jones was inspired. When Clay failed to make good on his call of a fourth-round win, the famously raucous New York crowd turned on him. The bout went the distance with little to recommend it. The judges gave Clay a **narrow win**, scoring it five to four in his favour, with one round shared. The referee came down with an unlikely eight-to-one verdict for Clay with one even. Many of the crowd began to call the fight a fix.

Trying to save some face, Clay claimed his prediction had been correct after all: first he had called six rounds, and then four, which added up to 10. No one was fooled, but Clay remained philosophical. His next three fights would contain enough drama for a lifetime.

> "I'M CHANGING THE PICK I MADE BEFORE: INSTEAD OF SIX, JONES GOES IN FOUR"
> **Cassius Clay**

Cassius Clay VS Henry Cooper

18.06.63

Venue **Wembley Stadium, London, England**
Opponent's nickname **Our 'Enery**
Prediction **KO, round five**
Outcome **Won, TKO, round five**
Record **Fought 19 Won 19 Lost 0 Drawn 0**
Trivia **Speaking some years later, Muhammad Ali said of Cooper's left hook that knocked him down at the end of the fourth round: "He hit me so hard it jarred my kinfolk in Africa"**

C lay's first scrap with **Henry Cooper** began to make his legend: up-close shots of Cooper's face during the fight's blood-smeared finale remain among boxing's most famous and gory images, and one piece of quick thinking from **Angelo Dundee** probably kept Clay's career on track.

The fight was scheduled for the anniversary of the **Battle of Waterloo**. Cooper was a hero in Britain and especially in **London**. He was an old-school pro with a big left hook, known throughout the land as '**Enery's 'Ammer**. Clay's description of Cooper as "a tramp, a bum and a cripple" did not endear him to the British public, at least at first. The newspapers pronounced him "unsporting" and even the well-mannered Cooper was driven to note that "everyone in Britain hates his bloody guts…"

Undeterred, Cassius predicted a fifth-round win and then proceeded to visit various dog tracks and night clubs for the benefit of the press. He hadn't stinted on his preparation though, boxing almost 100 rounds in sparring with his brother **Rudy** and **Jimmy Ellis** and running miles through **Hyde Park**.

Jim Wicks, Cooper's streetwise manager, had organised some sparring of his own, bringing in **Alonzo Johnson**, who had taken Clay the distance in **Miami**, to tune up Cooper. Johnson not only had experience of Clay, he could produce an uncanny imitation of his style.

With **Wembley Stadium** practically wobbling with cheers for Cooper, the stage was set. **Clay** entered the ring wearing a robe and a crown, and he began regally. For the first three rounds he destroyed Cooper, who was fit and game, but outclassed. Clay began clowning: every time Cooper was on the verge of falling, he would step back and dance. **Bill Faversham** yelled at **Angelo Dundee** to stop Clay messing around, but to no avail.

By the end of round four, Cooper was bloodied and exhausted, the notoriously fragile skin around his eyes sliced open by Clay's flying leather. On his very last legs and right at the end of the round Cooper threw a historic punch, an example of 'Enery's 'Ammer at its finest. It caught Clay flush on the jaw and set him through the ropes and on to the apron on his backside. The huge crowd – 55,000 strong – roared and Angelo Dundee could see Clay had gone. He somehow regained his feet but stumbled forwards again, to be saved only by Dundee's hug and the bell.

Desperate to buy his man some time, Dundee alerted the referee to a split in Clay's gloves, from which **horsehair** was protruding. The futile search for a replacement gained Clay an extra minute on his stool. With his powers of recuperation, it was all he needed.

When the fight resumed, he began to butcher Cooper, opening horrific gashes over both eyes. With Cooper effectively blinded, Clay launched a sustained assault: "Few men have absorbed such a beating in such a short space of time," the *New York Times* reported. Cooper's head and shoulders were covered in blood, as were Clay's gloves. The crowd screamed at the referee to stop the fight, which he did with 45 seconds of the fifth round left.

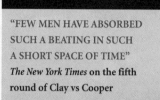

"FEW MEN HAVE ABSORBED SUCH A BEATING IN SUCH A SHORT SPACE OF TIME"
The New York Times **on the fifth round of Clay vs Cooper**

Dundee's quick thinking entered boxing history, with the story becoming embellished to the point it was claimed he opened the glove up with a **razor blade**. In fact, as he told Ali's biographer Thomas Hauser, Angelo had noticed the split after the first round and had told Clay to keep his fist closed. After the knockdown, he simply pushed a finger into it to open it a little more and then showed it to the ref. It was enough.

The fight had been dramatic and Cassius Clay had become the most talked about fighter in the game. He received a visitor in his dressing room immediately after the fight. It was **Jack Nilon**, manager of **Sonny Liston**. "I've flown three thousand miles to tell you we're ready," Nilon said. Cassius Clay was to fight for the title that he so fervently believed was his destiny.

PROFILE **The amateur years** Cassius Clay 1956-1960

How Ali began boxing is a tale that is often told. As a skinny 12-year-old, in his hometown of Louisville, he had his bicycle stolen. The young Cassius vowed to catch up with the perpetrator and "whup him". He reported the theft to local policeman Joe Martin, who invited him to train at the gym in his precinct. Martin supervised the training of young boxers and had a television show called *Tomorrow's Champions*.

Ali's natural flamboyance often masked the serious fighter inside, but statistics don't lie. They show that he triumphed 100 times in 108 bouts. Impressively, included in those victories were six Kentucky and two national Golden Gloves, as well as two AAU (Amateur Athletic Union) championships.

His crowning glory came in Rome in 1960, when he won gold at the Olympic Games, taking the light-heavyweight title, aged 18. He cheekily admitted afterwards that he had chattered to his opponents constantly in an attempt to distract and frustrate them.

Ali was fired up by the crowd booing Eddie Crook, who won a split decision to win the middleweight gold. "I knew I had to leave no doubts," said Ali. Saying he would keep his blood-spattered trunks as a souvenir, he announced: "I'm turning pro, but I don't know exactly how. I want a good contract with a good manager."

Cassius Clay VS Sonny Liston | 25.02.64

Venue **Convention Hall, Miami Beach, Florida**
Opponent's nickname **Big Ugly Bear**
Prediction **"He will go in eight, to prove I am great"**
Outcome **Won, TKO, round seven**
Record **Fought 20 Won 20 Lost 0 Drawn 0**
Trivia **The day after winning the championship, Cassius
announces he will no longer be answering to the "slave name"
of Cassius Clay. Instead he takes the "waiting name" of Cassius
X while Nation of Islam leader Elijah Muhammad decides on
a name for him**

f the **Brownsville** projects hadn't thrown up **Mike Tyson**, it would be harder to convey the fearsome mystique that **Charles 'Sonny' Liston** inspired in the America of 40 years ago. As Brownsville obliged with Iron Mike, imagine a less eloquent, equally destructive and furious man, a man whose strength appeared implacable. When Cassius Clay came to challenge him, Liston was considered unbeatable. The only uncertainty surrounding the fight would be whether Clay would exit the ring alive.

Liston had in fact been beaten. In 1954, he had lost on points to a heavyweight named **Marty Marshall**, a defeat he made good with a KO some months later. But that was when he still had to strip the rough edges of the prison yard from his technique. Prison was where Sonny had begun to fight, legally at least, while serving time at the **Missouri State Penitentiary** on two counts of robbery and larceny. Successive prison chaplains, Edward Schlattmann and Alio Stevens, encouraged him to box.

Liston possessed a natural power that couldn't be taught: you either have it or you don't. Sonny had it – he was knocking men out with his left jab. Another inmate was **Sam Eveland**, a former **Golden Gloves** amateur champion serving time for stealing cars. "Sonny was the real thing right away," Eveland told **David Remnick**, author of **King of the World**. "You'd show him a punch or technique and by the end of the day he had it down. But poor, poor Sonny. He could fight and that was it. He had the mind of an 11-year-old kid…"

It was a measure of Liston's life that he actually liked prison. The food was better than he'd had outside, and as Remnick wrote, "He started out with less than nothing." He wasn't even sure exactly when he'd been born; he guessed at either 1932 or 1933, although it was more likely to have been 1927 or '28. He wasn't sure where he'd been born, either. All he knew was that it was in one of the **Arkansas cotton farming** towns where his father Tobe worked in the fields. Before Sonny, Tobe Liston had 11 children with Sonny's mother, Helen. And before that, he'd had 12 with another woman. Later, Sonny said: "We grew up like heathens. We hardly had enough food to keep from starving, no shoes, only a few clothes and nobody to help us escape from the horrible life we lived."

By the time he was 16 years old, Sonny was already over 6ft tall and weighed around 210lbs. At 22, he was in jail, where he showed his potential as a fighter in an organised sparring session with a decent enough pro heavyweight called **Thurman Wilson**. After four rounds with big, bad Sonny and his iron bar of a left hand, Wilson was a broken man.

Liston's early career was sandwiched between another prison stint, when he went to the workhouse for a year for assaulting a police officer, but by 1958, he was ascending. He had beaten the well-regarded **Cleveland Williams** and **Zora**

Folley inside the distance, two of several fighters dropped by Sonny's giant fists.

Outside the ring, Liston fell into the hands of the **Mob**, first in the mid-West and then in New York. He became the subject of an extraordinary contract that was divided thus: 52 per cent to **Frankie Carbo**, the most powerful man in boxing; 12 per cent each to **John Vitale** and **Frank 'Blinky' Palermo** and 24 per cent to **Joseph 'Pep' Barone**. It didn't leave a whole lot for Sonny, who accepted his fate. He didn't have much else he wanted to do, anyhow. It was Sonny Liston's destiny to be the last of the fighters controlled by organised crime; Cassius Clay would be the first not to be.

Liston took the heavyweight title from **Floyd Patterson** on 25 September 1962. Patterson was outgunned physically and psychologically; he was a natural light heavyweight, weighing around 190lbs. Liston was 214lbs. Patterson was a man tortured by doubt; for every fight he packed what he called his loser's suitcase, containing things like a false beard and spectacles to wear to disguise himself should he suffer the shame of defeat.

Cassius Clay was one of 19,000 people at Comiskey Park in Chicago when Liston took Patterson's title in two minutes and six seconds of **controlled mayhem**. Patterson offered little resistance. He'd lost before he stepped through the ropes. The rematch, six months later in Las Vegas, lasted just four seconds longer than the first. Liston had barely even bothered to train. The boxing writers and the television commentators saw him as invincible. It was said that Sonny would remain champion for as long as he cared to be, or at least until old age robbed him of his power.

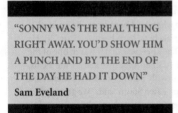

"SONNY WAS THE REAL THING RIGHT AWAY. YOU'D SHOW HIM A PUNCH AND BY THE END OF THE DAY HE HAD IT DOWN"

Sam Eveland

The contract for the Liston-vs-Clay bout was signed in November 1963. Liston knew that Clay was the biggest money fight out there. While both camps negotiated the deal, Clay began to study Liston hard. "The big thing for me," he told **Playboy** magazine, "was to observe how Liston acted outside of the ring. I read everything I could where he had been interviewed. I talked to people who had been around him or had talked with him. I would lie in bed and put all of the things together and think about them, and try to get a picture of how his mind worked."

While everyone obsessed over Liston's size and strength, Clay went to work on his head. He began a sustained and audacious campaign of intimidation. He nicknamed Liston **Big Ugly Bear**. He was pictured with **Angelo Dundee** and **Bundini Brown** reading a book entitled *Psychological Warfare*. He showed up at the gym when Liston was sparring and yelled at him. Liston began to question Clay's mental state. Before Sonny's second fight with Floyd Patterson, Clay stepped up his campaign. He travelled to Las Vegas with Angelo Dundee, and found Liston in a **casino** shooting craps. There are varying accounts of the exchange that followed – one even has Clay shooting a water pistol at Liston – but they agree on the result. The exchange the pair had backfired on Clay. Sonny Liston scared the hell out of him.

Liston was losing at the craps table. As he rolled the dice, Clay appeared, yelling, "Look at the Big Ugly Bear, he can't even shoot craps. He can't do nothin' right."

Liston was angry. He threw down the dice and walked up to Clay. "Listen, you nigger faggot," he said, "if you don't get out of here in 10 seconds, I'm going to pull that big tongue out of your mouth and stick it up your ass."

Later, Liston saw Clay on the casino floor again. He walked up to him and slapped his face.

"What was that for?" Clay asked.

"'Cause you're too fucking fresh…"

Liston said to his friend **Jack McKinney**, "I got the punk's heart now."

In his interview with *Playboy*, Clay admitted it was true. Liston had frightened him. "I ain't gonna lie. That was the first time since I known Sonny Liston that he scared me. I just felt the power and the meanness of the man I was messing with."

> **"I'M GOING TO PULL THAT BIG TONGUE OUT OF YOUR MOUTH AND STICK IT UP YOUR ASS"**
> **Sonny Liston to Cassius Clay**

It was a **miscalculation** on Clay's part. He had picked the wrong battleground. Liston was from the streets, Clay was not. Intimidating people in casinos came easily to a man like Sonny. By contrast, Clay was an athlete. His natural arena was the ring. But he had achieved something, nonetheless, because Liston was becoming convinced Clay was crazy. After all, who, other than a lunatic, would treat Sonny Liston in such a way?

Clay wasn't finished yet, however. He drove his bus to Liston's house in the middle of the night and had **Howard Bingham** get out and ring the doorbell. When Liston arrived at Miami airport to begin his final preparations for the fight, Clay goaded him into throwing a punch ("he missed by a country mile," Clay crowed). He then took a bus full of screaming girls to Liston's training HQ at the Surfside Community Centre. And finally, when the big day finally came, he really **freaked Liston out**.

At the morning weigh-in, Clay arrived first and went through his usual routine, coming up with the inspired rhyme "When the crowd laid down their money/They didn't dream they'd see a total eclipse of the Sonny…" and making a prediction: "Round eight/To prove I'm great!"

When Liston showed up, though, Clay went berserk. He screamed at Sonny – "You chump, you ugly bear, I'm gonna whip you…!" He became manic. His heart-rate was measured at 110 beats per minute, up from its usual 54. The fight doctor, **Alexander Robbins**, proclaimed that Clay was "emotionally unbalanced, scared to death and liable to crack up before he enters the ring".

Adding to the hysteria were rumours of a fix, along with the dawning realisation that Clay had joined the **Nation of Islam**, or at least was preparing to. And yet once the throng dispersed and the weigh in was over, Clay's vital signs were utterly normal once more. He was calm. Sonny Liston had returned to his hotel convinced he was fighting an unhinged man who might do anything.

All the excitement had not had its usual effect on the fight fans of Miami, though. The expectations of a mis-match, combined with some absurdly high ticket prices – ringside seats went for $250 – left the fighters with a half-empty arena in which to compete. There were 8,297 paying customers in a hall that held 15,744. Clay was paid $630,000, Liston $1,360,500.

Away from the hype, in the sanctuary of the dressing rooms, Angelo Dundee and Cassius Clay understood the test they were facing. "I won't lie," Ali admitted to **Thomas Hauser** in 1991. "I was scared. Sonny Liston was one of the greatest fighters of all time. He hit hard and he was fixing to kill me. But I was there, I didn't have no choice but to go out and fight."

Dundee thought Clay would win as long as he didn't become intimidated by Liston. "I felt he'd win because he had the speed to offset **Liston's jab** and Liston's jab was the key to everything. Liston had a jab that was like a battering ram. If he got you at the end of that jab, you were gone. But Cassius was able to surround the jab, side to side, either side, with quickness and agility."

"HE WAS SUPPOSED TO KILL ME. WELL, I'M STILL ALIVE "

Cassius Clay at the end of round one

Called to in the ring for the referee's instructions, Clay met Liston's gaze as Angelo had instructed him to do. In a final act of bravado, he whispered to Liston, "I got you now, Chump." The fight began.

Liston came out of his corner almost running, so eager was he to button the Lip. Clay, low-slung and loose, dodged a couple of big lefts with ease.

"He was jabbing with his left but missing," he said later. "And I was back-pedalling, bobbing, weaving, ducking. He missed me with a right hook that would have hurt me. I just kept running, watching his eyes. Liston's eyes tip you when he's about to throw a big punch."

Clay survived the first round, something Floyd Patterson had twice failed to do. He'd even bamboozled Liston with a flurry of punches towards the bell.

"I got back to my corner thinking, 'he was supposed to kill me,'" Clay told **Alex Haley**. "'Well, I'm still alive.' I was thinking something like, 'you old sucker. You try to be so big and bad!' He was gone."

"Who won the round?" Clay asked his cornerman **Bundini Brown**.

"You did," Bundini replied.

> "I REMEMBER THINKING, ALL I GOTTA DO IS KEEP THIS UP"
>
> **Cassius Clay on the second round with Sonny Liston**

Liston bulled forwards at the start of round two, determined or desperate or both. He got Clay on the ropes but couldn't pin him there. He hit him with a hard body shot that Clay rode out. He threw the big left hook. Clay spun away and Liston's fist struck the rope. **The rope!** Liston was being embarrassed.

Clay got to work. He flicked his jab into Liston's heavy face. Those at ringside could see a welt beginning to rise under the champion's left eye. The unthinkable was happening. Liston no longer looked unbeatable.

"He hit me some, but I weaved and ducked away from his shots," Clay told *Playboy* after the fight. "I remember thinking, 'all I gotta do is keep this up…'"

Clay noticed the welt under Liston's eye and went to work on it. A cut began to open. He was concentrating so hard on an inch or so of Liston's face he didn't see the long left hand that caught him flush on the jaw towards the end of the round. The punch shook him up, "but he either didn't realise how good I was hit, or he was already getting tired and he didn't press his chance."

In the third, Clay opened the cut on Liston's face with a good left-right combination. Liston dabbed it with his glove and saw red. It was the first time **Sonny's blood** had ever been spilled in the ring.

The fight had turned decisively Clay's way, or so it seemed. Throughout rounds three and four, he bossed Liston. The champ hadn't trained for a long fight and he was tiring quickly. Towards the end of the fourth, though, Clay began to have trouble with his eyes. They were stinging badly, and began to **stream with tears. Angelo Dundee** guessed that liniment from Liston's shoulder or the coagulant his corner had used to stem the bleeding from the cut under his eye had been transferred into Clay's eyes via Liston's gloves. Many years later, **David Remnick** uncovered hearsay evidence that Liston's gloves had been juiced by his cornerman **Joe Pollino**, a tactic they'd also used against **Eddie Machen** and **Cleveland Williams**. Pollino was said to have used an astringent that blinded a man just long enough for Liston to lay some leather on him.

Whatever the truth, only Dundee's clear head prevented disaster.

Clay collapsed on his stool, shouting: "I can't see. Cut the gloves off, we're going home!" Some black fans at ringside began shouting that Dundee himself was responsible for Clay's discomfort. Dundee remained cool. If he hadn't, there might have been no **Muhammad Ali** – Liston would certainly not have offered a rematch had he won. With mayhem all around, and Cassius panicking, Angelo dabbed his finger into Clay's eye and put it in his own. It burned. Quickly, Dundee sluiced Clay's eyes with a sponge and yelled at him, "Cut the bullshit, we're not quitting now. You gotta go out there and run."

> **"I CAN'T SEE. CUT THE GLOVES OFF, WE'RE GOING HOME"**
> Cassius Clay to his cornermen at the end of round four

What followed was an exhibition of rare skill and courage: for this alone Clay deserved the title. He was still unable to see much at all: some kind of **internal radar** kept him away from Liston's best punches. While he did so, Angelo showed the **Black Muslims** at ringside the water in his bucket and let them feel his sponge. "I want to win this as much as you do," he told them.

Midway through the round, Clay's eyes cleared. He had come through. The fight was fair once again and the better man prevailed. For the rest of the fifth and the sixth rounds, Clay hit Liston at will. He broke him up and he broke his heart. Liston slumped on his stool at the end of the sixth. He was finished.

Howard Cosell, providing radio commentary, began to yell: "Wait a minute… Wait a minute… Sonny Liston is not coming out! The **new Heavyweight Champion** of the **World** is Cassius Clay!"

Liston had quit on his stool. His face was bloodied and he claimed a shoulder injury was giving him too much pain to continue. The truth was, his spirit was broken and Sonny knew he would soon be knocked out.

Bedlam erupted. The ring filled with bodies. Clay ran to the ropes and climbed on them, screaming at the crowd and at the reporters who hadn't yet absorbed what they just witnessed.

"I am the greatest! I am the greatest! I'm the king of the world!"

Twenty-six years after the fight, Ali told **Thomas Hauser**: "Did Liston really hurt his shoulder? I can't say for sure, but I don't think so."

He also recalled a strange incident that occurred before the penultimate fight of his career, with **Larry Holmes**. A man had approached him and offered him a yellow substance, which, he told, Ali would temporarily blind Holmes if Ali rubbed it into his gloves. Ali refused, of course, but he thought back to his first fight with Sonny Liston and wondered.

Muhammad Ali VS Sonny Liston II | 25.05.65

Venue **St Dominick's Arena, Lewiston, Maine**
Opponent's nickname **Big Ugly Bear**
Outcome **Won, KO, round one**
Record **Fought 21 Won 21 Lost 0 Drawn 0**
Trivia **Ali claimed that his so-called 'anchor punch' that felled Liston was developed with the assistance of veteran comedian Stepin Fetchit (real name Lincoln Perry) who was taught the shot by Jack Johnson, the first black heavyweight champion of the world**

A li had been surreptitiously attending **Black Muslim** meetings for three years by the time he beat **Sonny Liston**, scared he would be prevented from fighting for the title should his involvement become public knowledge. **Malcolm X** and the **Black Muslims** had been visible in Ali's camp in the build-up to the fight. On the day after the scrap, with the title safely in his possession, Ali told the press explicitly that he was a follower of **Islam**.

Elijah Muhammad, leader of the **Nation of Islam**, gave **Cassius Clay** the name **Muhammad Ali** soon afterwards. White America did its best to reject it, and Ali. "The prevailing attitude," wrote Thomas Hauser, "was not to take him seriously. Sports figures were supposed to be one-dimensional quasi-cartoon characters. Now here was a young man a lot of people were starting to dislike. His carnival act seemed suddenly sinister to them."

The media attacked him. Some of the older commentators refused to call Ali by his new name, while the Nation of Islam itself was being torn apart by a rift between Elijah Muhammad and Malcolm X. Ali sided with Elijah Muhammad.

Ali's life took on further change. He visited **Africa** for the first time, he met **Sonji Roy**, who was to become his first wife, and he had a new manager, **Herbert Muhammad**, son of Elijah.

Amid all of this upheaval, a rematch with **Sonny Liston** was agreed, with Liston immediately installed as favourite to win back his title. There were two prevailing views on the first fight: it was a fluke or it was fixed. Either way, Sonny would shut Ali up this time: his fists would restore the natural order not just to boxing, but to society.

The bout was originally scheduled for 16 November 1964, but was postponed at three days' notice when **Ali** suffered a severe hernia that required an operation to correct. There was a delay of almost six months while Ali healed, during which time a fire of unknown origin blazed in his apartment, Malcolm X was assassinated and the Nation of Islam's headquarters in New York were bombed. Chaos simmered. Amid threats of violence and wild rumours that Ali himself might be assassinated, the fight was moved to a small provincial arena in **Maine**.

In effect, Liston and Ali were different men when they came to face each other again, but while Ali had moved forwards, Liston had slipped backwards. The writer **Robert Lipsyte** recalled going to visit Liston on the eve of the fight. Sonny was slumped in front of the television, watching the movie **Zulu**. **Dick Gregory**, who had gone with Lipsyte to see Liston, said to him: "His mind is blown. He's gonna lose fast."

Lewiston, Maine was so far off the beaten track that many of the boxing writers claimed not even to know where it was. Its location and the hysteria surrounding the fight, meant that on 25 May 1965, the smallest audience ever to see a modern world heavyweight championship bout – just 2,434 – witnessed the ring **debut of Muhammad Ali**. In another quirky twist, Ali and Liston were joined in the ring by another man who had held the world heavyweight belt, **Jersey Joe Walcott**, who was to referee.

Jersey Joe presided over a fight that even today still contains a mystery, a short fight that has become the most written about and talked about of all-time. It lasted one minute and 42 seconds only. Ali threw three punches of note, Liston none at all. The first came almost before the bell had finished ringing, a stiff right cross. The second was a clip to Liston's head, again with the right hand that appeared to stun him. The third, which practically no one, including Liston himself, even saw in real time, was a flashing right hand that lifted Liston's left leg and sent him to the canvas for a long count.

The punch, which Ali was quick to call the **anchor punch**, has been analysed endlessly. Seen now, with the benefit of slow-motion technology, it is exquisitely timed and certainly concussive, almost like the blow of a martial artist. Liston shakes and slumps to the floor. Only Sonny would ever truly know what effect it had.

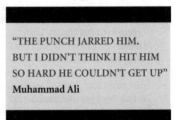

"THE PUNCH JARRED HIM. BUT I DIDN'T THINK I HIT HIM SO HARD HE COULDN'T GET UP"
Muhammad Ali

The punch had certainly duped the crowd. The columnist **Jimmy Cannon** proclaimed from ringside that "it wouldn't have dented a grape…" The audience became convinced the fight was fixed, a view that became popular over the following months. "Boxing wants no more of Liston," intoned **The Ring** magazine. Ali himself said afterwards: "The punch jarred him. It was a good punch, but I didn't think I hit him so hard he couldn't get up."

Ali stood over Liston, screaming at him to stand up and fight. Sonny couldn't, or wouldn't. Jersey Joe Walcott failed to get Ali to a neutral corner. Transfixed by Ali's manic behaviour, Walcott didn't realise Liston had been on the floor for a full 17 seconds by the time he finally got to his feet.

Walcott wiped down Sonny's gloves and ordered the fighters to resume. Only when a journalist at ringside alerted him to the fact Liston had been counted out by the timekeeper did Walcott signal the fight was over. For the second time, an Ali-vs-Liston bout concluded in chaos.

Two years later, Sonny Liston did speak about the fight. "Ali knocked me down with a sharp punch. I was down but not hurt… Ali is waiting to hit me, the ref can't control him. I have to put one knee and one glove on the canvas to get up.

You know, Ali is a nut. You can tell what a normal man is going to do, but you can't tell what a nut is going to do and Ali is a nut."

Rumours about the fight being fixed will never be stilled. **FBI agents** in Maine did question a number of informants but their testimonies were inconclusive. Liston was said to have told a trainer he worked with, a man named **Johnny Tocco**, that "it was the way the fight had to go." Liston's wife **Geraldine** maintained the fight was straight right up until her death in 1997. Ali too, does not believe the bout was fixed.

Sonny Liston was found dead in his **Las Vegas home** on the evening of 5 January 1971 by Geraldine, who had been away visiting her mother. Police estimated Liston had died six days before, but they couldn't be sure. The most prevalent theory on his end is that he was murdered, perhaps by a former police detective, but, as with the **anchor punch**, no one knew for sure except Sonny.

PROFILE **Ali's scariest opponent** SONNY LISTON

Legend has it that Charles 'Sonny' Liston's boxing career masked a much darker reality – that he was connected to the Mafia. Although he had one of the best jabs in boxing and knockout power in each fist, it has often been said that his best weapon was intimidation. Liston exuded brooding menace: one baleful scowl often had an opponent on his way to defeat before the first bell.

Born one of 25 children, Liston led a troubled life and learned boxing while in prison for armed robbery. He turned pro in 1953 and ascended the heavyweight ranks with some speed, slowed only by the occasional suspension and, in 1957, serving six months in jail for allegedly beating up a policeman.

He became world heavyweight champion on 25 September 1962 when he crushed Floyd Patterson in one round. He granted Patterson a rematch 10 months later but the result was the same – a knockout in the first round.

The idea of Liston being indestructible was shattered when he quit on his stool against challenger Cassius Clay in 1964.

In the rematch a year later, Liston was put down and out in the first round with Ali's infamous 'anchor punch'. Many at ringside thought he took a dive, leaving his reputation tarnished forever.

In his last bout in 1970, Liston beat future Ali opponent Chuck Wepner with a knockout in the tenth round. He seemed on the brink of a very unlikely comeback but was found dead in his Las Vegas apartment in December 1970, the alleged cause of his death being a drugs overdose. He was found with a syringe in his arm, which puzzled friends who knew he had a phobia of needles.

Ring magazine ranks Sonny Liston as the 15th-best puncher of all time.

Ali VS Floyd Patterson

22.11.65

Venue **Convention Center, Las Vegas, Nevada**

Opponent's nickname **The Rabbit**

Prediction **"I'll make him pay for insulting my religion"**

Outcome **Won, TKO, round 12**

Record **Fought 22 Won 22 Lost 0 Drawn 0**

Trivia **Patterson and Ali engaged in a bitter war of words before the bout, yet Patterson was one of the fighters who spoke up for Ali during the early days of his exile from the ring**

Since being defeated twice by **Sonny Liston**, **Floyd Patterson** had rebuilt both his career and his confidence. He had beaten **Sante Amonte**, **Eddie Machen**, **Charlie Powell**, **George Chuvalo** and **Tod Herring**.

Ali did not take Patterson lightly. The prevailing climate in America was against him. Floyd was seen as the white-establishment's choice for champion. Patterson had said he was going to win the title back "for America." This infuriated Ali, who took the remark to mean that as a Muslim he was somehow not American.

Ali trained hard. He brought in **Cody Jones** to spar with him; Jones was able to imitate Patterson's style. Patterson relied on the same strengths as Ali, he was quick, light on his feet and noted for his hand speed, yet Ali remained confident that Patterson could not match him in these areas; they were a young man's skills.

On the morning of the fight, **Frank Sinatra** summoned Floyd Patterson to his hotel room to tell him that many people in America were behind him, hoping he would win the title back.`

The fight marked one of the few occasions where Ali appeared cruel in the ring. He was riled and ready to take it out on his opponent. Patterson was not helped by back spasms that began to afflict him early in the bout, but his main problem was Ali, who as a boxer, was reaching a rare peak. He fired punches of all styles from all angles. He danced around Patterson, hitting him at will. As he did so, he called Patterson an **"Uncle Tom"** and shouted **"No contest! Get me a contender!"**

Ali was annoying the referee with his chat and was frustrating **Angelo Dundee** in his corner, who was shouting at him to knock Patterson out and finish the fight. Ali would not, even when Patterson took a count of five in the fifth round.

The referee almost stepped in during the 11th round, but Patterson refused to quit. Ali mounted a strong assault in the 12th and then the referee did intervene. Patterson admitted later that he had wanted Ali to knock him out, to bring an end to the pain. "I wanted to go out with a great punch," he said.

Afterwards, the crowd booed Ali. They felt he'd treated Patterson with cruelty, disrespecting a **respected fighter**. Writing for a newspaper the following day, **Joe Louis** said: "He could have knocked Patterson out whenever he really went to work. Let's face it, Clay is selfish and cruel."

Ali VS George Chuvalo | 29.03.66

Venue **Maple Leaf Gardens, Toronto, Canada**
Opponent's nickname **The Washer Woman**
Outcome **Won, decision, round 15**
Record **Fought 23 Won 23 Lost 0 Drawn 0**
Trivia **Billed as only a "heavyweight showdown" due to Ali's problems with the draft**

Ali's first marriage, to **Sonji Roy**, was dissolved in January 1966. On 17 February he made his comment about the **Vietnam** war: "I ain't got no quarrel with them Vietcong." The statement was particularly shocking as it came at a time when there was still little opposition to the war in America.

Ernie Terrell, who held a lesser version of the heavyweight championship was due to fight Ali next, but his association with **Bernie Glickman**, a man under investigation by the **FBI**, meant he was refused a licence to fight in New York.

Ali was banned from fighting in Chicago and Louisville after his comments on Vietnam led to protests and demonstrations. The protests rolled out over other mooted venues, too, until it became apparent Ali would have to fight outside America. **Toronto** accepted an offer to host the bout, but Terrell pulled out, citing contractual problems. **George Chuvalo**, a tough Canadian, stepped in. Ali had considered him as an opponent before, but Chuvalo's star had faded somewhat, especially after a defeat by Terrell. He had lost 12 times in all, but boasted that he had never been knocked out. Indeed, **Rocky Marciano** had said, "If all fights were 100 rounds, Chuvalo would be unbeaten in any era."

Chuvalo's corner devised a strategy based on draining Ali's speed. A concerted body attack, they reasoned, would take away his mobility in the later rounds, when George planned to batter a fading champion. Overhearing their plan, Ali deliberately exposed his torso to George's punches, effectively giving the challenger 10 free shots while exhorting him to hit harder.

But Ali was exceptionally strong. Chuvalo hit Ali hard but made little headway, although Ali would later claim Chuvalo was tougher than either Liston or Patterson. In truth, the fight was one-sided, except for a brief rally from Chuvalo in the later stages. The judges gave the challenger just one round of the 15 and even Chuvalo's close family might have had trouble recognising him afterwards, such were the lumps raised by Ali's punches.

Ali VS Henry Cooper II | 21.05.66

Venue **Highbury Stadium, London, England**
Opponent's nickname **Our 'Enery**
Outcome **Won, TKO, round six**
Record **Fought 24 Won 24 Lost 0 Drawn 0**
Trivia **Ali's contract stipulated an outsized ring for the bout – 20 feet square**

The trip to Canada was the first time a heavyweight title fight had left America in **five decades**. Next, as his case against his **draft reclassification** moved slowly through the courts in the US, Ali took the title to the UK for two fights, the first a rematch with **Henry Cooper**. The British public was captivated by the fight. Cooper was even more of a hero after his showing in their first encounter, and the fact he had dumped Ali on his backside led to the hope that **Our 'Enery** might have a chance. Ali received a terrific welcome on his return to Britain. His words about Cooper had helped, too: "He's an English gentleman and a worthy challenger for my title," Ali said.

Highbury Stadium, home to Arsenal FC, was full come fight night. Cooper was giving away over a stone in weight and was some eight years older than Ali. The scar tissue around his eyes was worse, too.

Ali was initially content to keep away from Cooper's left hand, but he was soon settling into his rhythm, letting Cooper chase him around the outsized ring and firing punches from all angles. During the sixth round, Ali flashed a right cross on to Cooper's left eyebrow and the fragile skin burst open. "It was the worst cut I ever had in boxing," Cooper remembered. Once again, both challenger and champion were covered in gore. The referee had no choice but to end it.

Ali VS Brian London
06.08.66

Venue **Earls Court, London, England**
Opponent's nickname **The Blackpool Tower**
Outcome **Won, KO, round three**
Record **Fought 25 Won 25 Lost 0 Drawn 0**
Trivia **Herbert Muhammad becomes Ali's manager after the fight**

The Cooper fight proved profitable and so promoters were keen to have Ali back, even if the best opponent they could find was **Brian London**, another veteran heavyweight known as the **Blackpool Tower**.

London's record was unimpressive. **Henry Cooper** had beaten him three times, **Floyd Patterson** had stopped him and **Ingemar Johannson** said that London would have struggled to beat his sister. Earls Court was only half full and not even Ali could make London look a worthy opponent. Instead he fooled around for a couple of rounds before jabbing the Briton into unconsciousness at **Angelo Dundee**'s insistence.

Ali VS Karl Mildenberger
10.09.66

Venue **Wald Stadium, Frankfurt, Germany**
Outcome **Won, TKO, round 12**
Record **Fought 26 Won 26 Lost 0 Drawn 0**
Trivia **Ali's first professional outing against a southpaw**

Ali continued his European tour against **Karl Mildenberger**, another long-odds challenger. In truth, he was tired and stressed by a return to the US to **continue his fight** against the draft and was far from his best in Germany. He cut Mildenberger in the fourth and dropped him in the fifth, but the German thrived on the adversity, rallying to cause Ali some discomfort as the champion laboured to finish off the fight. It was not until the 12th round, with Mildenberger on the ropes, that referee **Teddy Waltham** called a halt. Ali must have been grateful: at the airport next day, Waltham had his fee of £1,000 stolen. When Ali heard, he gave Waltham the money in dollars from his own pocket.

Ali VS Cleveland Williams

14.11.66

Venue **Astrodome, Houston, Texas**
Opponent's nickname **Big Cat**
Prediction **"He's way over the hill. I've got myself a pushover"**
Outcome **Won, TKO, round three**
Record **Fought 27 Won 27 Lost 0 Drawn 0**
Trivia **Ali made a concerted effort to end the bout early in the hope he could spare Williams lasting damage. The fight is considered to be Ali's greatest technical performance, convincing critics still sceptical of his punching power that he was the real deal**

The Fights

After two breezy European shows, the clamour grew to have Ali back in America to fight **Cleveland 'Big Cat' Williams**, a once-formidable fighter. Cleveland hailed from Texas and there was little objection to the bout going ahead in his home state. New York looked on with

"THAT NIGHT HE WAS THE MOST DEVASTATING FIGHTER WHO EVER LIVED" **Howard Cosell**

interest: it seemed likely they'd license an **Ali-vs-Terrell** fight there if the Williams bout passed without incident.

Williams was the epitome of a hard man. He'd been shot in the stomach by a policeman, attacked by a girlfriend with a meat cleaver and slugged it out toe to toe with **Sonny Liston** twice. He'd come through it all, but the cost had been high. Before he'd been shot, Williams had been a thrilling puncher, but how much of his ability remained after such travails was unclear. He'd won impressively enough in his comeback fights, but in reality Williams had little left for a man of Ali's skill.

Ali became concerned that Williams might be badly hurt if the bout went on for any length of time. **Jerry Izenberg**, alone with Ali the night before the fight, advised him to KO Williams quickly to avoid causing any lasting damage.

The fight was watched by an indoor **record 35,460** fight fans. What they witnessed was, in Ali's own words, "The night I was at my best."

During the first round, Ali remained elusive. Williams tried to cut the distance between them, but Ali's superior footwork kept him beyond his challenger's punches, although Williams did show flashes of his old power when he landed a shot or two. "He caught me a couple of times and really shook me up," Ali confided to **Cus D'Amato** years later.

Ali opened the second with two jabs to Williams' stomach before back-pedalling as Cleveland came on strong, then from nowhere he threw a one-two combination that sent the **Texan** to the canvas. Gathering himself during the mandatory eight count, Ali loosed a 16-punch barrage that rocked Williams back on to the seat of his pants. Gamely, **Big Cat** rose but five punches later, he was back on the deck and saved by the bell.

Enter the **Ali shuffle**. Some thought it a gimmick, but as Ali explained to Cus D'Amato, "When I do the shuffle, whatever you have planned, you're either gonna forget or look at my feet." In the third, his feet flew, a counterpoint to his fists. Williams was down again and the referee spared him more hurt.

Broadcaster **Howard Cosell** told **Thomas Hauser**: "The greatest Ali ever was as a fighter was against Williams. That night, he was the most **devastating** fighter who ever lived." Even Muhammad Ali's fiercest critics outside of the ring now saluted his dominance within it.

Ali VS Ernie Terrell

06.02.67

Venue **Astrodome, Houston, Texas**
Opponent's nickname **The Octopus**
Prediction **"At the sound of the bell, Terrell will catch hell"**
Outcome **Won, decision, round 15**
Record **Fought 28 Won 28 Lost 0 Drawn 0**
Trivia **Terrell maintained that his loss was due in part to Ali thumbing him in the eye and then exacerbating the problem by dragging the injury on the top rope. Ali denied any foul play**

The fight against **Ernie Terrell** returned Ali to **Houston** to again break all attendance records for an indoor fight – this time **37,321** bought tickets. Terrell held the **WBA Heavyweight belt** – which had been taken from Ali after his conversion – and was on a five-year, 15-fight unbeaten run. He was a tall fighter who Ali nicknamed **Octopus**. Unfortunately, Terrell decided to irk Ali in the same way **Floyd Patterson** had, refusing to refer to him by any name other than **Cassius Clay**. Ali would be just as heartless once more.

Ali opened with a flurry of hooks, then showed his disdain for Terrell's skills by alternately circling his opponent, hands down and daring him to land a shot, then slapping him one-handed. Terrell's best work was done in clinches he gained by advancing behind a high guard and weathering Ali's combinations. The fight became a **brawl** along the ropes when Terrell could force Ali there for whatever respite he could gain, and something of a nightmare for him when business was conducted from the centre of the ring. Ali had fractured a bone under Terrell's left eye early in the fight, and also damaged his retina. By the middle rounds, Terrell was finished, flinching every time Ali drew back his fist. Terrell suffered terribly as Ali carried him through all 15 rounds, taunting him the whole time: "What's my name, **Uncle Tom**? What's my name?"

> **"IT WAS A WONDROUS DEMONSTRATION OF BOXING SKILL AND A BARBAROUS DISPLAY OF CRUELTY" Tex Maule**

After the fight, **Tex Maule** wrote: "It was a wonderful demonstration of boxing skill and a barbarous display of cruelty."

Ali VS Zora Folley

22.03.67

Venue **Madison Square Garden, New York City**
Opponent's nickname **The Scientist**
Prediction **"I'll end it once you have enough film"**
Outcome **Won, KO, round seven**
Record **Fought 29 Won 29 Lost 0 Drawn 0**
Trivia **The first heavyweight title for 16 years at Madison Square Garden, New York's most famous boxing venue**

The **Terrell** fight turned the media back against **Ali** after their grudging approval of his win over **Cleveland Williams**. As **Thomas Hauser** pointed out, such cruelty looked bad while Ali was claiming in court that he was a conscientious objector to the war in **Vietnam**. Shortly before his fight with **Zora Folley**, Ali lost his appeal against an **A-1 classification** for the draft and was ordered to appear in **Louisville** on 11 April for induction into the **US Army**.

It was remarkable that Ali was able to prepare properly to fight in such circumstances, but he did. The Garden was to stage its first heavyweight title bout for a decade and a half, and Folley was old enough to have fought in that one, too. He was almost 35 and had been a pro since 1953, surviving by virtue of his technique.

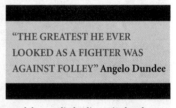

"THE GREATEST HE EVER LOOKED AS A FIGHTER WAS AGAINST FOLLEY" **Angelo Dundee**

Folley was a student of the sweet science and he studied Ali meticulously, watching film of all of his fights.

In response, Ali began with a style Folley had never encountered. He dropped his hands and beckoned Folley in before **blitzing** him with fast punches from strange angles. In the fourth round, he dropped Folley, who did well to beat the count. Ali knocked Folley out in the seventh with a right hand of similar speed to the one that had finished **Sonny Liston**.

"The greatest fight he ever looked was against Folley," **Angelo Dundee** said. "**Cleveland Williams**, that was great… But against Folley he was fantastic. And if he had gone on from there? There's no telling…" Ali had disposed of every credible opponent and was not yet in his prime. He seemed to be getting better as he approached his physical peak. The three years he was to lose as a result of his refusal to be drafted were potentially his greatest, but as Ali made clear, some things were far more important than boxing.

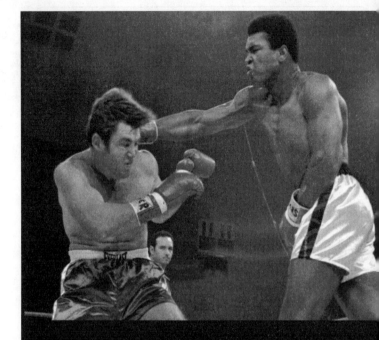

Ali VS Jerry Quarry

26.10.70

Venue Municipal Auditorium, Atlanta, Georgia
Prediction Angelo Dundee wrote "round three" inside Ali's gloves
Outcome Won, TKO, round three
Record Fought 30 Won 30 Lost 0 Drawn 0
Trivia Drew 'Bundini' Brown, Ali's cornerman, called on the spirit of Jack Johnson, the first black heavyweight champion, to inspire his man. Bundini could be heard throughout the fight telling Ali, "Jack Johnson's watchin' you"

The Fights

During his **exile** Ali had grown bigger than the sport of boxing. The fight game had lumbered on anachronistically while its most famous exponent was at the centre of a movement that had forced America to confront itself. Even Muhammad Ali himself had doubted that he would ever enter the ring again.

As he prepared to fight **Jerry Quarry**, Ali told **Sports Illustrated**'s **Mark Kram**, "It's been so long, I never thought I'd be back in my old life."

Ali was under no illusions about the burden he brought back to boxing. "I'm not just fighting one man," he told Kram. "I'm fighting a lot of men, showing them here is a man they couldn't conquer. If I lose, for the rest of my life I won't be free. I'll have to listen to all this about how I was this bum, how I joined the wrong movement and they misled me. I'm fighting for my **freedom**."

Ringside, Ali was supported by many influential members of the black community, **Sidney Poitier**, **Jesse Jackson**, **Julian Bond** and **Bill Cosby**

"I'M FIGHTING A LOT OF MEN. SHOWING THEM THERE WAS ONE MAN THEY COULDN'T CONQUER" **Muhammad Ali on the significance of his return to the ring**

included. He had become a figure comparable to earlier black sporting icons **Jack Johnson** and **Jackie Robinson**.

Facing Ali was Jerry Quarry, a rough and tough white heavyweight who had known plenty of hardship in his life. Quarry wasn't intimidated by Ali, or by the crowd. For the first time, Ali was in with a man younger than himself, a man certainly good enough to fight for the heavyweight title, by now held by **Joe Frazier**.

Plenty of people had advised Ali to take an easier fight on his return, yet their fears looked unfounded as Ali set about Quarry from the first bell like the **dancing master** of old, circling and flashing out his jab. For the opening three minutes, it seemed as though Ali had spanned the years of inaction unscathed.

But in round two, Quarry, a pressure fighter, bore in with solid body shots and forced Ali on to the ropes where he seemed content to stay. It was a tactic Ali would continue to use in his return from exile – though it was one that traditionally signalled a fighter's route to the canvas. Early in the third round, Ali got the better of a close exchange of infighting. When Quarry stepped back, there was a deep cut above his left eye. The referee, **Tony Perez**, halted the bout when Quarry's cornerman failed to close the cut during the interval between rounds three and four. Quarry was bitterly disappointed and rushed towards Ali, only to be stopped by **Bundini Brown**.

Ali's **comeback** fight had posed as many questions as it had answered.

Ali VS Oscar Bonavena

07.12.70

Venue **Madison Square Garden, New York City**
Opponent's nickname **The Beast**
Prediction **"The Beast is mine and tonight he falls in nine"**
Outcome **Won, TKO, round 15**
Record **Fought 31 Won 31 Lost 0 Drawn 0**
Trivia **Ali's prediction almost backfired as he was nearly KO'd himself in the ninth**

A li and the **Civil Liberties** organisation the **NAACP** had to get a court order to allow him to fight in New York, where the **New York Athletic Commission** was still resisting his comeback. But just six weeks after defeating Jerry Quarry, Ali was back in the ring to fight another rugged competitor, Argentinian **Oscar Bonavena**.

Bonavena, who had a reputation throughout his career for disregarding his trainer's advice, was prepared for the fight by the experienced **Gil Clancy**. Clancy told Bonavena not to chase Ali, but to wait for Ali to come on to him and then to hit him as hard as he could. For three rounds the advice seemed moot as Ali boxed beautifully, but by the fourth he had tired and gone to the ropes. Bonavena attacked to the body and the bout crawled to a halt as both men allowed the fight to become a slow-moving brawl. The crowd hooted derisively.

> "I'VE DONE WHAT JOE FRAZIER COULDN'T DO. I'VE KNOCKED OUT OSCAR BONAVENA. I WANT JOE FRAZIER!" **Muhammad Ali**

Ali had predicted a ninth-round win, and when he tagged Bonavena on cue, he moved in for the finish. Instead, Bonavena threw a desperate left hook that shook Ali all the way down to his toes. "I was numb all over," he admitted later. With the crowd shouting for '**Ringo**' (Bonavena was said to resemble The Beatles drummer Ringo Starr) Ali danced away from danger.

When the final round came, both men were exhausted and swung wildly at one another. Bonavena realised he needed a **KO** to win, but it was Ali who landed the decisive punch, a heavy left hook. Bonavena crumpled to the canvas. He beat the count, but Ali dropped him twice more. "I've done what **Joe Frazier** couldn't do... I've knocked out Oscar Bonavena," Ali proclaimed afterwards. "Now where is he? I want Joe Frazier!" Thus began one of the most ferocious rivalries in sport.

PROFILE **Ali's strangest fight** vs ROCKY MARCIANO

Who was the greatest heavyweight who ever lived? Close behind Ali must come Rocky Marciano, the only heavyweight champion to retire without losing a fight. He reigned from 1952 to 1955, making six defences of his title.

In 1969, promoter Murray Woroner approached Marciano and Ali with a proposition. He wanted to film a fight between them, using a computer to decide the final outcome.

Filming took place in a Miami boxing gym in front of a small audience. Seventy one-minute segments were filmed, then split into three-minute rounds, which included seven possible outcomes. All data on the two boxers, their fights and results, was fed into a computer to decide the winner.

On 20 January 1970, the fight was played in over 600 locations in America. It ended with Marciano as the winner by knockout in the 13th round.

Sadly, five weeks after filming Marciano died in a plane crash. During their time together the two had become friends. Ali revealed years later that he was closer to Marciano than any other white boxer he knew.

PROFILE **Ali's unwisest fight** vs ANTONIO INOKI

After stopping Richard Dunn in May 1976, Ali was offered $6m to contest 'the Martial Arts Championship of the World' against Antonio Inoki, a professional wrestler. The bout, in Japan on 25 June 1976, was supposed to be fixed, with Ali pounding on Inoki until the tables were turned and Inoki would jump him.

Ali's religion forbade such trickery and so the pair fought for real. Despite Ali claiming to have an "acupunch" to deal with Inoki, the fight was dreadful. Inoki was terrified of being hit and so crab-walked around the ring kicking Ali's legs. After 15 dull rounds, a draw was declared. The kicks to Ali's legs left him with blood clots and he was hospitalised on his return home. His cheque came in short, too; he only received $2.2m.

Ali VS Joe Frazier

08.03.71

Venue Madison Square Garden, New York City
Opponent's nickname Smokin' Joe
Prediction KO round six (Ali), KO round 10 (Frazier)
Outcome Lost, decision, round 15
Record Fought 32 Won 31 Lost 1 Drawn 0
Trivia Frazier and Ali each spent time in hospital as a result of the 'fight of the century' but split a purse of $5m in compensation – an unheard of sum for a prizefight in 1971

Thomas Hauser wrote: "Over four-and-a-half years, **Ali** and **Frazier** fought three fights that have become the pyramids of boxing." Perhaps Hauser, as Ali's biographer, is slightly biased – they aren't the three greatest fights ever – but taken as a whole, Ali versus Frazier is a major narrative in the history of the sport and in both of the fighters' lives.

Henry Cooper produced a succinct analysis of **Joe Frazier**'s style: "You could hit Frazier with your Sunday punch and you could break your hand," Cooper said. "He'd shake his head and come on after you."

Revelling in his nickname of **Smokin' Joe**, Frazier was an old-fashioned slugger in the tradition of **Rocky Marciano** and **Sonny Liston**. His idea of a fight was to get close enough to his opponent to "leave my beard hairs in his chest" and to then tap into his apparently limitless reserves of strength and courage.

Frazier's toughness came from his background: he had far more claim to having suffered the hardships endured by descendants of the southern slave trade than Ali ever did, yet this was the ground Ali seized upon, reaping the bitter harvest of the rage and hatred his attacks provoked in Frazier. It became easy to see why.

Frazier was one of 13 children born into a dirt-farming family in **South Carolina**. He was married at 15 and moved to Philadelphia to work in a slaughterhouse. He had won the **Olympic heavyweight gold** medal at Tokyo in 1964 with a broken thumb. Trained by the canny **Yank Durham**, Frazier became the **WBA** heavyweight champion during Ali's exile. When Ali returned, Frazier had won 26 fights in a row, 23 of them by knockout or stoppage. He was the dominant heavyweight of the day, as rich and powerful as he'd once been poor and powerless. And yet Frazier still burned. The title would not be truly his until he had beaten Ali.

The fight became a landmark event, not just for its ferocity and sporting excellence, but for the promotion that surrounded it. The men were to split $5m, a purse unheard of before.

During Ali's exile, Frazier had supported him by engaging in some pre-arranged publicity appearances, allowing Ali to remain in the public eye as a boxer and to earn some money on a lecture tour. Ali had said he viewed Frazier as a friend, joking he could see them sitting on a porch together as old men, talking about their lives. But as the upcoming fight began to grip public imagination worldwide, Ali turned up the hype and the relationship between the fighters deteriorated. "Ali turned Frazier into a black white hope," Frazier's friend **Dave Wolf** said.

Ali called Frazier an **Uncle Tom** and suggested that any black person who supported **Smokin' Joe** over him was effectively a traitor to their race. Given Frazier's background, it was easy to see how affecting such criticism was, made worse because it came from a man who Frazier had considered a friend and also from a black man who had a lot of white men working with him.

In addition, although Frazier was Ali's equal as a fighter, he was no match for Ali as a self-promoter. He found it hard to express himself publicly, which compounded his frustration. Dave Wolf told **Thomas Hauser**, "The damage he [Ali] did to Joe was never undone."

As the fight approached, Frazier trained like never before. Here, Ali was at a disadvantage. He had been inactive for three-and-a-half years before fighting Jerry Quarry. His doctor, **Ferdie Pacheco**, felt Ali had got himself back into fighting shape via the tough bout with Oscar Bonavena. "He should have let his body recuperate…" Instead, with the court case over his military induction still not resolved (Ali could theoretically be jailed should his pending Supreme Court appeal fail) and a huge purse on offer, Ali committed to fight Frazier.

It was sold as the **Fight of the Century** and Ali-vs-Frazier did indeed have a claim to that title. Both men were unbeaten. It was the time-honoured match-up of boxer versus slugger, plus the bout took on a symbolic quality, thanks to Ali's taunting of the champion.

There were unprecedented scenes at Madison Square Garden on the night of the fight. **Frank Sinatra** had to gain admission with a press pass (and actually took the photo that appeared on **Life** magazine's cover).

Both men stepped through the ropes sure that they would win. Ali had announced he would dance, run Frazier ragged, but the early rounds belonged to the smaller man. Each was closely fought, but Frazier landed more blows and his were the more telling. The intensity grew with every three minutes as the fighters became absorbed by one another.

Ali gave away points by lying on the ropes, apparently gathering himself for the battle still ahead; Frazier was ruthless and relentless throughout. He hit so hard to the body that the area around Ali's hip bones later swelled so badly he could barely walk.

In the 10th round, the referee, **Arthur Mercante Snr**, accidentally caught Frazier in the eye with his little finger while breaking up a clinch, but Frazier continued unfazed. Both men were becoming exhausted and their faces bore each other's marks. The fight swung between them: Ali had jolted Frazier in the ninth, Frazier almost dropped Ali with a left hook in the tenth and Ali had to hang on as Frazier became even more ferocious in his efforts. Neither man would yield and

"THAT NIGHT, ALI WAS THE MOST COURAGEOUS MAN I'VE EVER SEEN" **Ferdie Pacheco** as the 15th round began, the fight was still in the balance. Ali was utterly exhausted – exile had extracted its price on his fitness. Then Frazier produced a venomous left hook. "He hit him as hard as man can be hit," referee Mercante recalled and Ali's right leg buckled under him. The fight should have been over, yet Ali's desire drew him back to his feet even before Mercante could begin a count. "That night, Ali was the most courageous fighter I've ever seen," said Pacheco.

Ali even fought well during the remaining minutes of the fight, but Mercante and the two ringside judges awarded Frazier the decision, the referee by the slimmest possible margin of one round. Frazier had earned his victory, a point Ali would later acknowledge.

Both men were badly beaten up, both were bone-tired and weary. But Joe Frazier was still **champion**, and Muhammad Ali had lost for the first time in his professional career after a thrilling contest of almost warlike intensity.

Ali's enemies were jubilant, but Ali brushed them off. "The world goes on," he said. "You'll all be writing about something else soon."

Ali VS Jimmy Ellis | 26.07.71

Venue **Astrodome, Houston, Texas**
Opponent's nickname **The Sparring Partner**
Prediction **"If Ellis even dreams he can beat me, he better wake up and apologise"**
Outcome **Won, TKO, round 12**
Record **Fought 33 Won 32 Lost 1 Drawn 0**
Trivia **Angelo Dundee worked in Ellis's corner as Ellis was Ali's stablemate and long-time sparring partner. Ali faced the two men who knew him best**

Ali quickly rationalised his defeat by **Joe Frazier**, reasoning that he had lost just once in 32 bouts and the loss had not been an overwhelming one. Indeed, a little more activity in the middle rounds where he'd gone to the ropes might have been enough to give him the fight and his title. He was buoyed, too, when the **Supreme Court** finally overturned his draft conviction and quashed his **five-year prison sentence** a month before the bout.

He picked **Jimmy Ellis**, one of his sparring partners, as the fight to begin rebuilding his boxing career. Ellis had briefly held the **WBA** belt, and was a hard-hitting fighter. He had grown up in Ali's shadow: both were born in Louisville, and he had first fought Ali as an amateur (a fight Ellis claimed to have won easily). He had sparred more than a thousand rounds with Ali. Ellis even had

Angelo Dundee in his corner, with Ali's blessing, and so Ali used **Harry Wiley**, who had trained his hero **Sugar Ray Robinson**.

Between them, Ellis and Dundee knew more about Ali's methods than any partnership, yet Ali still won the fight with a punch they feared. After the expected fast start from Ellis, Ali threw a straight high right hand past Ellis's jab in the fourth round. "It hurt me so bad, I couldn't really fight my best after that," Ellis admitted. Ali treated the rest of the fight as an extended sparring session. In the 12th he threw the high right again, following up with a strong combination and only the ropes kept Ellis up. Ali pulled back and the referee stepped in.

Ali VS Buster Mathis | 17.11.71

Venue **Convention Hall, Miami Beach, Florida**
Opponent's nickname **The Whale**
Outcome **Won, decision, round 12**
Record **Fought 34 Won 33 Lost 1 Drawn 0**
Trivia **Buster had trained under Cus D'amato and adopted the peek-a-boo style used by D'amato's world champions José Torres, Floyd Patterson and 'Iron' Mike Tyson**

F lorida was the venue for Ali's next fight, against **Buster Mathis**, a genial character and a genuine heavyweight – he "resembled nothing more than a dancing elephant", according to one observer. This somewhat unequal contest required some selling – at one point Ali even suggested the promoters fake his **kidnapping** to generate interest, while he attempted to raise Mathis's ire with his usual round of poems and jokes, only to find Mathis laughing happily along with everyone else.

Ali barely bothered to train for the fight, and came in at his heaviest weight to date, 227lbs. He was intent on not hurting Mathis, even when he knocked him down once in the eleventh round and then three times in the last with punches that were barely more than gentle jabs.

"I GOTTA SLEEP AT NIGHT"

Muhammad Ali answering criticism of his "carrying" Buster Mathis

Ali received some criticism from the press for not finishing Buster off, but responded by saying that he would not hurt a man badly just for the benefit of the assembled writers.

"I gotta sleep at night," he said.

Ali VS Jurgen Blin

26.12.71

Venue **Hallenstadion Arena, Zurich, Switzerland**
Outcome **Won, KO, round seven**
Record **Fought 35 Won 34 Lost 1 Drawn 0**
Trivia **Ali took a trip to Saudi Arabia after the fight**

O n Boxing Day 1908, **Jack Johnson** had fought **Tommy Burns** for the heavyweight championship in **Sydney**, Australia, the first time the title had been contested between a black man and a white opponent. Johnson defeated Burns, to the horror of smug white society. Ali's own **Boxing Day** date was with a white fighter, too, a former Hamburg butcher **Jurgen Blin**.

Blin wasn't good enough to share a ring with Ali, and the fight was poorly attended, despite Ali's popularity throughout Europe. The German began quite well, with Ali content to clinch and lean on the ropes, but in the seventh, Ali decided to impose himself and dropped Blin with some snappy punches. Blin gamely regained his feet, but his corner had thrown in the towel.

PROFILE **Ali's toughest opponent** SMOKIN' JOE FRAZIER

History has been unfair on Joe Frazier's talent. A stocky heavyweight, he was as tough as he was powerful. He fought in a perpetual forward motion, never giving his opponents time to breathe (hence his nickname Smokin'), relentlessly trying to land his trademark left hook.

Philadelphia's favourite boxing son won a gold medal at the 1964 Olympics and had the somewhat unfortunate role of succeeding Ali as champion after the US government stripped Ali of his title for refusing the draft. Frasier won the title against Buster Mathis in 1967.

When Ali finally returned to the ring on 8 March 1971, Frazier floored him on the way to a 15th-round decision. His triumph was marred, slightly, by a three-week stay in hospital, during which the rumour that he had died swept across America.

Frazier couldn't match George Foreman, however, and lost his title in two devastating rounds in 1973. Foreman was the only opponent in a career spanning 37 fights that Frazier did not get close to beating: he lost the rematch in five rounds in 1976 after which he retired.

Like Foreman, he staged a comeback but Smokin' Joe's wasn't as memorable. After defeat against Jumbo Cummings in Chicago in 1981, he gave up boxing, though he still trained young fighters.

Ali VS Mac Foster | 01.04.72

Venue **Martial Arts Hall, Tokyo, Japan**
Outcome **Won, decision, round 15**
Record **Fought 36 Won 35 Lost 1 Drawn 0**
Trivia **Foster was another of Ali's former sparring partners**

Ali's uninspiring replication of **Joe Louis**'s famous **Bum of the Month** club continued with a trip to Japan to fight **Mac Foster**. Ali charmed his hosts, who were just glad to have the great man among them and willing to compete. The payday would prove useful to Ali, who had been stuck with a court order to give his first wife Sonji $44,000 in alimony payments.

Foster, like Jimmy Ellis, was a former sparring partner of Ali's and the pair fought out one of the least auspicious bouts of Ali's career. Ali won an easy points victory in a scrap devoid of excitement, but 1972 was to prove a difficult year for Ali as he encountered perhaps the first lull of his pro career.

Ali VS George Chuvalo II | 01.05.72

Venue **Pacific Coliseum, Vancouver, Canada**
Opponent's nickname **The Washer Woman**
Outcome **Won, decision, round 12**
Record **Fought 37 Won 36 Lost 1 Drawn 0**
Trivia **Chuvalo concluded that Ali was better pre-exile**

Ali had already beaten **George Chuvalo** on a decision in an utterly one-sided bout in 1966. The Canadian's greatest quality remained his ability to take sustained punishment without folding. However, his granite chin had finally met its match in the heavyweight division's fearsome newcomer – the glowering giant **George Foreman**. Just three rounds at the mercy of the fists of Foreman had, it was said, left Chuvalo's wife screaming at the referee to save her husband from Foreman's assault.

Ali didn't possess such power. He was still a **headhunter**, rarely dipping to throw to the body and his punches relied on their zinging, cumulative effect – he was no one-shot KO man. Also in question was Ali's **desire** to inflict true harm. A religious man, he was loath to burden his conscience with a bad injury to an opponent, especially those who obviously posed no threat to him. Foreman and **Joe Frazier** were untroubled by such concerns.

Chuvalo survived as Ali hit him almost at will. The fight looked set for the distance from the start; the decision, though, was never in doubt.

Ali VS Jerry Quarry II

27.06.72

Venue **Convention Center, Las Vegas, Nevada**
Outcome **Won, TKO, round seven**
Record **Fought 38 Won 37 Lost 1 Drawn 0**
Trivia **Soon after the fight, Ali began negotiations to star in a movie remake of** *Here Comes Mr Jordan* **called** *Heaven Can Wait.* **Francis Ford Coppola wrote the screenplay but the projected foundered**

A li had stopped **Jerry Quarry** on a cut in the first bout of his comeback and Quarry had been so disappointed when the referee halted the contest that he had to be restrained by **Bundini Brown** as he crossed the ring to confront Ali. The rematch lacked any of the mystery and tension of Ali's initial return to professional boxing – Ali knew he had Quarry's measure, while the rugged Californian's determination could only take him so far.

Ali looked the more imposing of the two fighters from the off and set about convincing Quarry that he had no chance. He used the same **psychological tactics** used in the first fight with **George Chuvalo**: "Your punches don't hurt me and I have no respect for you."

Ali made his point as the rounds ticked by, first smothering Quarry's attacks by tying him up then landing some swift combinations.

> "THIS IS AN EASY WAY TO MAKE A LIVIN'" **Muhammad Ali, at the end of the fifth round in his second fight with Jerry Quarry**

By the fifth Ali had seen off any threat and was entertaining the crowd with some shouted asides, informing the ringside press, "this is an easy way to make a livin'." In round six, Ali decided to try to close the show with hurtful combinations, but the ever-game Quarry remained on his feet. The fight was stopped 20 seconds into round seven as Ali, seeing his opponent had little left, waved the referee in to halt the contest.

Ali VS Al 'Blue' Lewis

19.07.72

Venue **Croke Park, Dublin, Ireland**
Prediction **KO, round five**
Outcome **Won, TKO, round 11**
Record **Fought 39 Won 38 Lost 1 Drawn 0**
Trivia **Ali was delighted to meet actor Peter O'Toole ("Come in, Lawrence")**

The promoter **Harold Conrad** had always wanted to put on a heavyweight fight in Ireland and did so, obtaining a guarantee of $200,000 for Ali to fight **Al 'Blue' Lewis**, a game ex-con from Detroit.

Ali charmed an entire country during his one-week stay. Arriving at the airport to claim he had a grandfather named **Abe Grady** who had emigrated to America a hundred years before, he proceeded to meet and greet everyone who was anyone in Ireland, from the Taoiseach **Jack Lynch** to the civil rights campaigner **Bernadette Devlin** and hellraising actor **Peter O'Toole**.

Conrad remembered Ali phoned him the day after he'd arrived in Ireland and asked, "Hal, where are all the niggers in this country?"

"There aren't any," Conrad had explained.

Ali contracted flu before the bout and should really have pulled out, but being Ali, he didn't want to disappoint. For his part, Harold Conrad was dismayed to find that around seven thousand fans had crashed the main gate and got in to the spectacle without paying.

> "HAL, WHERE ARE ALL THE NIGGERS IN THIS COUNTRY?"
> "THERE AREN'T ANY" **Ali and Hal Conrad discuss the Irish question**

The actual fight was a good one compared to some of Ali's lacklustre comeback bouts. He dropped Lewis in the fifth – the round he had predicted for a win – but then took his time in moving to a neutral corner. The referee extended the count to 15 seconds and Lewis survived.

The ninth round proved pretty exciting too, as first Ali, then Lewis landed heavy shots. At the end of the tenth though, Ali told **Angelo Dundee** he was desperate to pee and a sustained attack at the start of the 11th halted Blue's resistance.

Ali's plans to reach the dressing room toilets quickly to end his discomfort were stymied by an invasion of the ring. It was a further 25 minutes until he finally reached sanctuary.

Ali VS Floyd Patterson II   20.09.72

Venue **Madison Square Garden, New York City**
Opponent's nickname **The Rabbit**
Outcome **Won, TKO, round seven**
Record **Fought 40 Won 39 Lost 1 Drawn 0**
Trivia **Ali pays $200,000 for a Pennsylvanian hilltop training camp**

The fight Ali sought was a return with **Joe Frazier**, but Frazier was proving elusive. Ali was becoming despondent until his friend **Gene Kilroy** showed him a mountain-top property for sale in **Deer Lake**, Pennsylvania.

It was the ideal location for Ali's long-held dream to build a training camp like the one **Archie Moore** had owned in California and he bought the place for around $200,000 and christened it **Fighter's Heaven**. He installed cabins and a gym, and painted the names of the great heavyweights on the giant boulders that were scattered around the mountainside.

Fighter's Heaven lifted him and became his sanctuary. The long training runs through the hillside tracks afforded him time for reflection. The sprawling camp offered a place for Ali and his entourage to stretch out and build the family atmosphere he loved so much. Anyone who could get to Deer Lake was welcome and people came from miles around to watch Ali at work.

Ali trained for his rematch with **Floyd Patterson** at Fighter's Heaven, although he felt no need to go all out. Patterson was now 37 years old, and he had been beaten by **Jimmy Ellis** during Ali's exile, yet the match-up attracted more than 17,000 fans to Madison Square Garden.

A pre-fight appearance in the ring by Joe Frazier seemed to energise Ali more than the prospect of beating up poor old Floyd once more. Frazier took a bow and ignored Ali's attempts to rile him, smiling as Ali pretended to be restrained by his cornermen.

Ali soon had to stop clowning, however, as Patterson, fighting more freely than he had for years, took several of the early rounds and began to frustrate Ali with his **peek-a-boo** defence.

A sixth-round right hand from Ali turned the fight back his way, opening a cut on Patterson's eyelid. Another round's work left Patterson on his stool at the start of round eight, with the referee insisting the doctor take a look at his eye.

Over Patterson's protests the last meeting between these two former champions was called to a halt and Ali moved a step nearer to a **title shot**.

Ali VS Bob Foster

21.11.72

Venue **High Sierra Theater, Stateline, Nevada**
Opponent's nickname **The Giraffe**
Prediction **KO, round five**
Outcome **Won, KO, round eight**
Record **Fought 41 Won 40 Lost 1 Drawn 0**
Trivia **Ali suffers a cut eye for the first time in his career**

A s Ali's year drew to a close, he had little doubt it had been his worst in pro boxing. The **Frazier rematch** was no nearer, and he was finding it difficult to lift himself for fights like the one with **Bob Foster** that took place in a nightclub where the fans sat around dinner tables. It felt more like a second-rate cabaret attraction than a sporting contest.

Foster wasn't even a genuine heavyweight; Ali outweighed him by almost 40lbs. He had been a light heavyweight champ, though, noted for his stinging jab and he felt his speed would trouble Ali.

It didn't. Ali played with Foster until the fifth round, in which he had predicted victory. He **floored Foster** four times, but Foster survived and even opened a small cut above Ali's eye – the first time Ali had ever been cut in the ring. Two more knockdowns in the seventh preceded the end, which came a round later, to the relief of everyone.

Ali VS Joe Bugner

14.02.73

Venue **Convention Center, Las Vegas, Nevada**
Outcome **Won, decision, round 12**
Record **Fought 42 Won 41 Lost 1 Drawn 0**
Trivia **Ali admitted to liking Joe Bugner and predicted great things for him**

A li's staid fight with Joe Bugner was played out against a radically changed heavyweight scene. On being woken on the morning of 23 January 1972 to be told **George Foreman** had destroyed **Joe Frazier** in their bout in **Jamaica**, knocking him down six times in two rounds and becoming the new champ, Ali had wryly remarked: "My my, there goes $5m out the window…"

Frazier's defeat spurred Ali from the torpor that had threatened to stall his career. He signed for two fights, the first against the British heavyweight Bugner and the second against **Ken Norton**, a little-known former US marine who had quietly ascended the rankings.

Bugner was a source of great frustration to British fight fans. Descended from a Hungarian family, he was big and strong and a skilful technical boxer. Early in his career an opponent named **Ulrich Regis** collapsed and died a few days after Bugner had outpointed him at London's Shoreditch Town Hall. Many observers felt Bugner, consciously or otherwise, now held himself back. Nonetheless he was to box a combined total of **39 rounds** in fights with Ali and Joe Frazier and was not stopped by either.

The **robe** Ali wore to the ring, which had been given to him by **Elvis Presley**, turned out to be the flashiest thing on display all night. Over 12 slow rounds, Ali beat Bugner comprehensively without either man's senses coming under threat.

Ali VS Ken Norton I | 31.03.73

Venue **Sports Arena, San Diego, California**
Opponent's nickname **The Hour Glass**
Outcome **Lost, decision, round 12**
Record **Fought 43 Won 41 Lost 2 Drawn 0**
Trivia **Ali injured an ankle before the fight attempting to "revolutionise" the world of golf**

His last fight before taking on Muhammad Ali had earned **Ken Norton** precisely $300, but he sneaked up on Ali and on heavyweight boxing and irrevocably changed its order. His style was unrefined and his shape – huge shoulders and waspish waist – more suited to bodybuilding than boxing. He had been a sparring partner of Joe Frazier and become seasoned by the experience. He was also trained by **Eddie Futch**, who had plotted Frazier's defeat of Ali.

Futch instructed Norton to jab Ali to the ropes and work from head to body. Norton's jab was a powerful weapon and in round two, it forced Ali back into a corner. Once there, Norton nailed him with a straight right hand. It landed precisely at the point of Ali's jaw where he had lost two back teeth. Ali's mouth was slightly open at the moment of impact and these factors combined with Norton's power to **fracture the bone**.

Angelo Dundee realised immediately what had happened. "I asked him to let me stop the fight," Dundee remembered. "He said, 'No, I can beat this sucker. He won't touch my jaw.'" It was a remarkable display of courage from Ali, who fought for another 10 rounds, losing a narrow points decision.

Immediately after the fight, Ali had a 90-minute operation on the jaw. The bones were separated by a quarter of an inch and the surgeon who rewired them said: "I can't fathom how he could go the whole fight like that."

Ali said that in the heat of the fight he barely felt the injury. Indeed he claimed to have been troubled almost as much by his relative lack of fitness. He had missed out on fitness work after spraining an ankle while "revolutionising" the game of golf by trying to hit the ball on the run.

While Ali was again philosophical in defeat, his career had reached a crossroads. His 10-fight unbeaten run since the Frazier defeat took on a different note – he had fought no one of any note and now he had lost to a fighter most of the world had never heard of. **Howard Cosell** was among those who felt Ali's career was over: "It was the end of the road as far as I could see. So many of Ali's fights had incredible symbolism, and here it was again. Ken Norton, former **marine** against the **draft dodger** in San Diego, a conservative naval town. It seemed Ali would never get his title back."

> "I ASKED HIM TO LET ME STOP THE FIGHT. HE SAID, 'NO, I CAN BEAT THIS SUCKER' "
> **Angelo Dundee**

Ali VS Ken Norton II

10.09.73

Venue **Forum, Inglewood, California**
Opponent's nickname **The Hour Glass**
Prediction **"I'll bump Norton in four"**
Outcome **Won, decision, round 12**
Record **Fought 44 Won 42 Lost 2 Drawn 0**
Trivia **Ali called Norton "the man who shot Liberty Valance"**

Although Ali's defeat had thrown a doubt over his career in a sporting sense, it revived the interest of a flagging public. His rematch with **Ken Norton** easily overshadowed **George Foreman**'s first defence of his title, against the unheralded **José Roman**. Once more, Ali's power to polarise opinion galvanised the fans. He began a concerted campaign of hype: "Is he still the fastest and most beautiful man in the world," he shouted, "or is he growing old or slow? I took a nobody and created a monster. Now I have to punish him bad…"

In **Fighter's Heaven**, Ali whipped himself back into the sort of formidable

George Foreman's knockout of Joe Frazier in 1973 ranks among the most brutal demonstrations of power punching the sport has seen. Frazier was champion, but Foreman brought him to the canvas six times in less than two rounds.

Foreman made only two successful defences of his title, against José Roman and perennial Ali nemesis Ken Norton, both dismissed in two rounds. Text-book technique was not a prerequisite for Foreman at 6ft 3in and weighing 225lbs.

His amateur career culminated in Olympic gold in Mexico 1968 and he had won 40 straight victories with 37 knockouts by the time he faced Ali. Drained of confidence after losing the match, he squeezed in another victory over Joe Frazier in 1975, but retired in 1977 at 27 after losing to Jimmy Young.

Foreman returned to the ring 10 years later, billing himself as the 'Punching Preacher'. Nobody took this jovial, bald figure seriously. However, they were forced to when in 1994, at the age of 45, he became the oldest man to win a world title, knocking out the champion Michael Moorer who was almost 20 years younger.

Like Ali, Foreman had his own religious conversion, becoming a preacher at his local church, in Marshall, Texas in one spell out of the ring. Foreman idolised Ali as a youngster: "In 1962, just before the Liston fight, my brother and his friend and I would run around looking for a radio just to hear Ali speak. He shocked the world every time he opened his mouth."

shape he'd not been in since the fight with Frazier. He now understood what he faced when the time came to re-enter the ring. He began to figure out a way to beat Ken Norton. It was one of Ali's great gifts as a fighter – he would never lose a rematch with an opponent who had defeated him.

Ali began the fight well, although he still found Norton's style awkward. Norton was most vulnerable to big punchers who could force him backwards, but Ali was not that kind of fighter. He built up a points lead through the first half, but he had not been able to nail Norton often enough to slow him down. Throughout the later rounds, Norton came back at Ali, eating into his lead. As the final round began, the fighters were level on the scorecards. Taking the kind of instinctive decision that so often changed the course of his career, Ali abandoned his **stick-and-move** style and stood and traded with Norton for the last three minutes. Ali won the round quite clearly and the decision was his.

Norton disputed the decision but not his opponent's greatness. "Ali was a man who knew the ins and outs of boxing totally," he said later. "He could psyche you out mentally, he could psyche you out physically, and while you were doing certain things, he was a master of boxing and he would counter that.

Ali VS Rudi Lubbers

20.10.73

Venue **Senyan Stadium, Jakarta, Indonesia**
Outcome **Won, decision, round 12**
Record **Fought 45 Won 43 Lost 2 Drawn 0**
Trivia **The bursitis in Ali's hands that had plagued
him since exile flared up once more**

Ali faced one more low-key bout as negotiations for him to fight either **Joe Frazier** or **George Foreman** began. He travelled to Indonesia to face **Rudi Lubbers**, a mediocre Dutchman. The scrap itself was unremarkable as Ali eased through his paces without ever extending himself. What enlivened the contest was the rapt attention of the huge crowd – 35,000 watched the bout, with 10,000 more showing up at a brief exhibition Ali gave while in the country.

As his boxing career entered its most epic and resonant phase, his worldwide appeal remained unmatched by any other athlete. Far from being finished, the 32-year-old Ali was about to become the most famous man on earth.

Ali VS Joe Frazier II

28.01.74

Venue **Madison Square Garden, New York City**
Opponent's nickname **Smokin' Joe**
Prediction **"This may shock and amaze ya, but I will
destroy Joe Frazier"**
Outcome **Won, decision, round 12**
Record **Fought 46 Won 44 Lost 2 Drawn 0**
Trivia **Ali entered the ring as the 6-5 betting favourite**

While **Joe Frazier** had been champion and Ali had been unbeaten since their first bout, the mooted purse for each fighter in a second fight was $5m. Now, their market value had dropped quite dramatically, they were to receive $850,000 apiece. **George Foreman** was heavyweight boxing's brutal new king having destroyed Frazier, who had already beaten Ali.

There were other considerations, too. It was known that Frazier had been badly hurt by Ali in their first fight; he had been hospitalised with kidney damage for almost three weeks. He also had restricted sight in his right eye, a problem he had concealed for much of his career. Ali had recovered from his broken jaw, but it was apparent he would never again be the quicksilver genius he had been before his exile.

> "EVERYBODY KNOWS I WENT TO HOSPITAL FOR TEN MINUTES. YOU WERE THERE FOR THREE WEEKS"
> **Muhammad Ali to Joe Frazier**

Nonetheless, the bout was still big news, a superfight. Frazier and Ali even got into a wrestling match live on television while being interviewed by **Howard Cosell**. Frazier made a comment about Ali's trip to the hospital after their first fight and Ali became annoyed. "Why d'you say that, Joe? Everybody knows I went to hospital for 10 minutes. You were there for three weeks. You ignorant, Joe."

Given the history that existed between them, the taunt was too much for Frazier. He pulled his earpiece out and grappled Ali to the floor. Cosell was stunned and terrified. Ali just regarded it as horseplay to sell the fight, but Frazier did not and he wouldn't stop. Soon, the pair rolled into the audience and had to be separated by members of the crowd. They were **fined $5,000** each by the **New York State Athletic Commission**.

Frazier would not have to wait long for the chance to shut Ali's mouth with his fists. Almost 21,000 people filled the Garden as the pair went to the ring. As with his rematch win over Ken Norton, Ali had learned from defeat. He knew exactly what Frazier would bring to the fight. Round one went to Ali: Frazier barely touched him. In round two, Frazier built some rhythm, but Ali quickly shattered that. He clipped **Smokin' Joe** with a withering right, a big showy shot of the kind he rarely threw. Frazier was jarred by the punch and might have gone down under a follow-up, but Ali was denied the chance by **Tony Perez**, the referee, who thought – mistakenly – that the bell had sounded.

Ali continued to dominate the fight. He was throwing many more punches than Frazier, who was unable to lay his big shots on the elusive Ali. When Frazier did get in close, Ali grabbed him around the neck and held him safely until the ref broke the clinch. Frazier made more headway in the eighth and ninth rounds, keeping Ali pinned to the ropes with body punches. Then, as he had with Norton, Ali changed tactics and decided to trade, winning some hard exchanges. As the later rounds ticked by, Frazier realised he was done. Ali's **superior technique** had overcome his white rage. The older man had won comfortably.

Afterwards, Frazier claimed he had won every round, but in his heart he knew the truth. Ali had mastered him with something to spare. Now Ali would fight again for the championship that he had never surrendered in the ring.

Ali VS George Foreman

30.10.74

Venue **20th May Stadium, Kinshasa, Zaire**
Opponent's nickname **The Mummy**
Prediction **"If George don't get me in eight, I'm telling you, his parachute won't open"**
Outcome **Won, KO, round eight**
Record **Fought 47 Won 45 Lost 2 Drawn 0**
Trivia **President Joseph Mobutu, who put up most of the money for the fight, was too afraid of assassination to attend the bout. Instead he watched from his presidential compound on closed-circuit television**

Seven years after he had last fought for the title, Ali once more had his chance. And everything about the fight he christened the **Rumble in the Jungle** seemed designed to heighten the drama of his challenge. The setting was both awe-inspiring and heart-breaking, the cast packed with marquee names, the script a fabulous melodrama.

The central storyline was the match itself. Ali was a major underdog, boxing's faded prince at 32. Many of the writers and commentators who had followed him from his prodigious youth, who had seen him vanquish Liston, relinquish his title on principle and then twice overcome defeat, felt he had perhaps reached the end. For between Ali and the title stood a man who was bigger, younger and stronger, who had never lost and who had knocked out 37 of his 40 opponents. His last eight fights had all ended inside six minutes. He had destroyed **Joe Frazier** and **Ken Norton**, the two men who had beaten Ali. He was surely unbeatable, even more so than **Sonny Liston** had been.

"I know of a way to stop George Foreman," **Hugh McIlvanney** wrote, "but it involves shelling him for three days and then sending in the infantry."

The contest was at the core of a remarkable piece of promotion. **Don King**, a former numbers racketeer from Cleveland, had listened on the radio in a jail cell as Joe Frazier beat Muhammad Ali. King was serving a sentence for the manslaughter of **Sam Garrett**, whom he had stomped to death on the street in an argument over money. Just three years later, King put together the greatest purse any prize fighter had ever been paid: **$10m** to be split equally between Ali and Foreman.

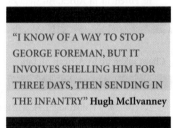

"I KNOW OF A WAY TO STOP GEORGE FOREMAN, BUT IT INVOLVES SHELLING HIM FOR THREE DAYS, THEN SENDING IN THE INFANTRY" **Hugh McIlvanney**

King had obtained the money from **Joseph Mobutu Sese Seko**, a third world dictator, a man who ran his country through fear, who had control of his people and whose hubris now demanded the acknowledgement of the world. Mobutu, who was known to his subjects variously as **le Clairvoyant** and **the Great Leopard**, paid for the fight from the **National Bank** and insisted the posters read: "A gift from Mobutu to the people of Zaire".

Zaire – which was previously and is now again, known as the Democratic Republic of Congo – offered an irresistible backdrop. It allowed Ali to fight for the title in **Africa**, and he became a hero there. His face was known even in the remotest areas. He learned something from the Zairian people, too.

"I used to think all African people were savages," he said. "But now that

I'm here I've learned that many Africans are wiser than we are. They speak English and two or three more languages. Ain't that something? We in America are the savages."

Along with the boxers, Don King and the music promoter **Stuart Levine** took a stellar line-up of black musicians to Zaire for a two-day music festival that would precede the fight. **B.B. King**, **Bill Withers**, **The Spinners** and **James Brown** were among the stars. They and the great retinue of press and media that included **Norman Mailer**, **George Plimpton** and **Hugh McIlvanney**, arrived to find many of their expectations of Africa confounded and many more reinforced. While the fighters and their entourages stayed in presidential splendour at **N'Sele**, Mobutu's retreat, the press resided in **Kinshasa**, some 30 miles away, where rats and cobras could be seen on the streets and many of Mobutu's grateful subjects endured penury.

Ali was soon settling in. He learned the phrase that became his mantra, "**Ali Boma Ye**" ("Ali Kill Him") a chant he encouraged everyone to join in. Foreman did not adjust as well. Surly and uncommunicative, he was soon losing the PR battle. Just as Ali painted Frazier as the outsider in his own land, he did the same to Foreman in Africa. Ali went out and met the people, Foreman remained secluded. Very quickly, Ali had the whole country behind him.

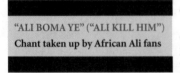

"ALI BOMA YE" ("ALI KILL HIM")

Chant taken up by African Ali fans

Then, eight days before the fight was due to take place, Foreman's sparring partner **Bill McMurray** accidentally caught the champion with an elbow and opened a cut over his right eye. The bout was off. Ali was distraught. He had got himself into his best shape since exile and had prepared himself mentally to face Foreman, although privately, he was longing to return to America after three weeks in Africa. In the hours after the accident, he demanded **Joe Frazier** be flown in to replace Foreman, but by the end of the day, he had accepted the delay. The fight would be **postponed** for almost five weeks and everyone would remain in Zaire while Foreman healed.

This of course gave Ali more time to work on his opponent. With a captive press corps, he characterised Foreman as **the Mummy**, and mocked his straight up-and-down style. He claimed he would dance rings around Foreman when fight night came. The weeks passed.

The weather before the fight was oppressive and sultry. The rainy season was near. At the 20th May Stadium, **Angelo Dundee** checked the ring and found the ropes were slack. He had them tightened, but they continued to stretch in the heat. The sponge mat had softened and so would be harder for Ali to move about on quickly. The mood in Ali's camp, already glum, darkened. **Wali Muhammad** said: "Before Ali fought Joe Frazier, we thought he couldn't lose. But we were wrong and against Foreman we were worried. George had been built up to be such a great fighter. People thought he'd kill Ali."

"WHAT'S THE MATTER? AIN'T NOTHIN' MORE THAN ANOTHER DAY IN THE DRAMATIC LIFE OF MUHAMMAD ALI"
Minutes before the fight

In the dressing room underneath the stadium, Ali had maintained almost to the last that he was going to dance around Foreman, but he had formulated another, counter-intuitive tactic. He looked around at the faces of his team. "What's the matter?" he asked them. "This ain't nothing but another day in the dramatic life of Muhammad Ali…"

The men went to the ring at four in the morning, to allow the satellite feeds to the US to be shown in prime time, to find 60,000 people awaiting them. Joseph Mobutu was not among them. His fear of assassination was so great that he watched the bout on closed-circuit television at his compound.

At the first bell, Ali seized the initiative with an audacious attack. He rushed at Foreman and landed a hard right hand. Then he hit Foreman with several right-hand leads – punches designed to confound the champ, which they did. Then Ali went to the ropes and allowed Foreman to hit him.

Ferdie Pacheco told **Thomas Hauser**: "Ali figured out that the way to beat George Foreman was to let Foreman hit him. Now that's some game plan…"

Archie Moore, who was in Foreman's corner, remembered: "Everything we'd planned was designed to get Ali on the ropes, where George could hit him. But once George got him there and Ali stayed there, George didn't know what to do."

In Ali's corner, even **Angelo Dundee** was unaware of Ali's plan. In between the first and second rounds, Ali steeled himself for what he realised lay ahead. Turning to the crowd, he raised his fist and led them in a chant of **"Ali Boma Ye!"**

He spent the second round on the ropes, which were by now very slack. Ali swung back into them to ride Foreman's punches. Others he absorbed on his arms and gloves. When the round was over, Dundee yelled at his man to start dancing. In the third, Ali ignored Dundee and repeated his **rope-a-dope** tactic. Wali Muhammad asked Dundee what was happening. "I don't know!" Dundee replied.

As Foreman continued to hit him, Ali began to talk: "Is that all you got, George? You disappoint me. My grandma punches harder than you do… You supposed to be bad…" After two more rounds, Ali's strategy was becoming clear. In the hot night, Foreman sucked at the heavy air. Ali began instructing Foreman to hit him harder. Then he opened his gloves and said, "George, now it's my turn," and unleashed some dizzying shots of his own.

Slumped on his stool after the bell, Foreman was attended by worried men. He hadn't had to fight for more than six minutes in a long time. In contrast, Ali had barely bothered to sit down. "I'll get him in a couple of rounds," he told Dundee.

For rounds six and seven, Ali continued to absorb punches, but landed more of his own. Foreman's swings grew desperate. In the eighth, Ali's moment came, as he had known it would. Foreman aimed one last slug and then staggered forward with the momentum of it. Ali sprang from the ropes, landing two beautifully timed straight rights, a concussive left hook and a last perfect right hand. Foreman flapped at him and then fell in a slow pirouette. As the count reached 10 he half-stood, only to feel the referee **Jack Clayton**'s warm embrace. It was over.

In seconds, the ring was full and Ali was engulfed. He had beaten the unbeatable for the second time and for a second time the sport's greatest prize was his.

Within an hour, the rains began, and the stadium was flooded.

On the bus back to N'Sele, Ferdie Pacheco said: "They just lucked out here in Zaire. They just happened to score the greatest fight in the last 20 years." The road back to the compound was lined with people, all wanting a glimpse of the new champ. "It was," said Pacheco, "like the return of a **victorious army**."

Ali VS Chuck Wepner | 24.03.75

Venue **Coliseum, Cleveland, Ohio**
Opponent's nickname **The Bayonne Bleeder**
Outcome **Won, TKO, round 15**
Record **Fought 48 Won 46 Lost 2 Drawn 0**
Trivia **Sylvester Stallone wrote the movie *Rocky* after watching the fight**

Where Ali had been a pariah, now he was king. People flocked to him, **Gerald Ford** invited him to the **White House**. He said: "Now that I got my championship back, every day is something special." His only sadness came when **Elijah Muhammad** died on 25 February 1975. Four weeks after that, Ali was back in the ring against charismatic journeyman **Chuck Wepner**, a fighter so prone to cuts his nickname was **the Bayonne Bleeder**. Wepner combined his boxing career with a full-time job as a liquor salesman.

The bout was promoted by Don King, who offered Ali the astonishing sum of **$1.5m**. Many promoters believed that King financed the fight with **Mob** money. However it was done, it was a classic King tactic. He was now firmly associated with Ali and a player on the heavyweight scene.

The fight was undistinguished. Wepner had none of the skills required to trouble Ali and Ali was content to coast. In the ninth round, Wepner landed a punch to Ali's chest and Ali went down. **Tony Perez** ruled a knockdown, although film footage shows Wepner standing on Ali's foot at the moment of impact, causing him to fall over.

> "HEY I KNOCKED HIM DOWN." "YEAH, BUT HE LOOKS REALLY PISSED OFF" **Chuck Wepner and manager after the ninth round**

Wepner went to his corner after the round and said to his manager, "Hey, I knocked him down."

"Yeah," Wepner's manager replied, "but he looks really pissed off…"

In the remaining rounds, Ali opened cuts over both of Wepner's eyes and broke his nose. With 19 seconds of the fight remaining, Ali knocked Wepner down for the first time in the Bleeder's career and Tony Perez stopped the fight.

There were two codas to the event. Firstly, Ali went on **Howard Cosell**'s *Wide World of Sports* show and accused Tony Perez of accepting money from the Mafia before Ali's second fight with Frazier, probably because he was upset Perez had ruled Wepner's chest-punch a knockdown. Perez launched, and lost, a $20m lawsuit, but he and Ali resumed their friendship years later. Secondly, ambitious young actor **Sylvester Stallone** watched the bout on closed-circuit TV and was inspired to write the script for **Rocky**, based on Wepner's gutsy challenge. Wepner would later sue Stallone, unsuccessfully, for a share of the profits.

Ali VS Ron Lyle | 16.05.75

Venue **Convention Center, Las Vegas, Nevada**
Prediction **KO, round eight**
Outcome **Won, TKO, round 11**
Record **Fought 49 Won 47 Lost 2 Drawn 0**
Trivia **"The man who will whup me will be fast, strong and hasn't been born yet"**

T he fight with **Ron Lyle** gave television viewers a rare chance to see Ali live (his fights were now mostly broadcast closed-circuit in cinemas, the earliest incarnation of pay-per-view), and Ali produced one of his finest finishes against the powerful opponent, who, like Sonny Liston, had learned to box in jail.

Ali began poorly and fell behind on the judges' **scorecards**. Lyle survived a flurry in the eighth round, which Ali had called for his win, and he kept himself in the fight. By the eleventh, Ali needed to do something and produced a straight right coming off of a **powerful jab** that sent Lyle skittering backwards, dazed and confused. Ali chased him, landing some heavy shots and beckoned to the referee to stop the contest. Lyle was battered, but with pride and brains intact.

Ali VS Joe Bugner II

30.06.75

Venue **Merdeka Stadium, Kuala Lumpar, Malaysia**
Outcome **Won, decision, round 15**
Record **Fought 50 Won 48 Lost 2 Drawn 0**
Trivia **Joe Bugner retired to Australia, where he made a comeback as 'Aussie Joe'**

Ali was lured to **Kuala Lumpar** by a $2m purse to resume hostilities with Briton **Joe Bugner**. He was also intrigued to be in Malaysia as it was only the second **Muslim** country he had fought in (Indonesia being the first).

The bout was a hard sell, however, as the pair's first encounter had been thoroughly predictable, dictated by Bugner's disinclination to become involved in anything approaching violence.

Ali was persuaded to announce to the press this might be his **last fight**, thus stirring up hype and hopefully shifting some tickets. Ali rehearsed some convincing lines about missing his family and wanting to go out on top, so that many reporters believed him. Until someone mentioned Joe Frazier.

"Joe Frazier?" Ali yelled. "I want him bad! How much money will I get for whupping Joe Frazier?"

Bugner once again proved himself a capable fighter, even if he didn't quite show the calibre that had prompted Ali to declare, after their first match, that Bugner could become the **World Heavyweight Champion**. He was a big man, hard to shove around and he was an adept boxer, strong in defence, but Ali built up a solid points lead throughout the fight and Bugner was unable to produce the aggression needed to upset Ali's rhythm.

The Briton had admitted, after the first fight, that it was hard to know how to fight Ali. Any plan you devised seemed to fall apart as soon as you entered the ring. Instead, he said, you had to rely on your instincts but here the challenger's instincts seemed to be all about survival.

The fight meandered to its inevitable conclusion, with the result never in doubt. Bugner had nonetheless fought **27 rounds** with Ali and had rarely been in any particular trouble.

Ali VS Joe Frazier III | 01.10.75

Venue **Araheta Coliseum, Quezon City, Philippines**
Opponent's nickname **Smokin' Joe**
Prediction **"I'm gonna put you away Joe. You just don't have it"**
Outcome **Won, TKO, round 14**
Record **Fought 51 Won 49 Lost 2 Drawn 0**
Trivia **Boxing bible *The Ring* voted the Thrilla the greatest fight in the magazine's 75-year history**

While Ali had beaten and befuddled **George Foreman**, and Foreman had annihilated **Joe Frazier**, Ali understood that Frazier would always bring him some hell in the ring. Aside from the enmity that fuelled their personal rivalry, Frazier had a style that troubled Ali; he had always been vulnerable to the left hook and Frazier's was the most devastating in the business.

Mike Katz, the doyen of New York's boxing writers, said: "These are two guys who would probably do it to each other if they fought in their eighties. That's just the way they are."

Although the fight would quickly assume the same iconic status as the **Rumble in the Jungle**, the announcement that Ali and Frazier had signed to meet for a third time was not met with immediate enthusiasm: the ringside cognoscenti considered both men to be past their best. Also, Ali had beaten Frazier comfortably in their rematch, which had not been able to replicate the drama or intensity of their first encounter. Yet there was the zing of greatness about the **Thrilla in Manila** from the start. Ali travelled to the Philippines with a 50-strong entourage, a vast circus of trainers, cornermen, gofers, friends, hangers-on and ne'er-do-wells who had attached themselves to him. Ali entranced Manila, even though he would soon have his problems there. Frazier travelled lighter – just 17 were in his party – but his was a heavy presence. He appeared dark and determined, a man bent on revenge and redemption, whatever the physical cost.

> **"THESE ARE TWO GUYS WHO WOULD PROBABLY DO IT TO EACH OTHER IN THEIR EIGHTIES. THAT'S JUST THE WAY THEY ARE" Mike Katz**

The promotion was another of **Don King**'s, and his presence had an electricity of its own. He had extracted a vast site fee from the regime of **Ferdinand Marcos** and his wife Imelda, who seemed to regard the country's money as their own. Ali received $4m guaranteed against 43 per cent of the gross, and Frazier $3m (Ali wound up with around $6m).

The build-up followed a now familiar pattern. Ali joshed Frazier and unveiled his famous poem: "It will be a killer/And a chiller/And a thrilla/When I get the gorilla/In Manila." Ali even produced a toy gorilla and began punching it.

Once again, Frazier was hurt. "Look at my beautiful kids. How can I be a gorilla?" Frazier began to turn all of his anger into fuel. "I want to hurt him," he told the press. "I don't want to knock him out, I want to take his heart out."

Before he engaged with Frazier, Ali had another conflict on his hands in Manila, and it was one of his own making. He had begun a relationship with a model, **Veronica Porsche**, and had taken her to Manila with him. It would have been fine had he not still been married to his second wife **Belinda**, or had he and Veronica been more discreet. But when Ali visited Ferdinand Marcos he took Veronica as his guest and when Marcos complimented him on having such a beautiful wife, Ali did not contradict him.

"THEY TOLD ME JOE FRAZIER WAS WASHED UP"
"THEY LIED, CHAMP, THEY LIED!"
Ali and Frazier in the sixth round

Soon Belinda was on her way to **Manila**, where she confronted Ali. According to **Leon Gast**, who made the film *When We Were Kings* about the Rumble in the Jungle, "People were talking about Belinda versus Veronica as much as they were talking about Ali versus Frazier."

Ali's marriage was something he would have to deal with back in America, however. Soon after Belinda's visit, Joe Frazier would be commanding all of Muhammad Ali's attention.

When the pair went to the ring for their rubber bout, there were 28,000 Filipinos there waiting for them, crammed in almost as tightly as for the cockfights that were the country's sporting obsession. The fight began at 10.45am to accommodate the closed-circuit feedback to the US. Ali stepped through the ropes with the words of **Herbert Muhammad** resounding within him: Muhammad had told him he was fighting not for himself, but for all of the **Muslims** who were praying for him. Ali could feel them; he drew strength from his mission.

Almost from the start, it became obvious to everyone in the arena they were witnessing greatness. Ali began best, reusing the tactic of throwing right-hand leads that had worked against Foreman. **Smokin' Joe**'s motor was cold and he got tagged several times before it warmed up. By the third, Ali's ringside crew were beginning to crow. **Bundini**'s ebullient voice rang out. But if they had forgotten about Frazier's desire, Ali had not. Frazier edged his way back into the fight with his iron will. Ali bust Frazier's mouth open in the fourth and Frazier just tossed back his head and kept coming. The fight became intense, ferocious, a two-headed drama played out before millions. In the sixth Frazier threw a left hook that **Angelo Dundee** rated as the hardest shot he'd ever seen thrown, and Dundee had seen a few. It thumped into Ali's jaw and spun his head round. Somehow, Ali swallowed the shot and said to his opponent, "They told me Joe Frazier was washed up."

"They lied, Champ, they lied!" Frazier snarled.

The fight began to turn Frazier's way. His body shots drove into Ali's kidneys,

"MAN, I HIT HIM WITH PUNCHES THAT WOULD BRING CITIES DOWN" Joe Frazier

his liver, his short ribs. They sucked the life from him. By the ninth, he was propped against the ropes waiting for the storm to blow out.

"Damn," Frazier said to his cornerman after the bell. "What's keeping that motherfuckin' fool up?"

The tenth round was almost Ali's last. Frazier was merciless and relentless. "Man," he would say later, "I hit him with punches that would bring cities down." Bundini pleaded with Ali to "go to the well one more time. " Ali drew himself from his stool and did so. Ali blasted Frazier's gumshield loose in his mouth, sending spit flying and still Frazier faced him down. It was clear this was an extraordinary fight: every good human quality was on display. As **Jerry Izenberg** said, "They were fighting for the championship of each other," and neither was willing to yield.

In the twelfth, Ali took the fight back his way with more right-hand leads. He had a second wind and he used it to change the shape of Joe Frazier's face. Ali's shots began to close Frazier's eyes and darken his brows. The vision in Frazier's left eye – never good – was now all but gone. Ali could hit him at will with right hands, and he did. The 13th round was dreadful for Frazier and his trainer **Eddie Futch** only let him go out for the 14th because he felt Ali might have used the last of his resources trying to finish his man during those three seemingly endless minutes.

Yet if the 13th was bad for Joe, the 14th was worse, one of the hardest rounds of boxing ever contested. From ringside, **Mark Kram** estimated that Ali threw 30 right hands into Frazier's ruined left eye. His right eye was now almost swollen shut, too, the topography of his face immeasurably altered. He existed on pure heart and guts. When the bell rang, the referee had to guide Frazier to the corner because he couldn't see where it was.

Ali went back to his stool not sure he could fight another round. "It was the closest thing to death that I could feel," he said.

He would not have to. In one of the great acts of sporting compassion, Eddie Futch stopped Joe Frazier with the words: "**Sit down, son, it's over**. But no one will ever forget what you did here today."

In the dressing rooms, both men bore the marks of the fight. Ali was grey with exhaustion. He had haematomas over both hips and welts and bruises all over his back and chest. Frazier could barely see through the slits of his brows. The Thrilla would extract its toll from them for months and years to come.

Although Joe Frazier took a long time to reconcile his feelings about Ali as a man, he was clear on his opinion of him as a fighter.

"We were gladiators. In the ring, I didn't ask no favours of him, and he didn't ask none of me," he told Thomas Hauser. "I don't like him, but in the ring, I got to say, he was a man."

For his part, Ali is now much more understanding of Frazier's anger. "He bought out the best in me and the best fight we fought was in Manila. That fight, I could feel something happening to me, something different from what I felt in fights before... So I'm sorry Joe Frazier is mad at me. I'm sorry I hurt him. Joe Frazier is a good man. And if God ever calls me to a holy war, I want Joe Frazier fighting beside me."

Ali VS Jean-Pierre Coopman | 20.02.76

Venue **Clemente Coliseum, Hato Rey, Puerto Rico**
Opponent's nickname **The Lion of Flanders**
Outcome **Won, KO, round five**
Record **Fought 52 Won 50 Lost 2 Drawn 0**
Trivia **Coopman was so happy to be fighting Ali, he drank champagne before the bout**

Ali followed one of his most sublime fights with one of his most ridiculous, against the Belgian heavyweight champion **Jean-Pierre Coopman**. Being heavyweight champion of **Belgium** was a bit like being the best darts player in Finland: all very well but no ringing endorsement of ability. As **Howard Bingham** put it: "By all accounts he was a very nice man. He just couldn't fight."

For Ali the bout was a little light relief, a breather before projected rematches with **George Foreman** and **Ken Norton**. For Coopman it was as though one of the religious statues he carved for a living had come to life and blessed him.

At the press conference to announce the fight, Coopman was so pleased to meet his hero he kept trying to kiss him.

"Get this guy away from me," Ali said. "How am I supposed to get mad at him?"

Soon Coopman had a new nickname, too, **the Lion of Flanders**, dreamed up by the American manager who had made the fight, **George Kanter**. Kanter's imagination was further taxed when everyone arrived in Puerto Rico. He organised some sparring against a washed-up fighter who hadn't been in a ring for seven or eight years. The guy smashed Coopman all over the place. Kanter declared that all Coopman's future workouts would be closed, as he had a "secret plan" to defeat Ali.

Desperate for a hook to sell the fight, Kanter found a voodoo **witch doctor** who he claimed would help Coopman win. It turned out the Belgian believed in witches and was delighted to play along as he was put into a deep hole and had water poured over him. Eleven thousand people turned up to watch the bout, a tribute to Ali's appeal after the Frazier fight. Kanter went into Coopman's dressing room to discover his man drinking **champagne** and kissing his wife, so delighted was he to be facing Ali.

> **"YOU GUYS ARE IN TROUBLE. AIN'T NO WAY YOU'RE GONNA GET ALL YOUR COMMERCIALS IN"** Ali conducting an impromptu TV interview between rounds

When the fight started, Ali went into his usual clinch to test out his opponent's strength. When he came out of it, he was laughing. He leaned over the ropes and said to one of the TV broadcasters, "You guys in are trouble. Ain't no way you're gonna get all your commercials in."

Ali somehow kept Coopman upright until the fifth round. As George Kanter remembered: "He was the happiest loser I ever saw."

Ali VS Jimmy Young 30.04.76

Venue **Capital Center, Landover, Maryland**
Outcome **Won, decision, round 15**
Record **Fought 53 Won 51 Lost 2 Drawn 0**
Trivia **Ali versus Jimmy Young was perhaps Ali's least distinguished bout**

The fight with **Jimmy Young** was precisely the kind of bout Ali should have avoided, but as **George Plimpton** observed, "He loved to fight." Even so, Ali's desire to entertain was becoming taxed. He went to the ring against Jimmy Young patently short of conditioning and at his heaviest weight ever of 230lbs. Always prone to gaining weight, in part due to his inability to refuse bowls of ice cream, his favourite dessert, Ali would usually slough the weigh off in the gym. For a fight like Young, though, he didn't bother. Ali's relative lack of fitness was matched only by Young's absence of ambition.

Ringsiders were agreed that Ali produced the worst performance of his career in outpointing an opponent whose sole aim was to survive. Several times during the fight, Young put his head through the ropes as Ali advanced on him, forcing the referee to **halt the action**.

The final bell, when it came, was a merciful release for all involved.

Ali VS Richard Dunn | 24.05.76

Venue **Olympiahalle, Munich, Germany**
Prediction **KO, round five**
Outcome **Won, TKO, round five**
Record **Fought 54 Won 52 Lost 2 Drawn 0**
Trivia **Dunn was the last opponent Ali would ever stop inside the distance**

British fighter **Richard Dunn** could probably have comfortably handled Jean-Pierre Coopman, but he was not a fighter of the quality of Henry Cooper or Joe Bugner. Again, Ali's special appeal in **Europe** rescued the promotion, but it was becoming clear that the champion was a winter king, a fighter whose sublime skills would soon be claimed by the passing years.

Dunn, tall and blond, had trained hard and gave Ali his best; there was no shame in his performance. He just wasn't good enough. Ali knocked him down **five times in five rounds**.

Ali had promised the gloves he'd used in the fight to British promoter **Mickey Duff**, who was raising funds for **Chris Finnigan**, a terrific fighter who had lost sight in one eye. When he passed his gloves to Duff in the ring, Ali told Duff to look inside. In one it was written, 'Ali wins', and in the other 'round five'.

Ali VS Ken Norton III | 28.09.76

Venue **Yankee Stadium, New York City**
Opponent's nickname **The Hour Glass**
Prediction **"Norton must fall"**
Outcome **Won, decision, round 15**
Record **Fought 55 Won 53 Lost 2 Drawn 0**
Trivia **Ken Norton and Joe Frazier are the only men who Ali fought three times**

Ali was no longer a god; he still looked the same, but his physical gifts were diminishing. **Richard Dunn** would be the last opponent he ever put on the canvas. Robbed of much of his power, with his speed in decline and his great love of training on the wane, Ali had become reliant on his **ringcraft** and his ability to take the punishment to win fights. Now he faced the man who, after Frazier, had claim to be his most difficult opponent – **Ken Norton**. Each of their

161

previous fights had been close and Ali knew a third scrap would prove a severe test, but it was a test he was paid **$6m** to take. Ali prepared as well as he could. He would need to be fit: in their first encounter, Norton had been unseasoned. Now he had added a fine defence to his aggression.

Events surrounding the fight were chaotic. Strike action by New York's police meant the **Yankee Stadium** was host to a rough crowd. The fighters were jostled on the way to the ring, a herald to an uncomfortable night for the champ.

Norton controlled the first half and after seven rounds, was comfortably ahead. Ali, with his accumulated experience, began to work his way back in, stealing rounds with bursts of effort and spoiling Norton's attacks. From the ninth until the fourteenth, he lost just one round. With the referee, **Arthur Mercante Snr**, and two ringside judges scoring, the fighters answered the final bell dead level. Mercante remembered **Angelo Dundee** exhorting Ali to give everything in the final three minutes; they felt he needed the round to win. Norton's corner, though, thought they were further ahead than they were. Their advice was to keep out of trouble.

It was to prove fatal to Norton's chances. Ali took the 15th and with it the fight. Norton was distraught – he was the fitter man and had the reserves to outpunch Ali in the final throes, but had held back.

Somehow, Ali had found a way through. His instinctive understanding of what was required to win maintained his unsteady hold on the championship.

Ali VS Alfredo Evangelista

16.05.77

Venue **Capital Center, Landover, Maryland**
Outcome **Won, decision, round 15**
Record **Fought 56 Won 54 Lost 2 Drawn 0**
Trivia **Before the fight, Ali appeared in the DC comic, *Superman vs Muhammad Ali***

The Capital Center had hosted Ali's dreadful fight with **Jimmy Young**. Here was another stinker, with **Alfredo Evangelista**, a man not fit to lace Ali's boots. Indeed, the WBC had pulled strings to gain Evangelista the ranking necessary to sanction the bout as a title fight. The fight was turgid, with Ali in no danger of either losing or of stopping his opponent.

The decline was apparent and Ali himself began to discuss **retirement** openly.

Ali VS Earnie Shavers

29.09.77

Venue **Madison Square Garden, New York City**
Opponent's nickname **The Acorn**
Outcome **Won, decision, round 15**
Record **Fought 57 Won 55 Lost 2 Drawn 0**
Trivia **Ali turned up with 50 friends an hour before the sold-out bout and demanded they be let in – or he wouldn't fight**

Ali had been in boxing for so long, and had become such a part of American life that he was now seeing fighters who idolised him staring over from the opposite corner. **Earnie Shavers**, a big-hitting man who threw the hardest single shots in the fight game, was one such. In 54 fights, Earnie had won by stoppage or KO 52 times. His plan was simple: he was going to hit his hero hard.

The Garden was sold out again, and a huge television audience tuned into the fight. Drama was inherent in almost all of Ali's bouts, but the emphasis had shifted as he grew older. Now, people watched to see if he could survive.

If Earnie Shavers had possessed the ability to read a fight in equal measure to the size of his punch, he would have defeated Ali and become champion of the world. In round two, he hurt Ali but failed to follow up. In an inspired piece of brinkmanship, Ali had convinced Shavers he was merely pretending to be hurt, and Shavers backed off.

Ali came through the second and built a steady lead. In a promotional gimmick, the television commentators at ringside were allowed access to the judges' scorecards at the end of each round, and so **Angelo Dundee** was able to gain access to the status of the fight. By the 12th, Ali was ahead by eight rounds to four. Shavers came on strong in the 13th and 14th rounds, rocking Ali with some big punches. A big last three minutes for the challenger might have seen him home, yet Ali came back from the edge yet again. He stole the centre of the ring and stung Shavers with some cutting punches. It was enough.

Ali had won again, but some of those closest to him were worried. **Teddy Brenner**, who had booked Ali at the Garden for so long, took a stand. He told the 35-year-old champion he would no longer put on his fights, that it was time for Ali to go. **Ferdie Pacheco** wrote to Ali to advise him that his kidneys were showing signs of damage and that he should no longer fight.

The response of **Herbert Muhammad**, and of Ali, was to look for an easy payday. In **Leon Spinks**, they thought they'd found one.

Ali VS Leon Spinks I

15.02.78

Venue **Hilton Pavilion, Las Vegas, Nevada**
Opponent's nickname **The Vampyre**
Outcome **Lost, decision, round 15**
Record **Fought 58 Won 55 Lost 3 Drawn 0**
Trivia **Ali named the loss to Spinks as the most disappointing moment of his career**

T he 1976 Olympic Heavyweight Champion **Leon Spinks** was a rookie pro with just five fights and a manager called **Butch Lewis** behind him.

Ali was cool on Lewis's advances until he figured out an angle on which to sell the fight. As well as being an Olympic champion himself, Ali had beaten the three other **gold medallists** of his era: **Floyd Patterson**, **Joe Frazier** and **George Foreman**. The raw and ill-disciplined Spinks offered the chance to beat another. Yet Spinks was considered too far beneath Ali for him to be taken seriously as a challenger. "I'll be a laughing stock if I fight him," the champ said. So Spinks fought out a draw with the mediocre **Scott LeDoux** before beating **Alfio Righetti** in order to gain a ranking high enough to challenge for the belt.

> "I'LL BE A LAUGHING STOCK IF I FIGHT HIM" **Muhammad Ali on Leon Spinks as an opponent**

Spinks was a major underdog with two things on his side: youth and fitness. Ali had neither. When the bout failed to attract much interest despite the Olympic angle, Ali lost enthusiasm, too. **Thomas Hauser** reported that he sparred just 20 rounds in preparation.

Still, Ali should have been able to handle Spinks, who went to the ring with pain-killing injections for a muscle tear in his side, yet the pattern of his most recent fights was repeated. He lay on the ropes while the challenger built a lead. Spinks wailed away unscientifically on Ali's arms and body and he did not tire of doing so.

But when Ali went to the well, he found it empty for the first time in his career. He could not erode Spinks's lead: neither could he engineer a stoppage. Adrenaline carried Spinks through the pain of his injury and the drama built as it became apparent Ali was going to lose.

The champ summoned something for the last round and drove Spinks into the ropes, but it was not enough. He lost a split decision, which, in its closeness, appeared a little kind to the beaten king.

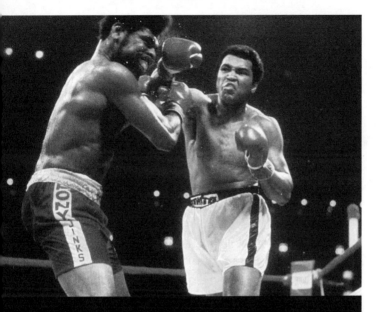

Ali VS Leon Spinks II

15.08.78

Venue **Superdome, New Orleans, Louisiana**
Opponent's nickname **The Vampyre**
Prediction **"I'm gonna put a whuppin on 'im"**
Outcome **Won, decision, round 15**
Record **Fought 59 Won 56 Lost 3 Drawn 0**
Trivia **Leon Spinks's younger brother Michael would later hold a version of the world heavyweight title and then lose it to Mike Tyson**

Ali was hurt by his loss. He remained gracious to **Spinks** but did not spare himself: "I was lousy," he admitted. Now, the promoters, managers and sanctioning bodies that had been forced to kowtow to the will of **Herbert Muhammad** for so long were in a position to freeze Ali out.

The public wanted a rematch with Spinks; it was the big-money fight for the new champion. But while Ali took a promotional tour of Russia, **Don King** had separated Spinks from the WBC belt without recourse to the ring. When Spinks refused to fight **Ken Norton** rather than Ali, he was stripped of that portion of the title, which would now be contested by Norton and **Larry Holmes** in a bout promoted by King.

Spinks and his ambitious manager **Butch Lewis** held firm, and signed to fight Ali again. The **WBA** belt would be on the line, as well as the linear championship.

Ali had given Butch Lewis his start in the game and Lewis now returned the favour.

> "NO TALKING, NO CLOWNING, NO ROPE-A-DOPE. THIS TIME I'M SERIOUS" **Muhammad Ali**

While Ali doggedly prepared to reclaim his title, Lewis had his work cut out controlling Leon Spinks. "I'm just a ghetto nigger," Spinks said. He was arrested for possession of cocaine (he had a five-dollar wrap in his hat-band) and he kept breaking training camp.

Without his championship, Ali had become even more of a draw. He was truly the people's fighter, and **64,000** packed the Superdome to see if he could become the first man to take the heavyweight championship three times.

Convinced this would be his last fight, Ali pushed himself through the rigours of training hoping to whip his ageing body into condition to go the distance on his toes if necessary. Ali didn't look good in his sparring sessions but he promised: "No talking, no clowning, no rope-a-dope. This time I'm serious."

Ali did ignore the ropes and fought from the centre of the ring but his timing was marginally off. By round five he'd found his range and began to tee-off on Spinks. Spinks countered by rolling from the waist in an attempt to bypass Ali's scoring jabs. When this brought him no joy he began charging at Ali who simply grabbed Spinks and held on until the referee broke them.

Ali took control and kept it. The fight was a slow one, devoid of thrills as Ali gave the inexperienced champion a lesson in ringcraft, but the drama grew steadily as Spinks tried to cut Ali's lead. As the last rounds dribbled away, the emotion of the moment took over. History was at hand. Ali took a clear decision and the title for a third time.

Nine months later, he announced his retirement from professional boxing.

Ali VS Larry Holmes

02.10.80

Venue **Caesar's Palace, Las Vegas, Nevada**
Opponent's nickname **The Peanut**
Prediction **"I promise you, it will be no contest. I predict a miracle"**
Outcome **Lost, TKO, round 11**
Record **Fought 60 Won 56 Lost 4 Drawn 0**
Trivia **Ali fails to go the distance for the first time in his professional career**

n his retirement, Ali travelled the world on goodwill missions. He went to India and then undertook what **Time** magazine called, "The most bizarre diplomatic mission in recent US history," travelling to Tanzania and Kenya on behalf of president **Jimmy Carter**, to raise support for the American boycott of the 1980 Olympic Games in Moscow. Yet he could not resist the lure of the ring – or the money it offered, which he now needed. Against all good advice, including that of his mother **Odessa**, Ali decided to end his retirement to fight the new champion, a former sparring partner of his named **Larry Holmes**.

Holmes had learned his trade at the fists of not one master, but two. As well as sparring with Ali for two years, he had helped **Joe Frazier** to prepare for his first fight with the champion. Now he was a champion himself, and a fine one at that, far too good for Ali in his dotage.

Yet Ali relished his return: he clowned around more happily than ever in training, sometimes sparring one-handed because, he claimed, that was all he would need to beat Holmes. Despite that, the truth was Muhammad Ali should never have been licensed to fight this bout. His speech had already begun to deteriorate and he was experiencing some difficulty in motor function, especially when tired. Beyond the medical evidence, it was clear to boxing people that Ali was a shot fighter.

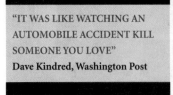

"IT WAS LIKE WATCHING AN AUTOMOBILE ACCIDENT KILL SOMEONE YOU LOVE"

Dave Kindred, Washington Post

Yet public interest was high. Could Holmes handle the pressure of fighting **The Greatest**, the three-times world champion? Ali tried to needle a reaction from his opponent in the build-up, but found Holmes wasn't playing the game.

Ali had very few competitive rounds left in him. He was lethargic and slow. His physical magnificence, still in evidence, was an illusion and some of the medication he'd been prescribed was exacerbating his condition. Even **Angelo Dundee** was clinging to the hope that Ali just looked bad in the gym, as he often had done, and would come through in the ring.

It was a false hope exposed by Holmes, who took little pleasure from beating Ali up. That beating does not need describing here. As ever, Ali's courage was boundless but, as **Dave Kindred** of the **Washington Post** told Thomas Hauser: "It was like watching an automobile accident kill someone you love." Angelo Dundee threw in the towel at the end of round eleven.

For his pain, Ali received a vote of thanks from **Don King**: a paycheck that was $950,000 short of the $8m he had earned at such a price.

Ken Norton was guaranteed worldwide fame when, in 1973, he became only the second man to beat Ali, breaking his jaw in the second round into the bargain.

Norton, who took up boxing when he joined the marines, had to suffer the corny nickname of The Black Hercules for a while. But he always seemed to save his best for Ali, countering his rapier combinations with a lack of regard and clubbing blows.

Their rubber match in 1976 was highly controversial, with most of the 30,000 spectators believing Norton had done enough to win. Ali had also got the better of him in the rematch.

In 1978, Leon Spinks failed to honour an agreement to defend his world title against Norton and the WBC awarded the belt to Norton. His reign lasted just three months, however, when he lost on points to Larry Holmes in one of the greatest heavyweight fights ever. "I felt I won that fight," he said. "I still feel I did enough to earn a split decision."

He retired in 1981, briefly acted in movies but was left permanently injured after a horrendous automobile accident.

Ali VS Trevor Berbick

11.12.81

Venue **Queen Elizabeth Sports Center, Nassau, Bahamas**
Outcome **Lost, decision, round 10**
Record **Fought 61 Won 56 Lost 5 Drawn 0**
Trivia **Mike Tyson became the youngest-ever champ when he KO-ed Berbick in 1986**

"I thought I should go out of boxing with a win," Ali said. "Or if not with a win, at least throwing punches." It was nonsense, of course. Almost 40, already damaged by the attrition of his profession and now the victim of another large financial scandal (see page 82), Ali took a bout with **Trevor Berbick**, who had just lost a decision to Larry Holmes in a title bout.

Manoeuvrings behind the promotion, run by **Nation of Islam** member **James Cornelius**, were internecine. Even Don King received a beating "for interfering with Muslim business" as he pressed a claim for a part of Berbick's end of the deal.

Berbick handed Ali another defeat, although Ali exited on his feet, which was as he had wanted. "I came out all right for an old man," he said in the post-fight press conference. "We all lose sometimes. We all grow old."

With those words, perhaps the greatest career in boxing came to an end.

Henry Cooper MBE Fought Muhammad Ali in 1963 and 1966

The **greatest tribute** I can pay Ali is that he was the best of his time. He took on and overcame all of the challenges put in front of him.

The greatest fighter I ever saw was **Sugar Ray Robinson**. He had everything: he was good looking, he had the best jab ever and he fought 201 times, winning 174. If I had to look at the heavyweights in historical terms then **Joe Louis** would be number one on my list. The reason I've gone for Louis is simple: he made a record number of successful defences (25) of the heavyweight crown. He was the fighter I looked up to. He was tremendously patient but a terrific finisher.

For me, Ali would come in just behind **The Rock**, Rocky Marciano. People never talk about Marciano and I don't know why. He is the only heavyweight to retire without losing a single fight. That's some feat considering he had 49 of them. I'd have given both Louis and Marciano a great chance of beating Ali even in his prime. They were experts at cutting the ring off and were such deadly punchers they were an instant danger. Louis, especially, was the most economical of all the heavyweights; never moving more than a foot or two to connect on his opponent.

You just have to have a look at the guys Ali struggled against and you will see they were the shorter guys with good left hooks, like **Joe Frazier**. Even though I was over six feet I was considered a small heavyweight and I had to get inside his enormous reach. And I did, knocking him down with a perfect left hook. A fighter called **Sonny Banks** knocked him down early in his career: again a smallish boxer with a dangerous left hook.

When I fought Ali, he wanted the biggest ring was available, which was over 20 feet square, so he knew the danger of being cornered. World champions back then could stipulate the size of the ring. When Marciano was champion he wanted the 18ft ring, so that the chances of him trapping and getting to his opponents increased.

Ali loved to fight the bigger guys like **Ernie Terrell**, **Sonny Liston**, **George**

Foreman, because he was so much faster and that would immediately put them at a disadvantage. He could control them with his jab, which was beautiful to watch – but not to feel, I can tell you. You could hurt Ali if you got inside and roughed him. I did this in our first fight in 1963: I gave him a bloody nose and thought "this kid has no idea how to fight on the inside."

He was a quick learner: in the rematch every time I went to slip and get inside he grabbed me so tight it felt like a vice. He was much bigger and stronger than he had been in the first fight and he could mix it a bit more. I think Ali's power is underrated. It wasn't until he slowed down that he got more leverage on his punches and hit with more force. He did pound a few guys and knocked out tough men like Liston and Foreman. He even stopped **Joe Frazier**, which seemed impossible for him to do. But then he often did the impossible.

Emmanuel Steward Trainer and founder of the Kronk Gym

Muhammad Ali would, undoubtedly in my mind, have beaten every heavyweight who ever lived. Regardless of all the defects they said he had, he succeeded so much at what he did. He was in such condition that just the tempo and pace of his fights in his prime meant no one could keep up with him. He was also one of the most intelligent men in boxing. He combined rhythm, movement and psychology to become one of the greatest fighters ever.

Comparing him to other heavyweights throughout history is difficult though, because I think in his prime he was far ahead of them.

Behind Ali I would rate **Larry Holmes**, who I think was never given his due credit. He was an intense fighter with a great jab, one of the best ever, and he was extremely tough and difficult to beat. Like Ali, he mastered two or three things to such a degree that nobody of his time could beat him.

George Foreman is my third choice. A lot of people might find that difficult to fathom, but I just couldn't see most heavyweights outside of Ali beating Foreman in his prime. Plus he achieved a hell of a lot considering that his career went flat after losing to Ali in 1974. My former fighter **Lennox Lewis** would be my next choice. Lennox is a big guy: his size means a lot. And there was his jab and his efficiency. He was a very good technician. Completing the top five heavyweights is **Sonny Liston**. Again some people may scoff at that, but in his prime – and I don't mean the old man that fought Ali twice – in 1958, '59 and '60 Liston was the most fearsome, awesome fighter I have ever seen.

The best heavyweight boxer I had ever seen prior to Ali was **Gene Tunney**. Ali's style had a lot of similarities to Tunney's, even though he tried to take after **Sugar Ray Robinson**. But Robinson never did much dancing: he would move

Ali was the first heavyweight to bring the movement and speed of lighter fighters up to the top division. " I am the fastest heavyweight with feet and hand."

Early in his career he wanted to box like his hero Sugar Ray Robinson, who was noted for the devastating speed of his combination punching and footwork.

The young Ali used his legs to keep himself out of the punching range of opponents while inviting them to attack his unprotected chin. With his uncanny reflexes he was able to pull back from the waist rather than block or duck and with his hands held low he was able to launch attacks from unconventional angles.

"Ali was very unorthodox," says Henry Cooper, who fought Ali twice. "He made you miss by slipping punches inside, leaning away. His movement was not heard of in those days: it was just a rhythmic glide all over the ring. He was undoubtedly the fastest moving heavyweight the world has ever seen. I think only Floyd Patterson, who I also fought, was faster with his punches."

Later in his career, Ali relied increasingly on his wonderful jab and his stiff, straight right hand, plus his ringcraft and the ability to take a punch. But perhaps his greatest asset was his mental strength: he always found a way to win, whether it was by foxing – George Foreman –or out-psyching – Sonny Liston.

and then explode with big vicious combinations. Tunney was cute just like Ali, and was he way too skilful for the men of his time in the 1920s. He could move well and shift directions and he had a fantastic jab.

Style-wise Ali mastered three things, which in my opinion, are what made him so great: he had a beautiful jab, which he timed immaculately. He had a beautiful right hand – he could throw that right over your jab with marksman precision – and from that he developed a left hook, which wasn't a power punch, but a tool used to expand his repertoire.

Ali would move, change direction, jab to the body, feint jab to the head and then move again… Most heavyweights are not used to moving. Not even great heavyweight champions like **Joe Louis** and **Jack Johnson**. These guys who fought Ali would just get exhausted, not just physically but mentally because of the tempo of the movement and the rhythm of the fight.

He couldn't punch to the body, he couldn't and didn't in-fight, nor did he throw a good uppercut, but it didn't matter. Remember too he had great mental strength. All those things he did, he did so well, and that's how he was able to become the greatest heavyweight ever.

Muhammad
Ali
social history

How Ali's developing political consciousness
influenced world opinion — and the course of a war

"HE'S CONFESSED HE'S A BELIEVER.
HE HAS ACCEPTED MUHAMMAD AS
THE MESSENGER OF ALLAH" **Elijah Muhammad**

Birth of the Nation

The morning after he defeated Sonny Liston for the first time and became heavyweight champion of the world, Cassius Clay acknowledged that he was a member of the **Nation of Islam** and adopted the **waiting name** of **Cassius X**. Up until that moment, he had been regarded as a brash, perhaps eccentric young man. Immediately afterwards, in the public eye he was perceived as something far more dangerous: a black man allied with a sinister cult that much of America feared and did not understand.

It was 1964. Ali had grown up in America's South, among people who didn't have to look back beyond their grandparents to see the days of slavery, who lived in cities divided along racial lines. In the course of Cassius Clay's political awakening, a disparate array of individuals, movements, philosophies and ideas would interact, almost randomly, as forces for change. Clay himself became a figurehead and catalyst for that change. This section looks at the people and groups involved, and how they came together during an era that changed the political and social landscape of America.

The man who would become known as **the Messenger** was born **Elijah Poole** in 1897, the grandson of Georgia slaves. His was a childhood of extreme poverty and fear in a time when black men were lynched with sickening regularity. At the age of 25, Poole moved to Detroit with his wife and three children to work on the assembly lines. Life in the city was no better and Poole began to look for some meaning beyond the grind of work and the escape of alcohol. He heard about the sermons of a preacher called **WD Fard**, a door-to-door silk salesman. Fard had drawn on a variety of ideas and stitched them together. From **Islam** he took the heritage, claiming black superiority going back thousands of years. From other **American churches** he drew in the concepts of strong moral behaviour and clean living. He also included notions of black pride from Marcus Garvey, a Jamaican who formed the **Universal Negro Improvement Association** and emigrated to America to spread his ideas. Garvey's central thoughts concerned the establishment of a black homeland in Africa, where black people had lived in civilised societies at a time when whites were still savages.

Fard took these ideas and formed the Nation of Islam with himself cast in the role of **Allah's spokesman**. Elijah Poole quickly became dedicated to Fard and to the Nation and rose within its ranks. Fard developed a credo that differed from that of the **Koran**, although he used the Koran as his holy book.

According to Fard and, later, **Elijah Muhammad**, the universe had begun 76 trillion years before. The earth had been formed from a single atom, and the **Original Man, Allah**, had come from the same atom. Allah then created the universe and the black race.

There had been no white people until 6,600 years before the beginning of Fard's account, when an evil scientist called **Mr Yacub** began preaching against Allah, whereupon he and 59,999 of his followers were exiled to an Aegean island called **Patmos**. There Yacub began killing off black men and creating a devil race by mating the lighter men and women. When Yacub died, there were no blacks left, and six hundred years later, the people of Patmos had become white devils, a sickly, stupid people who were exiled to **Europe** after trying to return to Islam. There, they lived as savages until **Moses** was sent to civilise them. Gradually they came to be dominant and began to import slaves from **Africa**, teaching them **Christianity**.

Redemption, Fard preached, would come only when a spacecraft half-a-mile wide, crewed by black men, flew down to distribute pamphlets telling Muslims where to hide from a forthcoming attack. Ten days after this event, the foretold brutal attack would leave only the righteous alive and America would burn in a lake of fire for 390 years.

Elijah Poole took over from Fard in 1934 and assumed the name **Elijah Muhammad**. He refused the draft into the US Army during World War 2, and was imprisoned for three-and-a-half years. When freed, he resumed his mission. The Nation, and other movements like it, found support in poor black communities. Some drew comfort from its stories of coming events that would improve the lives of black people. Others, mainly young men, were attracted to the Nation because of its message of black pride, discipline and self-sufficiency.

If the wilder theologies of Fard and Elijah Muhammad seem strange and distant almost a century later, they must be viewed within the context of the times. For millions of black people in America, life was a struggle from which there appeared little chance of release. Grinding poverty was an overriding theme. **Segregation**, especially in the South, was common and enforced by law. More than that, it was reinforced by the power of economics. Black areas were the poor parts of town. Black people sat at the back of buses and on separate benches and in different parks and theatres. Such divisions were bound into the social fabric, and removing them from the minds of the American people would be far harder than removing them from the statute books.

Against this background, churches and preachers, who were offering a message of pride, hope and solidarity found a natural constituency. One of the young men drawn to Elijah Muhammad and the Nation of Islam was

Malcolm Little, who became known as **Malcolm X**.

Malcolm was thrown into the struggle as a child. His father **Earl** was a follower of Marcus Garvey and an outspoken **Baptist minister**. While his mother **Louise** was pregnant with Malcolm, **Ku Klux Klan** riders galloped up to their home with rifles and chased them out of town. Another white supremacist organisation, the **Black Legion**, burned down their house.

In 1931, when Malcolm was six-years-old, his father was found dead on some streetcar tracks. The police ruled his death an accident, although the family were sure the Black Legion were involved. Louise never recovered from her loss and was committed to a mental institution, leaving Malcolm and his seven brothers and sisters to be split up and sent to various orphanages and foster homes.

Elijah Muhammad had an unusual interpretation of Islam

Malcolm was an excellent student with a powerful intellect, but became disillusioned when a teacher told him his idea of becoming a **lawyer** was "no realistic goal for a nigger". He dropped out, moved to **Harlem** and became involved in narcotics, prostitution and gambling rings. In 1946, he was sentenced to eight to 10 years in jail for burglary, and was paroled after seven. He began serving his time in Charlestown prison, where he had access to the library. Here, he devoured as many books as possible, beginning a process of **self-education** that would continue on his transfer to Norfolk Prison in Massachussetts.

In prison he was visited by his brother **Reginald**, who was a Nation of Islam member, and Malcolm became interested in what his brother had to say. On being freed from jail he joined up and replaced his slave name of Little with an X, to symbolise his lost tribal name.

Malcolm's passion and intelligence quickly marked him out. Elijah Muhammad made him a national spokesman for the Nation and Malcolm's fire increased membership from 5,000 in 1952 to 30,000 in 1963. This burgeoning organisation was the one **Muhammad Ali**, then Cassius Clay, was about to join.

Cassius Clay's awakening

Cassius first met Malcolm X in **Detroit** in **1962** at a diner next to a mosque at which Cassius and his brother Rudy were to attend a rally. As was his habit, Cassius introduced himself to Malcolm and they struck up an immediate rapport. Malcolm had no idea that Cassius was the best young boxer in America and a contender for the heavyweight title because he didn't follow the sport – Elijah Muhammad preached that **boxing** was an example of black men being subjugated for the entertainment of whites. But as Clay began his campaign to get **Sonny Liston** in the ring, Malcolm X sought him out at various rallies and spoke with him about the **Nation** and its aims.

During 1963 and 1964, Malcolm and Cassius developed a close bond. Malcolm was a mentor and advisor to the younger man, who found his rhetorical brilliance and the intellectual ferocity of his arguments highly persuasive.

While Cassius had not been exposed to anything like the horrors of Malcolm's childhood, he had been raised in a home where the social order was often questioned. Cassius Clay Snr had left school at the age of 14 and his dreams of becoming an artist had, he felt, been stymied by the limited opportunities available to black people. As a younger man, he had been a great admirer of Marcus Garvey, and supported his ideas of black pride and self-sufficiency. He often held forth at the Clay dinner table about his distrust of white people.

In tandem with his father's views, Cassius Clay was growing up in a divided city. **Louisville**, Kentucky was segregated along racial lines and subject to the so-called **Jim Crow laws**, passed in the Southern states after the Civil War in the

Malcolm X returns to his bombed home in February 1965

1870s. These laws, more than 400 separate pieces of legislation, kept society segregated, discriminating against black Americans with regard to attendance at schools, theatres, diners, and public facilities and spaces and on public transport. In some states, they even forbade inter-racial marriage.

During Cassius's childhood in the 1950s, the Jim Crow laws were slowly being repealed. The National Association for the

Advancement of Colored People (**NAACP**) campaigned for the end of segregation on trains and buses. The **Supreme Court** ruled such segregation unconstitutional on inter-state railways in 1952 and on inter-state buses two years later. Yet segregation continued, with blacks forced to sit at the back of buses on local rides.

The divisions were ingrained in minds as well as on the statue books. Cassius and Rudy soon learned which areas of Louisville would earn them shouts of "go home, nigger" if they ventured there. Cassius knew what it was like to see his mother refused a glass of water at a diner, and how it felt to have white people jump ahead of them in queues as if they didn't exist.

Just months after the court case that followed the murder of **Emmett Till** – in a sham trial two white men accused of the crime, Roy Bryant and JW Milam, were acquitted – **Rosa Parks** made a stand and refused to surrender her seat on a bus to a white person in Montgomery, Alabama. The subsequent **Montgomery Bus Boycott** led to the emergence of **Dr Martin Luther King** as a civil rights leader and set in action the chain of the events that led to the end of the Jim Crow laws.

Emmett Till had been just a year older than Clay when he died. The lesson was clear. Clay understood he was growing up in a country that might be hostile to him because of the colour of his skin and he, like many others, burned with the injustice of it. Clay first heard about the Nation of Islam and Elijah Muhammad while at a **Golden Gloves** tournament in Chicago in 1959. He read a copy of the **Muhammad Speaks** newspaper and found its sentiments chimed with his own experience. A year later he returned from Rome a hero, with an Olympic gold medal around his neck, but he later told his biographer **Thomas Hauser**, "I still got treated like a nigger."

In Miami in 1961, he met **Captain Sam**, the former **Sam Saxon**, who was recruiting for the Nation of Islam. He took Clay to a meeting, where he listened to a preacher named **Brother John** speaking. Brother John's words awoke something in Clay. "The first time I felt truly spiritual in my life was when I walked into that mosque in Miami," he told Hauser. "I liked what I heard. I respected Martin Luther King and all the other civil rights leaders, but I was taking a different road."

As the Civil Rights struggle raged, Ali met **Jeremiah Shabazz** and then Malcolm X. Everything about the Nation made sense to him, he even bought the stories about Yacub and the spacecraft.

"For three years, up until I fought Sonny Liston, I'd sneak into Nation of Islam meetings through the back door," Ali told Hauser. "I didn't want people to know I was there. I was afraid that if they knew, I wouldn't be allowed to fight for the title. Later on, I learned to stand up for my beliefs."

Conversion: from Clay to Ali

oon after Cassius met Malcolm X, a serious split opened up in the Nation of Islam. Malcolm discovered that Elijah Muhammad had been engaging in extra-marital affairs, with as many as six women within the Nation's organisation and had even had got two of his secretaries pregnant (this was not news to the FBI, who had known since 1959 and tried to discredit Elijah with a series of anonymous letters that were ignored by his followers).

Malcolm's faith was deeply compromised: he had taken Elijah's teaching as the moral centre of his life and remained celibate until his own marriage to **Betty Shabazz** in 1958. Now he had discovered **the Messenger** was a hypocrite, he began to question other facets of the Nation, such as the acquisition of real estate and luxury cars. He felt guilty about the thousands of men like him that he had recruited – apparently on the basis of a lie. Malcolm also found himself at odds with the Nation's theology, some of which went against **Muslim orthodoxy** in declaring WD Fard as Allah incarnate.

The division widened when Malcolm was suspended from the Nation for 90 days by Elijah Muhammad after he ignored Elijah's order not to make any public comment on the assassination of **John F. Kennedy** (he'd made a remark about "chickens coming home to roost"). Malcolm was torn by his exile and made a taped apology to the Messenger, who still refused to reinstate him.

Cassius Clay carefully avoided taking sides in the dispute. He invited Malcolm, Betty and their children to stay with him in **Miami** weeks before he fought **Sonny Liston** for the heavyweight championship. The **FBI**, who routinely kept individuals and organisations within the Civil Rights movement under surveillance, recorded the event. Cassius and Malcolm went to New York together, where Clay attended a rally, and when the men got back to Miami, the story of Clay's involvement with the Nation began to break in the press. On 3 February 1964, 21 days before the Liston scrap, Clay told the **Louisville Courier-Journal**: "Sure, I talked to the Muslims and I'm going back again. I like the Muslims." He went on to explain that he agreed with them that integration was wrong and as white people didn't want it anyway, everyone should be happy.

The following week, **Cassius Clay Snr** confirmed rumours that his son had joined the **Nation** in an angry interview with **Pat Putnam**, the **Miami Herald**'s boxing reporter. "They've brainwashed him," Cassius Snr said. Putnam received several death threats after the piece ran – threats that stopped only after Putnam told Cassius about them.

While Malcolm felt that delivering Cassius Clay as a new recruit might re-establish his power base within the Nation and even curry some favour with its leader. But Muhammad was ambivalent about Clay joining. He felt that a defeat to Liston would damage the Nation's image and he told Malcolm not to align himself too closely with Clay. Malcolm ignored Elijah's advice and instead helped Cassius to prepare mentally for the challenge of the forthcoming fight with Liston. They talked about **David and Goliath**, and how **God** would not allow someone who believed to fail. Their talks became important psychological tools for Clay as a person and as a boxer.

Clay's victory over Liston was so unexpected that his management, the **Louisville Sponsoring Group**, had no celebration planned. Instead, Cassius spent the hours after the fight in a hotel room with Malcolm, several other Nation activists and the football player **Jim Brown**, eating ice cream. The next morning, he confirmed to the press – and through them, to the world – that he was a **member** of the Nation of Islam.

Two days later, Elijah Muhammad welcomed Clay while addressing some five thousand people at a rally in Chicago. "I'm happy he's confessed he's a believer," Elijah said, going on to claim that Clay had beaten a tougher man "because he has accepted Muhammad as the messenger of Allah".

Within two weeks, Cassius Clay was no more. Subsequent to his adopting the waiting name of Cassius X, Elijah Muhammad called him **Muhammad Ali**. At the same time, Ali's brother **Rudolph Clay** became **Rahaman Ali**.

The name change was a great moment for Ali and yet most of the country refused to acknowledge it. To mainstream America, the Nation of Islam was an obscure sect of which they had barely heard, the name **Black Muslims** used dismissively. Cassius Clay had been an eccentric braggart; Muhammad Ali became something else entirely. Some people in the boxing world chose to believe that Ali wasn't serious about his name change. However, when the new champion was introduced to the crowd at Madison Square Garden on 20 March 1963 as Cassius Clay, he left in disgust, the boos ringing in his ears.

Ali's **conversion**, although a momentous event in his life, and now a significant and symbolic moment in a wider context, had a sad end as it led to the end of his friendship with Malcolm X. The **split** between Elijah Muhammad and Malcolm was widening. Ali had hitherto refused to side with Malcolm against the Messenger. However, on the night of the

"SURE, I TALKED TO THE MUSLIMS, AND I'M GOING BACK AGAIN. I LIKE THE MUSLIMS"
Cassius Clay

Martin Luther King with Nation leader Elijah Muhammad

Liston fight, he had confided in Jim Brown that he considered Elijah to be a great man and that he would continue to align himself with him. Ali's obvious affection for Malcolm was not enough to change his mind.

Malcolm, the **firebrand** who had once preached that death wasn't good enough for anyone who stood up against Elijah Muhammad, now did just that. He was open about the fact that in doing so, he felt he was contributing to his own doom. He stated publicly that he thought the Muslims would assassinate him. According to **Jeremiah Shabazz**, when questioned as to why, Malcolm replied, "because I taught them".

In the spring of 1964, Malcolm went on a **pilgrimage to Mecca** and his world view began to alter quite radically. "There I met blond-haired, blue-eyed men who I could call my brothers," he said. The quote was the exact opposite of his famous polemics of the 1950s, when he preached about **blue-eyed devils**.

After his return from Mecca, Malcolm began preaching to all races and took an integrationist view: "America needs to understand **Islam**, because this is the one religion that erases from its society the race problem…" He formed the non-religious, non-sectarian **Organisation of African American Unity**. In May 1964, he travelled to **Ghana**. By coincidence, Muhammad Ali was also there on a trip of his own. The pair crossed paths in the lobby of the **Hotel Ambassador**. Ali refused to acknowledge Malcolm, a man he had once revered. "He's gone so far out, he's gone completely," Ali told the press. "No one listens to Malcolm any more."

The writer **Alex Haley**, who knew both men, told Thomas Hauser of the results of Ali's actions: "[They] hurt Malcolm more than any other person turning away from him that I know of." The rift was never healed.

After surviving many attempts on his life, Malcolm X, the man who said, "We have to keep in mind at all times that we are not fighting for integration, nor are we fighting for separation, we are fighting for recognition… for the right to live as free humans in this society," was assassinated on 21 February 1965, shot 15 times at close range at the **Audubon Ballroom** in Manhattan. The three men convicted of his murder, Talmadge Hayer, Norman 3X Butler and Thomas 15X Johnson, all had connections to the **Nation of Islam**.

Cassius Clay in context

The Nation of Islam was just one of a disparate group of social and political influences in the America of the 1950s and 1960s. Before Malcolm X became involved, it was a tiny cult with a strict moral code.

The Nation offered a method of resistance that went beyond passive protest. But the Nation of Islam's message was extreme and separatist, and there were other philosophies, such as that of Martin Luther King. He preached a message of black pride, hope and non-violent protest, but it was inclusive rather than exclusive. While the Nation was still growing, King led the 381-day **Montgomery Bus Boycott** that saw the Jim Crow laws start to crumble. In 1963, at the **March on Washington**, he made the most famous and impactful speech of the **Civil Rights** movement. It encapsulated his world view: "I have a dream that my four children will one day live in a nation where they will not be judged by the color of their skin, but by the content of their character."

By 1964, as Cassius Clay became **Muhammad Ali**, King had won the **Nobel Peace** Prize and was influential on a scale beyond anything the Nation could consider. For the 13 years that he led the Civil Rights movement, King faced almost constant danger of assassination. **J Edgar Hoover's FBI** hounded him, even trying to force him to commit suicide after winning the Nobel prize.

In 1964, movements for social justice, like **NAACP**, the Congress of Racial Equality (**CORE**) and the Student Nonviolent Coordinating Committee (**SNCC**) began to register huge numbers of black voters, changing the demographic of the electorate. President **Lyndon Johnson** signed the Civil Rights Act that year, making segregation and discrimination in employment illegal. But still violence raged. In August 1964, three Civil Rights workers were murdered by the **Ku Klux Klan** in Mississippi. Malcolm X was assassinated in February 1965 and in March, police hospitalised 50 black protesters at a march in Alabama on what became known as **Bloody Sunday**.

Dr Martin Luther King was **assassinated** by **James Earl Ray** on 4 April 1968, nine months after the Supreme Court forced 16 States to repeal laws banning interracial marriage, and just seven days before Lyndon Johnson signed the Civil Rights Act of 1968, which outlawed discrimination in housing.

Set in the context of such far-reaching social upheaval, the impact of Ali's involvement with the Nation of Islam was, in the end, peripheral to the central struggle. It was with his refusal to be inducted into the **US Army** that Ali truly found a global voice.

"No Vietcong ever called me nigger"

When Ali failed to take a step forward to answer his name at the **US Army's Entrance Station** in Houston on 28 April 1967, he backed up his words with actions; he became a man of principle. He also became a catalyst, a man around whom opposing forces fought. Indeed, it was perhaps as a **global figurehead** as the embodiment of this struggle, that he had his greatest impact. When he took his stand with the words, "I ain't got no quarrel with them Vietcong," and later, by way of clarification, the even more explosive "no Vietcong ever called me nigger", Ali caught a particular moment and framed it in one sentence.

In the early days of his exile, Ali's arguments over **refusing the draft** were prone to confusion. Soon, though, the situation was clearer in his mind. The battle he wanted to win was the one being fought out in America, not in Vietnam. Martin Luther King encouraged him, both privately and publicly. Two days after Ali had refused the draft, King told his Alabama congregation, "He is giving up even fame. He is giving up millions of dollars in order to stand up for what his conscience tells him is right."

King had been advised that he was mistaken in allying the Civil Rights movement with the anti-war protests, yet the two were linked by the disproportionate amount of black Americans dying in the conflict and the lack of black representation on draft boards.

Ali's act, a stance that questioned the validity of the war, came during a year when America began to sustain heavy casualties, with no end to the bloodshed in sight. There were half-a-million US troops in **Vietnam**, and 10,000 of them died. In October 1967, a **Stop The Draft** week involved thousands of demonstrators, mostly white. The peace movement, full of hippies and white liberals, formed a strange alliance with Ali and Martin Luther King. Throughout 1968, their voices grew louder, even though Ali's own focus remained on the plight of black Americans in "a white man's war".

Ali remained a symbol to all. **Esquire** magazine ran a famous cover depicting Ali martyred, **Saint Sebastian**-style, his torso shot full of arrows ("The slings and arrows of outrageous fortune," the coverline read). He became revered for his courage in facing jail, and in the face of the almost constant threat of assassination, despite which he rarely used bodyguards. People throughout the world understood how much he loved boxing and being the champ, and yet he had surrendered it all on a matter of principle.

The shift in public opinion over the conflict was to become the overwhelming factor in his return to boxing and the eventual overturning of his conviction by the Supreme Court.

Late in 1969, the **National Baptist Convention** urged the government to show clemency to Ali in order to "lessen domestic tensions". Many black servicemen also now saw Ali as a leader, with 56 per cent of the black American population opposed the war. In

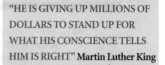

"HE IS GIVING UP MILLIONS OF DOLLARS TO STAND UP FOR WHAT HIS CONSCIENCE TELLS HIM IS RIGHT" Martin Luther King

October 1969, one million people of all creeds marched on Washington in protest at the conflict and by the summer of 1970, public opinion stood at almost 60 per cent against America's continued involvement in Vietnam.

In May 1970, four students were shot dead on the campus of **Kent State University**, near Cleveland, Ohio. More than four million people protested. America began to withdraw troops from Vietnam and by October, Muhammad Ali had returned to the ring. His conviction for draft evasion was quashed by the US Supreme Court on 28 June 1971. The last US **troops were withdrawn** from Vietnam on 29 March 1973.

Ali never really convinced anyone that his opposition to the war was entirely religious. It was in truth bound up in far more complex issues at the point where the Civil Rights and anti-war movements met. Yet Ali, whatever his motives, was an inspirational figure in those years. His public stand was applauded by Martin Luther King and **Stokely Carmichael**, the more militant black leader who coined the phrase Black Power, and helped highlight the inequalities in the way the draft for Vietnam was applied.

He was never as vociferous from the 1970s onwards but he did, in 1975, take an interest in the case of controversial black boxer Hurricane Carter, accused of murder. But in the 1960s, Ali's moral courage, and also his fame throughout the world, marked him out as a man of his age, a sportsman who transcended his sport, just as **Jack Johnson** and **Jackie Robinson** had done before him.

The struggle won

When Elijah Muhammad died in 1975, the Nation of Islam, under Elijah's son **Wallace**, rejected separatism and violence. Wallace aligned the Nation with the international Islamic community and opened it to members of all races. The Nation was renamed the **American Society of Muslims**, although a group of former members led by **Louis Farrakhan**, established a new organisation, bearing the original name, in 1977. The two groups finally declared an end to their rivalry in 2000.

Muhammad Ali's own faith changed as the Nation did. "Wallace taught us the true meaning of the **Koran**," Ali told his biographer Thomas Hauser in 1991. "He showed that colour doesn't matter. What I believe in now is true Islam."

Muhammad Ali became a symbol of an era of monumental change. He began it as a villain in the eyes of many and emerged as a hero to nearly all. When he lit the Olympic flame to open the Games of 1996 in Atlanta, three billion people watched, and, as Thomas Hauser wrote: "In all likelihood there has never been a time in the history of the earth when three billion people felt love at the same time. But Ali made it happen… He is not only a great man, he is a good one."

Muhammad Ali at prayer

Muhammad
Ali
the icon

Pretty as a picture and with a personality to match,
Ali created himself in his own image

"LOOK – THERE AIN'T NEVER BEEN ANOTHER FIGHTER LIKE ME. AIN'T NEVER BEEN NO NOTHING LIKE ME" **Muhammad Ali**

The icon

As his life and career gained momentum, **Ali's** circumstances, his personality, his *joie de vivre* and innate quotability drew TV crews, photographers, reporters, writers and artists to him. Until his exile, Ali had polarised opinion, with many of America's most influential media commentators against him. Afterwards, as he began to box again, his legend grew. His physical beauty, his love of performance and people, and the impact of his fights made him an obvious subject for the best reporters and photographers of the day.

As American involvement in **Vietnam** came under question and the **Civil Rights** movement asserted the rights of black Americans to live freely and equally, Ali's position in American culture was reassessed. There was a synergy between the great fighter and some great writers, who found they could use Ali as a lightning rod, a figure who might define the times in which he lived.

In turn, Ali was happy to have them as an audience. An ingenuous fellow, Ali was the exact opposite of the contemporary celebrity. He allowed the press access on a scale unthinkable today. He would talk to anyone (**George Plimpton** remembered waiting for his slot while Ali gave an interview to some students from a high-school newspaper), and he would answer any question they threw at him. Being a part of Ali's entourage was a joy: he would prove equally entertaining for a heavyweight writer like **Norman Mailer**, gonzo correspondent **Hunter S. Thompson** or a TV host such as **Michael Parkinson**. Ali's verbal jousts with the American TV presenter and boxing commentator **Howard Cosell** turned Cosell into a bigger celebrity, too.

The unequivocal outcome of a boxing match, the natural tendency to pitch the "good" man against the "bad," Ali's willingness to sell a fight in whatever way suited him best, and the brilliance of his contests, generated all the drama the media

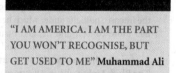

"I AM AMERICA. I AM THE PART YOU WON'T RECOGNISE, BUT GET USED TO ME" **Muhammad Ali**

could handle. Ali's encounters with **Liston**, **Frazier** and **Foreman** in particular came to represent more than just sports events. Their scale and impact turned them into cultural moments: people remembered where they were when they watched the **Thrilla in Manila** or heard the result of the **Rumble in the Jungle**. The images of his fights – Ali standing over Liston, shouting at him to "Get up!", Foreman tumbling to the canvas in **Kinshasa** – became snapshots from a century.

For some years, Ali was the most famous man on Earth, and one of the most photographed. His deeds in the ring, his political and religious convictions, his availability to the media and the growth of the **global village**, knitted together by television, all conspired to turn fighter into icon.

RECOMMENDED READS AUTOBIOGRAPHICAL ACCOUNTS

Muhammad Ali: His Life and Times

Thomas Hauser with the co-operation of Muhammad Ali (Pan, 1991)

Muhammad Ali: His Life and Times is rightly regarded as the major official work on Ali. While there is better writing about Ali, **Hauser's** is the definitive account of the life, and it comes alive as an oral history. On beginning the project in 1988, Hauser conducted almost two hundred interviews with Ali, his family, friends, opponents and those who took a role in his story. Ali emerges through these personal accounts, which are reported verbatim, allowing the reader, rather than the editor, to be the jury.

When Hauser first met **Muhammad** and **Lonnie Ali**, he was told that despite the coverage of Ali's life, "People still don't know the real Muhammad…" Perhaps it would be fairer to say that in Ali's later years his own perspectives had changed. His religious convictions became more devout and his Parkinson's Syndrome prefaced a gradual and natural withdrawal from the intense spotlight under which he had conducted his adulthood. His life now had more context and he, and many of the people involved with him, were allowed the benefit of hindsight and of the cultural shift of two decades.

Hauser, who had previously written an excellent book about boxing called **The Black Lights**, allows Ali's story to unfold chronologically, only occasionally inserting an author comment to offer some context or to set the scene. Ali comes alive in these pages and to his credit, he makes little attempt to disguise his faults. He speaks honestly about his womanising and about his association with **Elijah Muhammad** and the **Nation of Islam**. He expresses regret over his casual ostracism of **Malcolm X**, and he confronts his cruelty to **Joe Frazier**. He and Hauser allow others to freely express their opinions, too.

Yet the man that emerges from …His Life And Times is nonetheless a giant; a superhuman athlete, a charmer, a devout man devoted to helping others, a hero with spirit and purpose. His innate good-heartedness is apparent in his kindness. He honours all of his opponents (even, and especially, Joe Frazier), he stops his car to give money to strangers, he flies to Iraq to negotiate the release of American hostages with **Saddam Hussein**.

There are villains here, too. **Don King** exploits Ali and robs him blind after his loss to **Larry Holmes** in 1980. **Elijah** and his son **Herbert Muhammad** (Ali's manager) suffuse Ali's boxing career with their own agendas. Ali's extended coterie of hangers-on bleed and betray him. And yet Ali remains forgiving. He is as sure of his greatness as when his mouth allowed him to boast of it, and yet his condition has made him humble, too. Reviewers described the book – for which Hauser won the coveted **William Hill Sports Book of the Year Award** in 1991 – as "hilarious, sad, moving and hopeful".

It is all of these things and more. Anyone wishing to understand Ali should certainly begin here.

The Greatest

Muhammad Ali with Richard Durham (Random House, 1976)

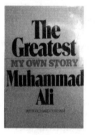

Ali's first attempt at autobiography is an odd affair, and a partial success at best. Ali was uninterested in the book – indeed, he didn't read it until it had been published. Worse, every page that **Richard Durham** produced had to be initialled by manager **Herbert Muhammad** before it could be submitted to the publisher. "I'm not sure the book is the true story of Ali's life," **James Silberman**, one of the book's editors later acknowledged.

The Greatest was part of a strong commercial drive following Ali's triumph over **Joe Frazier** in **Manila**. Its publication preceded a movie of the same name (see Ali on Film, page 205) in which Ali starred as himself, and a series of **DC comic books** (see Ephemera, page 248). There was a degree of speculation at the time that Ali might retire from boxing, and Durham, then an editor for the **Nation of Islam**'s *Muhammad Speaks* magazine, was hampered by the relative lack of time he got with Ali.

Durham makes what he had work hard, though, trying to flavour Ali's career with some insight into his lifestyle. Written in the first person (Ali), the book opens with Ali returning to **Louisville** after his points loss to **Ken Norton** in 1973, and it's a compelling account. There's some terrific fight detail, too: Ali describes the first match with **Sonny Liston** and his temporary blindness at the beginning of the fifth round. Later he claims to have a dream that predicts the **phantom punch** that ended the second meeting with Liston.

The Greatest is brought down, though, by the heavy hand of Herbert Muhammad – the text often seems to reflect many of his sensibilities rather than Ali's own – and also by the tone adopted by Durham as ghost author. It's strangely far removed from Ali's true voice, which, after all, had become familiar to millions of his fans across the world.

RECOMMENDED READS BOOKS ABOUT ALI

The Fight

Norman Mailer (Penguin, 1975)

By 1974, **Norman Mailer** had become the self-styled heavyweight champ of American letters. In a golden era for serious magazine writing, Mailer's stories for **Esquire** and his non-fiction work (especially 1968's **Armies of the Night**, which won the **National Book Award** and the **Pulitzer Prize**) had helped to define the 'new journalism'. Boxing was among Mailer's many passions and Ali, occupying a central role in America's sporting life and at least a peripheral one in its politics, was a natural subject for Mailer's flamboyant and florid pen (the famous opening paragraph of **The Fight** describes Ali, amongst other things, as '**the Prince of Heaven**').

Mailer threw some novelistic trickery into his mix. He cast himself in the narrative in the third person, adding another stylistic layer to the techniques of the non-fiction novel that Mailer, along with **Truman Capote** and **Tom Wolfe**, had developed. Taking not just the fight but the entire crazy experience of **Zaire** as his frame, Mailer turns the Rumble into a gripping event.

Both **Ali** and **Foreman** are nailed to the page. The extent of Ali's delicacy and uncertainty comes through all the bluster; Foreman's existential brute gives way to a bewildered wreck. But it is the characterisation of the supporting players that turns *The Fight* into a sporting classic. **Bundini Brown**, ebullient and emotional, contrasts with Foreman's stoic, streetwise trainer **Dick Sadler**.

Don King emerges in full, too. Throughout, Mailer essays some seductive detail: he watches Foreman play ping-pong and notes he uses the delicate pen-holder grip; he gets left behind while out jogging with Ali and thinks he's going to be eaten by a roaring lion that turns out to be in a cage in close by **N'sele zoo**.

Mailer's take on the fight itself is prescient. Writing immediately on his return, he could not have known quite how celebrated the encounter would become, but his style, heavy on symbolism and myth, is the perfect fit.

King of the World

David Remnick (Random House, 1998)

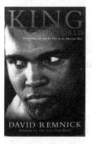

David Remnick had already won a **Pulitzer** Prize for **Lenin's Tomb**, his book about the collapse of the **Soviet Union**, and by 1998 he was about to be made editor of the **New Yorker**. So he brought a genuine intellectual rigour to his penetrating retelling of Ali's genesis. "I wanted to write about the way Ali had created himself," Remnick said, "the way a gangly kid from **Louisville** managed to become… a moulder of his age and a reflection of it."

And so **King of the World** is a book about a boxer rather than about boxing. Although the pivotal fights with **Liston** are here, Remnick is at his forensic best on events taking place beyond the ring. The young **Cassius Clay** is presented as a wilful innocent in an age defined by two obnoxious stereotypes: the "good negro", as represented by Floyd Patterson, and the "bad negro", embodied by Sonny Liston. Ali becomes, in his own words, "a new kind of black man".

Remnick sets Ali's rise in a political, rather than sporting, context. In making clear Ali's desperate desire from the age of 12 to become **heavyweight champion of the world**, Remnick illustrates the depths of Ali's sacrifice in his willingness to give up the title rather than go to **Vietnam**.

King of the World finishes at that point in 1967, as **Ali** disappears into exile, miserable and misunderstood. But Remnick has made plain his case that Ali had already achieved greatness. He had become a creation of his own imagination, a figure who frightened an old order that was about to be swept away. As the book opens, Ali emerges from the **Jim Crow South** into a corrupt sport run by the **Mob**. At its end everything is in the throes of precipitous change. As Remnick establishes, Ali had laid the foundations of his legend as a sportsman and had concocted a persona that made **America** face itself.

Ghosts of Manila

Mark Kram (Harper Collins, 2002)

Perhaps alone among those journalists who watched and covered Ali's career from ringside, **Sports Illustrated's** palindromic, iconoclastic **Mark Kram** saw Ali as a boxer and nothing more. "Hagiographers never tire of trying to persuade us that he ranked second only to **Martin Luther King** but… Ali was not a social force," Kram writes in his introduction to this powerful and bleak examination of the Ali-Frazier trilogy and in particular, the **Thrilla in Manila**.

The heavy price that the final fight drew from its combatants is apparent in Kram's brilliant opening, in which he visits Ali and Frazier decades after the Thrilla ended with both of them battered almost to oblivion. Ali's face is masked by his Parkinson's Syndrome, his verbal virtuosity now stilled forever. Frazier remains blisteringly bitter that his own greatness is being slowly forgotten: "I made him (Ali) what he is," he hisses at Kram. "Take that any way you want…"

As he excavates the roots of a feud that drove both men to the brink in the ring, Kram portrays **Ali** as less than saintly: he womanises, he is manipulated by the **Nation of Islam**, he is full of empty rhetoric.

Worse, Ali belittles a proud man who was unable to fight back with words. While Ali saw his "gorilla" taunts as harmless fun designed to sell a rivalry, Frazier felt the pain of a lifetime's ostracism. When Ali painted himself as the true black man and Frazier as an **Uncle Tom**, Frazier thought of the whip scars on his grandfather's back.

But while Kram makes Frazier's rage almost palpable, he is less clear on portraying the forces that Ali draws upon in order to win in **Manila**. Having revised Ali the man, he can offer only that Ali was a great fighter whose ring strategy enabled him to fend off Frazier's concentrated fury on two occasions out of three. It's Kram's least convincing theory.

That aside, **Ghosts of Manila** deserves to be read along with **Hauser** and **Mailer**. It is a revisionist history that offers a well-argued, valuable alternative view of Ali's impact, and of Frazier's own role in his story, as seen by a man on the front lines when it happened.

Redemption Song: Muhammad Ali and the Spirit of the Sixties

Mike Marqusee (Verso, 1999)

Where **David Remnick's** *King of the World* concerns itself with Ali's emergence as a political and social figure as well as an athlete, **Mike Marqusee** goes a step further in examining **Ali's** role within the radical politics of change. Where Remnick's book ended with Ali's refusal to be inducted into the **US Army** in 1967, Marqusee pushes the story forward, reinterpreting the **Rumble in the Jungle** and adding an international dimension, as Ali's travels in Africa and around the world begin to affect him as well as those fans who watched and loved him. Central, too, are Ali's relationships with **Malcolm X**, **Martin Luther King**, **Joe Louis** and **Jackie Robinson** as he takes the fight to the establishment and becomes a symbol of civil rights and the anti-war movement. Here, in the synergy of the times, Marqusee illustrates well how this eclectic, unrepresentative group of personalities came together to lend momentum to momentous change.

The Tao of Muhammad Ali

Davis Miller (Vintage, 1997)

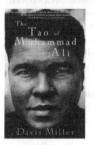

Davis Miller's quirky, thoughtful memoir sprang from an extraordinary piece he had written for **Sport** magazine in 1989 entitled **My Dinner With Ali**. Having spent most of his life idolising the fighter, Miller found himself driving past Ali's mother's home in **Louisville**, Kentucky. Ali's trailer was parked outside. Miller knocked on the door and ended up spending an evening with **Ali**, his mother and his brother **Rahaman**.

Ali does magic tricks, eats cookies and sits with his family while they watch a video of his fights that he and Miller drove into town to rent. Then, with everyone else in bed, the 46-year old Ali rises to his feet and tells **Miller** he is planning a comeback. With his 1971 fight with **Frazier** flickering on the TV in the background, he begins to dance around the living room, flashing punches. "Now do you believe?" Ali asks Miller, who is astonished by the athleticism Ali is displaying. "I believe," Miller admits, before Ali gleefully tells him "April fool..."

Encouraged by a **Pulitzer prize nomination** for the magazine piece, Miller expanded it into **The Tao of Muhammad Ali**, the strangely affecting story of how Ali's benign, distant presence inspired a North Carolina kid to transform himself from "short, skinny and scared" into a champion **kick-boxer**. His first meeting with Ali actually comes in 1975, when Miller – then 23 – is called out of a crowd at Ali's training camp in Pennsylvania to spar with the Champ. Just when Miller's speed has him thinking he has the better of 33-year-old Ali, Ali swats him effortlessly – a reminder of who's boss.

Warmly told, *The Tao of Muhammad Ali* works best as an example of the effect Ali's personality has had on successive generations. Through this one story in microcosm, you get a clear view of his extraordinary reach.

I'm A Little Special: A Muhammad Ali Reader

Edited by Gerald Early (Random House, 1998)

To collect just 30 articles among the thousands written about **Ali** was some task, and one which respected cultural critic **Gerald Early** achieved with style. Here, from voices as diverse as a young **Tom Wolfe** and the punchy newsroom prose of **AJ Liebling**, a rich and rounded vision of Ali emerges.

In his introduction to the collection, Early notes that there's a danger that Ali could become "overesteemed". If that happens, he argues, his great achievements may become diminished by his celebrity. With that in mind, Early's selection is eclectic: two pieces of a dark hue, Mark Kram's **Great Men Die Twice** for *Esquire* and Joyce Carol Oates's **The Cruellest Sport** from her book *On Boxing,* are followed by Gay Talese's **Boxing Fidel**, a marvellous account of Ali's trip to **Cuba** in 1996, where he performed his magic tricks for a delighted **Castro**. Elsewhere, **Norman Mailer**'s monumental story for **Life** magazine, *Ego*, previews Ali's first bout with **Frazier** in apocalyptic style, while **George Plimpton** hangs out with Ali and **Malcolm X** for **Harpers magazine**.

Early divides the selection by decade, and here, shifting perceptions of Ali are most noticeable. In the 1960s, his brashness and the disregard he invokes in the old stagers yields to a grudging respect as he backs up his boasts with his fists. The 1970s are epic, as Ali's career becomes almost mythical, defined by those unforgettable fights. The 1980s see him slip into his post-boxing life, while in the 1990s he is reborn as the **cultural icon** that Early fears for.

In all, an absorbing document, stitched together with great thought and skill.

THE BEST WRITERS ON MUHAMMAD ALI

ALI ALLOWED WRITERS UNPARALLELED ACCESS – WITH FABULOUS RESULTS

Norman Mailer Before publishing *The Fight* in 1975, Mailer contributed two superb, lengthy magazine pieces – *Ego*, for *Life* magazine and *King of the Hill* for *Esquire* – that bookended that first Frazier match. A boxer himself (often outside the ring), Mailer has been involved in almost as many well-publicised fights as Ali (although he doesn't shuffle so much a brawl). Somehow, his extravagances – many wives, many divorces – only add to the wild appeal of his masculine prose.

George Plimpton Often a foil for his friend Mailer, the urbane Plimpton (who died in 2004), had a reputation as a dilettante.It was undeserved. His writing was effortless, but he invented participatory sports journalism, and was always found where the action was. Plimpton had a strong bond with Ali, reflected in the fondness of his writing on him. And he credited Ali with lifting boxing from the moribund, Mafia-run, state it was in before The Greatest turned professional.

Hugh McIlvanney The boxing correspondent for *The Observer* and then *The Sunday Times*, McIlvanney covered almost all of Ali's career. His brilliant reportage, often phoned in from the ringside a mere hour or so after a fight, stands as some of the best sports writing of the century. His book *McIlvanney on Boxing* contains much of his best writing on Ali. In 1970, for *The Observer*, he wrote that Ali was"an historic figure in boxing, the last of its truly universal geniuses".

Budd Schulberg Son of the film producer BP Schulberg, journalist Budd, born in 1914, was a friend and contemporary of F Scott Fitzgerald and Ernest Hemingway. A lifelong fight fan, he also wrote a great boxing novel, *The Harder They Fall* (which Thomas Hauser lists as one of the great boxing books) a good Hollywood novel, *What Makes Sammy Run*, and the screenplay for *On the Waterfront*, for which he won an Oscar. For Schulberg, Ali, not the soccer player George Best, was "the fifth Beatle".

Mark Kram Kram, who died in 2003, was another quixotic figure, but one who never subscribed to the common view on Ali, on whom he reported for *Sports Illustrated* for 11 years."Ali was no more a social figure than Frank Sinatra," he wrote. "Seldom has such a public figure of more superficial depth been more wrongly perceived." He admitted that he could see why some found the first Ali-Frazier fight a mild technical disappointment, and found some of Ali's infight antics 'bizarre".

GOAT (Greatest Of All Time) – A Tribute To Muhammad Ali

Edited by Helmut Sorge (Taschen, 2004)

Maverick German publisher **Benedict Taschen** has founded his reputation and his business on confounding conventional wisdom, and he's broken the mould once again with **GOAT**, certainly the most expensive book ever published on Ali. A limited edition of nine thousand cost $3,000 each. An even more limited run of a thousand, which have exclusive artwork by **Jeff Koons** and four tipped-in gelatine prints from **Howard Bingham**, retail at $5,000.

But then everything about *GOAT* is excessive. It is 780 pages long, comes in its own display case and weighs in at 34kgs (75lbs). It features more than 3,000 pictures. Every copy has been personally signed by Ali, and it's bound by the book-binders used by the **Vatican**.

Its contents include fight cards, Ali's own writing and drawing, and some unique testimony from his family and friends. The major essays come from **Norman Mailer** and **Thomas Hauser**, while Ali's closest friend and personal lensman **Howard Bingham** serves as the principal photographer and editorial consultant. The result is certainly spectacular.

Perhaps the most pertinent comment about *GOAT* came in a review in the German newspaper **Der Spiegel**: "This is not a book," it wrote. "This is a monument on paper, the most megalomaniacal book in the history of civilisation, the biggest, heaviest, most radiant thing ever printed – **Ali's last victory**."

For those lacking the cash for a copy (and you may have to fight for the heavyweight championship in order to afford it) visit **www.taschen-goat.com** for an excellent showcase.

I Am King

David King (Penguin, 1975)

I Am King was published very soon after Ali had regained the heavyweight title with his victory over **George Foreman** in **Zaire**. Still available from online retailers, it's become something of a memorabilia piece.

Ali's victory over Foreman caught many on the hop. In the days before the **alphabet belts** of the boxing title sanctioning bodies, the heavyweight crown was rarely regained once lost: **Floyd Patterson** had been the only man to have done so. The fact that Ali had overcome such great odds – Foreman had humiliated **Joe Frazier** and **Ken Norton**; Ali had lost to both – made his achievement all the more rare. To exploit the post-fight fervour, **David King** put together some standard text, with Ali's life retold by those close to him.

But where **I Am King** really scored was in its selection of pictures and in how they were used by some excellent graphic artists. Making use of grainy blow-ups, powerful action shots and some off-beat stuff (including a full-page, life-size shot of Ali's fist), *I Am King* puts across a little of the essence of Ali. One double-page spread of Ali with a horrifically broken jaw (courtesy of **Ken Norton**) catches both the brutality of the contest and the concern of **Bundini Brown**, who looks, if anything, worse than Ali.

It's interesting to note that *I Am King* demonstrates that Ali was already the most famous sportsman in the world, even before he fought Frazier in Manila, or before he regained the heavyweight title for the third time three years later.

Muhammad Ali: A 30-Year Journey

Howard Bingham (Robson, 1991)

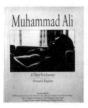

Howard Bingham first met Ali when he was assigned to do a photo shoot with the then Cassius Clay by the **Los Angeles Sentinel** in 1962. Almost 30 years later, Bingham began to collate the extraordinary images that he took of the world's best-known athlete. Bingham and **Ali** are close friends, and Bingham's love for his subject comes through. While he may not have taken the definitive images of Ali – **Sports Illustrated**'s **Neil Leifer** can best lay claim to those –

Bingham – who has a naturalistic style – is certainly responsible for the most intimate. Many of these pictures reflect just the moment in which they were shot. Their power comes from the subject, whether he's reclining on a sofa or standing in a stadium in front of thousands.

Muhammad Ali In Perspective

Thomas Hauser (Collins, 1997)

Hauser followed his epic authorised biography **Muhammad Ali: His Life and Times** with this excellent collection of pictures, many previously unseen. They're stitched together with some thoughtful text consisting of quotes from Ali, and from the great and good who have come into contact with him throughout his epic life.

There are some beautiful and candid shots here: Ali is pictured bowing to the tiny figure of Nation of Islam leader **Elijah Muhammad**. **The Beatles** are clearly delighted to be throwing punches in the Champ's direction; Ali poses underwater for **Life** magazine, after fooling a photographer into believing that punching against water improved his power.

While Ali always looked tremendous when he knew he was within range of a camera, some of the best images come from the less guarded moments. The look on **Sonny Liston's** face – part doleful, part fearful – as Ali attempts to interrupt his weigh-in before their second fight, is priceless. If this picture had been published before the fighters took to the ring, few would have been surprised at the outcome.

There's another shot of Ali, this time pictured in a crowd, somewhere near Piccadilly Circus in London as he alights from a cab. The effect of his sudden appearance is obvious, too. The entire gathering, which must number a few hundred, is smiling. Elsewhere, there's a terrific full-page shot of Ali teasing **Joe Frazier** by appearing at a window at Frazier's training camp, and another extraordinary one of the first day that he encountered the girl who would, many years later, become his fourth wife, **Lonnie Ali**.

Ali even reveals his favourite picture of himself. It's a snapshot of three men sitting on a bench. One is Ali, and the others are his boxing heroes **Sugar Ray Robinson** and **Joe Louis**.

In all, this makes a fine companion to *Muhammad Ali: His Life and Times*.

Muhammad Ali: The Glory Years

Felix Dennis and Don Atyeo (Ebury Press, 2002)

A labour of love for Australian journalist **Atyeo** and British multi-millionaire publisher **Dennis**, **The Glory Years** is a handsomely produced edition that will delight Ali fans in search of another warm retelling of the tale. Produced to high standards and utilising a silvertone process to enhance many of the well-researched pictures, it's at least an affordable alternative to **Taschen's GOAT.**

Atyeo and Dennis draw on their excellent 1975 biography of Ali (**The Holy Warrior**) but augment their own experience with contributions from **José Torres** (the World Light Heavyweight champ and writer of the Ali biography **Sting Like A Bee**), music writer **Victor Bokris** (who produced the overwrought **Muhammad Ali In Fighter's Heaven**) and boxing historian **Mark Collings** (who edited **Muhammad Ali: Through The Eyes Of The World**).

The text remains lively and informative, especially for those lacking any great knowledge of Ali's career, but the pictures score best. There are some thrilling action shots – what's noticeable throughout is the concentration on Ali's face – and some old favourites get lavish re-runs. **Leifer's** classic aerial shot of Ali with arms raised in one corner of the ring and **Cleveland Williams** spreadeagled and unconscious on his back in the other gets a full page, as does **Warhol's** famous screenprint of Ali. The **Norton** broken jaw shot is reproduced across another spread and remains a shocker.

Also out there

Facing Ali: The Opposition Weighs In
Stephen Brunt (Pan, 2003)
Fifteen fighters who faced Ali talk about the experience, a simple idea that works well. While some of the best-known, such as Joe Frazier, are covered better elsewhere, there are some terrific recollections from lesser lights, including Ali's first pro opponent Tunney Hunsaker. His is a sad chapter, as Hunsaker's  wife helps Canadian writer Brunt draw the story from the ailing fighter. The couple also reveal Ali's numerous visits to their hometown for benefit dinners. With the exception of Frazier, these fighters are grateful for their role in Ali's epic tale.

Sting Like A Bee: The Muhammad Ali Story

José Torres (McGraw Hill, 2001)

Torres became Light Heavyweight Champion of the World three years before Ali took the heavyweight crown. A first world champion for Cus D'Amato, who would later train Mike Tyson, Torres has the inside track on boxing and offers this occasionally quirky yet rewarding take on Ali's career, first published in 1971. As with his later book on Tyson, *Fire and Fear*, Torres is prone to placing himself in his subject's story, but this technique yields some interesting asides here. Norman Mailer's foreword adds some weight, too.

Muhammad Ali: In Fighter's Heaven

Victor Bokris (Cooper Square, 2000)

Bokris is best known as a music and pop culture journo, but in 1973 and 1974 he visited Ali's training camp as Ali prepared to fight George Foreman. The result is offbeat and uneven, inexpert in the face of much of the great writing on Ali, but Bokris can at least base it on first-hand experience and a love of his subject.

Muhammad Ali: Through The Eyes of the World

Edited by Mark Collings (Sanctuary, 2001)

Collings collated an eclectic cross section of opinion on Ali, from sources as diverse as Maya Angelou, Dustin Hoffman, Billy Connolly, B.B. King, Tom Jones and Billy Crystal, plus some people actually involved in boxing, including Angelo Dundee, José Torres and Hugh McIlvanney. Much of the comment is from the companion DVD of the same name, produced by Transworld.

Muhammad Ali: Ringside

Edited by Aaron Kenedi and John Miller (Bulfinch, 1999)

Art press Bulfinch, established by Kenedi and Miller, pulled together this beautifully presented collection of pictures and memorabilia with a slightly different perspective to many of the coffee-table books on Ali. They have a sharp eye for evocative ephemera: many fight cards and posters, the X-ray of the jaw broken by Norton and the media's betting pool for the Rumble in the Jungle add more flavour. The supporting text comes from the usual suspects – Mailer, Oates et al – but it at least has brevity on its side.

RECOMMENDED READS BOOKS FEATURING ALI

McIlvanney On Boxing

Hugh McIlvanney (Mainstream, 2002)

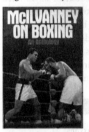

This collection of **McIlvanney's** boxing journalism charts the history of boxing since the 1960s. Inevitably, it's closely linked with **Ali**, but it covers other fights as well, including **George Foreman's** brutally efficient demolition of **Ken Norton** in **Caracas**, and ends with a selection of more recent articles.

McIlvanney is a superb writer and his observations, normally made from the ringside, give the book an almost palpable immediacy.

The 12 Greatest Rounds Of Boxing: The Untold Stories

Ferdie Pacheco (Sportclassic, 2000)

Known as **The Fight Doctor**, **Pacheco** worked in **Ali's** corner for 17 years. Rounds from the **Thrilla in Manila** and the **Rumble in the Jungle** are nominated, but the book also includes unexpected choices as well as a great range of anecdotes, such as the story about two muggers who made the mistake of attacking an old, but far from infirm, **Jack Dempsey**.

The Devil And Sonny Liston

Nick Tosches (Little, Brown, 2000)

Tosches explores the idea that when **Liston** traded prison for the ring, he made a Faustian pact that placed him under the control of **organised crime** for the rest of his life. He doesn't seek to excuse Liston's vices, but does make him a more sympathetic figure than his image as a two-dimensional thug allows. Tosches touches on the notion that the second fight with **Ali** was fixed, but provides no hard evidence from his investigations – we'll probably never know now.

Shadow Box: An Amateur In The Ring

George Plimpton (Lyons Press, 2003)

Like a **PG Wodehouse** character who has wandered into the wrong book, the eloquent and self-effacing **Plimpton** opens with an account of an ill-fated sparring session with Ali's former trainer and opponent **Archie Moore**. The Mongoose bloodies Plimpton's nose, but bloods an ongoing friendship between fighter and writer too. Plimpton proceeds to marry his love of boxing and literature, travelling through Ali's era in the company of Hemingway, Mailer and Frazier alike.

BOOKS BY ALI'S FAMILY

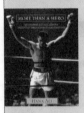

More Than A Hero: Muhammad Ali's Life Lessons
Hana Ali *(Pocket Books, 2000)*
A slim volume containing poetry, aphorisms and quotes from Ali and his daughter Hana. Much of Ali's fighting spiel is here, as is a good deal of of homespun fridge-magnet philosophy. Most worthwhile are the reruns of some of Ali's speeches from the 1960s and 1970s, while Hana's own recollections of her father are charmingly intimate, if (understandably) reverential.

The Soul Of A Butterfly
Hana Ali *(Bantam, 2004)*
Due in 2004, this is a second collection of Ali's thoughts, speeches and journals, bound together as a "spiritual memoir" by Hana Ali.

Reach: Finding Strength, Spirit And Personal Power
Laila Ali with David Ritz *(Hyperion, 2002)*
Ali's boxing daughter offers some thoughts on her own motivations for defying convention and forging a path in the shadow of a famous parent. Most interesting is her account of her childhood with Ali and her mother, Veronica Porsche, when she's honest on her feelings of isolation as the world claims ownership of her father. Rough times, including a jail stint, are overcome as she finds solace and success in the disciplines of gym and ring.

Sparring With Hemingway: And Other Legends Of The Fight Game

Budd Schulberg (Robson, 1997)

The veteran boxing correspondent and **Oscar-winning** screenwriter collects the best of his fight journalism. Ali, **"Our sweet prince,"** is here, as are **Mike Tyson**, **George Foreman**, **Sugar Ray** and the titular **Ernest**, who asks **Schulberg** to step outside in his usual macho style when the two cross swords at Papa's Cuban retreat. As Hemingway discovers, Schulberg was schooled in the history of the ring from boyhood and he has almost a century's worth of memories by now.

MOVIES FILMS FEATURING ALI

When We Were Kings

Director *Leon Gast* (1996)

Completed and released more than 20 years after it was filmed, **When We Were Kings** is the story of the **Rumble in the Jungle**, Ali's 1974 fight with **George Foreman** in Kinshasa. Vibrant and funky then powerful and moving, and blessed with characters and a storyline that scriptwriters would reject as too unlikely, it is a landmark sporting documentary.

Director **Leon Gast** travelled to **Zaire** with the fighters, promoter **Don King**, the musicians who would perform at the accompanying pop festival as well as the entire retinue of writers, blaggers and hangers-on. He returned with many hours of footage and no money to finish the film. It languished for two decades, a hidden treasure. When finance was ultimately secured Gast was able, with the help of producer **Taylor Hackford**, to cut the tapes and to add the interviews with the likes of **Norman Mailer** and **George Plimpton** that give the film new context.

There seems little doubt that *When We Were Kings* is a better movie because of the gap. In those two decades, the fight had assumed its role in the pantheon of 20th-century sporting encounters. Ali's place in American life had become greatly different, but Foreman's had become even more so. The George Foreman of 1974 was a brutal misfit, a fighter who defined himself by his ability to KO men and spread fear. The awe in which his power was held is exemplified by the story that **Norman Mailer** tells to camera. When Foreman hit the heavy bag in the gym, **Ali** would avert his eyes as he walked past, not wishing to look at the grapefruit-sized dent Foreman's fist had put in it. Mailer's implication is clear.

Foreman is an implacable presence in *When We Were Kings*. Huge, brooding and with a German Shepherd for a companion (a mistake; it reminded the Zairian people of the occupying Belgians who used the dogs to subdue unrest), Foreman spreads discomfort wherever he goes. One French TV reporter asks him what will happen if he loses to Ali. "I beg your pardon?" Foreman replies. Thinking **Foreman** can't understand his accent, the reporter asks several more times. He is met with the same answer until Foreman's meaning dawns upon him.

The effect the Rumble had on Foreman's life is astonishing, as **George Plimpton** points out. For two years, he entered a spiralling depression. His boxing career petered out. But he found his faith, reinvented himself as **The Punching Preacher**, regained the heavyweight title aged 46, made another fortune from his "lean, clean grillin' machine" and had eight children, all also called George. As Plimpton puts it, "It's hard to think of a more avuncular figure in American life."

With perhaps the most dramatic boxing match of all time at its heart, *When We Were Kings* could hardly fail. But it has more. Zaire, with its Conradian undertone and the touching innocence of its people, becomes a character in the story, too.

Ali runs on its roads, surrounded by children. He walks by the Congo in the evenings, and he comes to understand that African people have something that Americans do not. After the fight, as if cued by the gods, a Biblical rainstorm floods down, immersing the stadium where the fight took place.

But beyond all this majesty lies the true heart of darkness. The country's recidivist dictator, the repulsive **Joseph Mobutu**, uses the rooms under the stadium where the fight will take place to torture and kill his people, while he hides in his palace, unwilling to attend the fight for fear of assassination.

Foreman smiles after his two round demolition of Joe Frazier earns him the heavyweight crown

When We Were Kings conveys not just the weighty significance of the Rumble, but the sense of theatre that surrounded it. **Don King** and music promoter **Stuart Levine** stage a black **Woodstock** in the days before the fight, featuring **James Brown**, **B.B. King** and a terrific cast of musicians who arrive in Zaire to party and proceed to do so. When the fight is delayed for six weeks by Foreman's cut, the whole circus just stays in town and rolls on, adding to the story.

The climax is the fight itself. **Mailer** establishes the brilliance of Ali's strategy, and, despite knowing the result, it's impossible not to feel your heart pounding as the denouement approaches. Gast's film was voted **Best Documentary** at the **1997 Academy Awards**, and sports movies don't come much better than this.

Ali Frazier I: One Nation... Divisible

Director *Dave Anderson* (2000)

Produced by American cable TV network **HBO**, **One Nation... Divisible** (an inversion of a line from the Pledge of Allegiance) focuses on the genesis of the **Frazier-Ali** rivalry and on their first scrap on 8 March 1971, won on points by Frazier and described as **The Fight of the Century**. But much as **Mark Kram** does in his **Ghosts of Manila** (see page 194), **Dave Anderson** uses the totemic figures of Ali and Frazier to embody the deeper divisions of American society. The fight became a highly charged political event as well as an indelibly brilliant sporting contest, and *One Nation... Divisible* establishes both points equally well. Ali has maintained that his motives in riling Frazier by calling him a "gorilla" and an "Uncle Tom" were down to nothing more than his usual drive to sell the fight. But they burned within Frazier, who understandably bridled at being tagged "The white man's champion" by Ali. Frazier, who had picked cotton as a boy in South Carolina, had a better claim to a life close to that of most African-Americans than Ali did.

Once Ali had seized that ground, though, his cruelty fired Frazier the fighter. For fifteen rounds they stood toe to toe, united by their athletic brilliance and unyielding will. What *One Nation... Divisible* makes clear beyond the greatness of the contest, is the injustice done to **Frazier**. He had offered **Ali** his unconditional support during Ali's exile, and he had been Ali's friend. No wonder he burned so. Anderson shows well how his plight has been worsened by the media beatification of Ali down the years.

One Nation... Divisible builds a strong case for injustice done. Ali's "jokes" no longer come across as such, and a wrong is at least partially righted by this film.

Ali

Director *Michael Mann* (2001)

Michael Mann's heartfelt **Ali** must represent one of the few big-budget **Hollywood** biopics in which its star – in this case a gallant **Will Smith** – is less handsome, less charismatic and less talented than the figure they are portraying. In an era when many actors became sure that a convincing impression of a public figure would lead to an **Oscar** nomination – it had worked for **Jim Carrey** as Andy Kaufman in **Man In The Moon** and **Denzel Washington** as boxer Rubin Carter in **The Hurricane** – Smith's decision to play The Greatest could have been folly. Who does not know Ali, one of the century's most famous figures? But the likeable Smith, abetted by Mann's taut screenplay and muscular film-making, fails only narrowly. *Ali* is a good picture, slightly overwhelmed by its subject.

Mann did a fine job in condensing Ali's story: the recreations of the **Liston** and **Foreman** fights are particularly good, while Smith's impression of Ali's verbal athleticism is uncanny – if you can overcome the ears. **John Voight's Howard Cosell** almost steals the movie, and Smith's partner **Jada Pinkett** pops up as Ali's foxy first wife **Sonji Roy**. Boxers **Michael Bentt** and **James "Lights Out" Toney** appear as **Liston** and **Frazier**, adding realism to the fight scenes, traditionally a weak point in boxing flicks. Smith got his **Academy Award** nomination, but ultimately the movie shrinks rather than expands on Ali's life.

The Greatest

Director *Tom Gries* (1977)

In its own way, **The Greatest** was as disappointing as the autobiography of the same name (see page 191). Ali played himself with pizzazz opposite **Ernest Borgnine** as **Angelo Dundee**. **James Earl Jones** is **Malcolm X** and **Howard Bingham**, **Bundini Brown**, **Lloyd Wells** and **Rahaman Ali** appear as themselves. While Ali lights up the screen, this strange mix recreates his key moments all too stagily.

This would be acceptable but for the fact that many of these events had already been captured on film for real, a problem that also reoccurred with **Michael Mann's** biopic some two decades later.

Muhammad Ali: King of the World

Director *Tom Gries* (1997)

A made-for-TV biopic based on **David Remnick's** book, *King of the World* (see page 193), charting Ali's rise and move into exile. **Terrence Dashon Howard** takes the title role.

MOVIES ALI AS AN ACTOR
ALI HAD VISIONS OF BECOMING THE SELF-STYLED "DARK GABLE." HE WAS PRETTY ENOUGH, AS HE OFTEN REMINDED EVERYONE, BUT HE WAS ALWAYS TO BE A BETTER FIGHTER THAN AN ACTOR...

Freedom Road Jan Kadar (1979)
Made-for-TV movie in which **Ali** plays the lead role of **Gideon Jackson**, a slave in 1870s Virginia who wins freedom, gets elected to the **US senate** and battles with the owners of his former plantation to grant sharecroppers the rights to the land on which they worked. Ali plays opposite **Kris Kristofferson** in a soggy melodrama undermined by its unlikely plot.

The Greatest Tom Gries (1977)
Ali plays himself, a role he's eminently qualified for: "I been rehearsing it all my life," he said. Pity, then, that the rest of the production isn't quite world championship class. The makers were simply too willing to trust that Ali's incredible charisma would do their work for them. Despite the presence of such acting pros as Ernest Borgnine, this isn't as forceful as it could be.

Requiem For A Heavyweight Ralph Nelson (1962)
Ali's first film appearance, a cameo as himself. **Cassius Clay** knocks out **Anthony Quinn's Mountain Rivera**, sending the veteran heavyweight into ignominious decline, and a career as a wrestler.

TELEVISION ALI ON TV

ALI'S RISE TO FAME COINCIDED WITH THE SPREAD OF TV'S AVAILABILITY ROUND THE WORLD. HERE ARE 50 OF HIS MOST NOTEWORTHY AND QUIRKY SMALL-SCREEN APPEARANCES...

1 **Rome 1960: Games of the XVII Olympiad** (1960)
Credited as Cassius Clay

2 **Tonight Show with Johnny Carson** (1960) His first Carson appearance, as Cassius Clay

3 **The Superfight** (1970)
The "computer fight" between Ali and Rocky Marciano (see page 131)

4 **AKA Cassius Clay** (1970) Documentary

5 **Ali The Fighter** (1971) Documentary

6 **Black Rodeo** (1972)
Documentary about a rodeo in Harlem, at which Ali appears

7 **Malcolm X** (1972)
Documentary with archive footage

8 **Money Talks** (1972)
Candid Camera-style comedy show in which Ali appears in a sketch where he refuses to sign for a COD package

9 **Funny Girl to Funny Lady** (1975)
Ali appears as a presenter in a Barbra Streisand tribute

10 **The Big Fight: Ali vs Frazier** (1975)
Fight film on the Thrilla in Manila

11 **The Barbara Walters Special** (1976)
The TV diva devotes a show to Ali

12 **The 49th Academy Awards** (1977)
Ali presents the Best Supporting Actress Oscar to Vanessa Redgrave

13 **I Am The Greatest** (1977)
Animated series in which Ali does the voiceover duties for his own character.

14 **Vegas** (1978)
Television drama. Ali appears as himself in episode 11

15 **Diff'rent Strokes** (1978)
Ali appears as himself in the iconic US sitcom, in episode two of season three, titled "The Hero"

16 **Muhammad and Larry** (1980)
Documentary on Ali and Larry Holmes

17 **Body and Soul** (1981)
TV drama. Ali appears as himself

18 **Wrestlemania** (1985)
Ali introduces tag team Hulk Hogan and Mr T in the first of the popular series

19 **Doin' Time** (1985)
Ali and Bundini Brown make special appearances in this prison flick

20 **1960s Music Memories and Milestones** (1988)
Archive footage of Ali and other 1960s icons including Neil Armstrong, The Beatles, Fidel Castro and George Best

21 **Eyes on the Prize** (1990)
Mini-series on the Civil Rights struggle

22 **Desert Storm: The War Begins** (1991)
Documentary that includes Ali's role in bringing hostages back from Iraq

23 Muhammad Ali's 50th Birthday Celebrations (1992)
Tribute show with Dan Aykroyd, Whitney Houston and Arnold Schwarzenegger

24 Fame in the Twentieth Century (1993)
Documentary series examining the nature of contemporary fame

25 Legend to Legend Night: A Celebrity Cavalcade (1993)
Celeb fest starring Tony Bennett, Angie Dickinson, Sugar Ray Leonard and more

26 Malcolm X: Make It Plain (1994)
TV documentary with archive Ali footage

27 Touched by an Angel (1994)
Ali appears as himself in an episode called "Fighting The Good Fight"

28 Idols of the Game (1995)
Sports documentary in which Ali contributes to the segment titled "Inventing The All American"

29 Sonny Liston: The Mysterious Life and Death of a Champion (1995)
Includes archive footage of Ali

30 Atlanta 1996: Games of the XXVI Olympiad (1996)
Ali lights the flame in an unforgettable moment in Atlanta

31 Muhammad Ali: The Whole Story (1996)
Documentary following on from interest reawakened by his Olympics appearance

32 The Real Las Vegas (1996)
Ali appears in this documentary on the history of Vegas

33 The Journey of the African American Athlete (1996)
Documentary with archive footage

34 The Cold War (1998)
Documentary series on Russo-American relations, with archive Ali footage – both sides liked him...

35 Best of the Dean Martin Celebrity Roasts (1998)
Archive footage of Ali on Martin's series of TV specials

Ali makes a guest appearance in the American TV series *Diff'rent Strokes*

36 **Howard Cosell: Telling it Like it is** (1999)
TV documentary spinning off the back of
Jon Voight's then forthcoming turn as
Cosell in Michael Mann's *Ali*

37 **Kings of the Ring: Four Legends of
Heavyweight Boxing** (2000)
Ali appears in an excellent documentary
on the careers of himself, Jack Johnson,
Jack Dempsey and Joe Louis

38 **Hendrix** (2000)
Ali appears in archive footage in the
story of the celebrated guitarist

39 **Liberace: Too Much of a Good Thing
is Wonderful** (2000)
Ali appears in archive footage of the
flamboyant pianist

40 **Legends Icons and Superstars
of the Century** (2000)

Turn-of-the-millennium documentary
also featuring Mahatma Ghandi, Babe
Ruth and more

41 **Fidel** (2001)
Documentary on the Cuban leader, in
which Ali appears along with Nelson
Mandela, Harry Belafonte and more

42 **Breaking The Silence: The Making
of Hannibal** (2001)
Ali shows up at the New York premiere of
Tony Scott's cannibal flick

43 **Pinero** (2001)
Archive footage of Ali in a documentary
on American playwright and actor
Miguel Pinero

44 **America: A Tribute to Heroes** (2001)
Ali appears in this tribute to the victims
of the September 11 attacks

45 **The Making of Ali** (2001)
Documentary on the making of Michael
Mann's movie starring Will Smith

46 **Greater Than The Greatest** (2001)
Another tribute, this time narrated by
Chris Eubank

47 **Muhammad Ali's All-Star 60th Birthday
Celebrations** (2002)
Nice tribute programme featuring family
members, plus John Travolta, Sylvester
Stallone and more

48 **Second Annual BET Awards** (2002)
Ali receives Black Entertainment TV's
Humanitarian Award

49 **Best of Bert Newton** (2002)
Archive footage of Ali on the Aussie
icon's chat show

50 **The Fight** (2004)
Archive documentary footage on the
seminal 1938 Joe Louis vs Max
Schmeling fight

The icon

As Ali himself observed, Yorkshire-born journalist and television presenter **Michael Parkinson** was "just like Johnny Carson over there". Indeed he was. On his long-running BBC1 Saturday night talk-show, Parkinson interviewed the world's great and good: everyone from **Peter Sellers** to **Paul McCartney** appeared. But his four interviews with **Muhammad Ali** – the first in 1971, two in 1974, pre and post Zaire, and the last in 1981 – became amongst the most celebrated moments on British television.

"Muhammad Ali was the most singular human being I ever met, no contest," Parkinson recalled. "He was not only an athlete, he was a part-time comedian, sometime poet and a man who made a robust contribution to relations between black and white people".

Ali's first appearance was startling enough. Just out of exile, he was relaxed and regal. He began by telling the story of his meeting with the wrestler **Gorgeous George** in Las Vegas just before he fought **Duke Sabedong** in 1961. Both Parkinson and the studio audience roared as he imitated George's outrageous hype and described how he appropriated it for himself. "He was real conceited and arrogant," Ali said, deadpan. "I thought, 'this is a good idea'..."

"In America," he went on, "they got a little saying. The nigger talks too much..."

Ali began an impassioned defence of **Elijah Muhammad** and his "white men are devils" remarks, going on to describe how black people "have been robbed of our names, our culture, our history. We are walking dead men."

It was the kind of speech that in America had been met with hostility. In Britain, it was met with applause.

Parkinson travelled to America in January 1974 to interview both Ali and **Joe Frazier** together with US host **Dick Cavett**. The interview was a knockabout affair designed to publicise the forthcoming rematch at Madison Square Garden. Frazier and Ali squared up twice.

After defeating Frazier and then **George Foreman**, Ali was back in Britain for what became one of the most famous moments on British television. After Parkinson quoted **Budd Schulberg** questioning Ali's denunciation of white people when he had many white men in his camp, Ali became enraged.

"I'm not just a boxer," he said. "Your **Oxford University** offered me a professorship in philosophy and poetry. You do not have enough wisdom to tackle me on wisdom. I mean that. How you gonna trap me on TV? You can't beat me physically or mentally. You're a joke."

By 1981, Ali's deterioration was marked. His speech quiet and slurred, Parkinson described their meeting as "sad and dispiriting". Even more shockingly, Ali would fight once more. Yet as Parkinson said, "when I think of Ali now, it's with **a smile on my face**."

THE FIGHTS ALI ON DVD

The Fighters: Muhammad Ali and Joe Frazier (1971)
Now available on DVD, this package charts the build-up to their first fight, along with film of the fight itself.

When We Were Kings Leon Gast (1996)
(See page 205). A new DVD edition of the movie contains fights two and three with **Joe Frazier** as extras, as well as the full **Rumble in the Jungle**.

Champions Forever Dimitri Logothetis (1989)
A terrific documentary, still available and worth seeking out, that focuses on

the fights and careers of Ali, **Larry Holmes**, **Ken Norton**, **Joe Frazier** and **George Foreman**. All five took an active role in the making and promotion of this collector's piece, which features crucial action from their major bouts.

Ali: The Greatest William Klein (2002)
Klein filmed Ali's fights with **Liston**, **Foreman** and more, and stitched them together for this documentary, which was released around the same time as the movie, *Ali*. This is better.

Muhammad Ali: Through The Eyes of the World (2002)
Documentary that spawned the companion book (see page 202). Personalities from **Tom Jones** to **Spike Lee** discuss Ali's influence. Intercut with plenty of good fight footage.

Ali v Spinks Fights I and II (2002)
Both fights, plus background on how Ali lost and regained the heavyweight title against the erratic but likeable **Leon Spinks**.

The Last Hurrah: Muhammad Ali v Trevor Berbick (2002)
Film of **Ali's** last, desperately sad fight against **Berbick** in the **Bahamas** in 1980.

THE WORLD'S MOST FAMOUS MAN
AT TIMES IT SEEMS AS THOUGH ALI HAS MET EVERYONE IN THE WORLD.
HIS CELEBRITY ENSURED THAT OTHERS IN THE STARRY FIRMAMENT
SOUGHT HIM OUT…

Muhammad and the most famous No.10 of all time: Pelé

Former fighter John Huston, director of boxing movie *Fat City*, spars with Ali in Dublin in 1972

Pop artist Andy Warhol shoots Ali at the champ's Deer Lake training camp

101 reasons to love

Poems, predictions and hollering -- the famous Ali wit
lit up not only boxing but the world

"HE USES THE ENGLISH LANGUAGE LIKE AN ELIZABETHAN," CRITIC KENNETH TYNAN SAID OF ALI'S VERBAL SKILLS. BUT HIS INCISIVE WIT, FAR FROM BEING MERELY THE TRIUMPH OF STYLE OVER CONTENT, OFTEN CONTAINED A SERIOUS MESSAGE. THE WORLD STILL ADORES HIM FOR IT

"Float like a butterfly, sting like a bee"
This phrase, coined by cornerman Drew "Bundini" Brown became Ali's catchphrase and was invoked by Ali and other members of his camp throughout his career, often with extra lines, including "Rumble, young man, rumble" and "Your hands can't hit what your eyes can't see"

2 **"My name is Cassius Marcellus Clay Junior. I'm the Golden Gloves champion of Louisville, Kentucky. I won the Pan American Games a month ago and I'm going to win the Olympics and I wanna talk to you"**
Ali's first words to future trainer Angelo Dundee

3 **"Hey Floyd! I seen you! Someday I'm gonna whup you! Don't you forget, I am the greatest!"**
Meeting heavyweight champion Floyd Patterson during the 1960 Olympic Games in Rome. Five years later, Ali made good his promise

4 **"I'm running down Broadway and all of a sudden there's a truck coming at me. I run at the truck and I wave my arms, and then I take off and I'm flying… and all the people are standing around and cheering and waving at me. And I wave back and keep on flying. I dream that dream all the time"**
Sharing his dreams of stardom with reporter Dick Schaap after returning from the Olympics

5 **"I love to see my name where everyone can read it. Someday I'm gonna see it in bright, bright lights"**
Discussing his ambitions with a local reporter

6 **"When I lay a man down, he's supposed to stay down! I should be champ before I'm 21… you write that down in your notebooks"**
To reporters after beating Willie Besmanoff. Ali had knocked his opponent down but Besmanoff struggled back up – only for Ali to knock him down again

7   **"Archie's been living off the fat of the land**
     I'm here to give him his pension plan
     When you come to the fight
     Don't block the halls and don't block the door
     'Cause ya all going home after round four"

On the upcoming fight with former trainer and legendary light heavyweight Archie Moore.
His prediction proved to be accurate – the referee stopped the fight in the fourth round

8   **"Marcellus vanquished Carthage**
     Cassius laid Julius Caesar low
     And Clay will flatten Douglas Jones
     With a mighty, measured blow!"

Still fighting under his original name, Cassius Marcellus Clay, Ali predicts the outcome of
his fight with Doug Jones in March 1963. It lasted for ten gruelling rounds and the mighty,
measured blow never came – Jones lost on a controversial points decision

9 **"I'm not the greatest, I'm the double greatest. Not only do I knock 'em out,**
I pick the round. I'm the boldest, the prettiest, the most superior,
most scientific, most skilfullest fighter in the ring today"

After his first fight against Londoner Henry Cooper, in June 1963. Ali had won in the five
rounds he had predicted, although Cooper had succeeded in knocking him down
with a left hook known as 'Enery's 'Ammer

10 **"I said I was the greatest, not the smartest"**

On failing the mental aptitude test used to determine candidates' eligibility for being
drafted into the US armed forces, January 1964

11 **"Sonny Liston is nothing. The man can't talk. The man can't fight.**
The man needs talking lessons. The man needs boxing lessons.
And since he's gonna fight me, he needs falling lessons"

Before the first Liston fight in February 1964

12 **"He's too ugly to be the world's champ!"**

On Sonny Liston

13 **"I'm the prettiest thing that ever lived"**

From the build-up to the Liston fight

14   "Now Clay swings with a right,
      What a beautiful swing,
      And the punch raises the bear
      Clear out of the ring.
      Liston is still rising
      And the ref wears a frown
      For he can't start counting
      Till Sonny comes down"

*From the build-up to the Liston fight.
Ali referred to him as 'The Bear'*

15 "Why, chump, I bet you scare yourself to death just starin' in the mirror.
You ugly bear! You ain't never fought nobody but tramps and has beens.
You call yourself a world champion? You're too old and slow to be champion!"
Taunting Sonny Liston at Liston's own training camp.

16 "Eat your words! Eat your words! I am the greatest"
*To reporters after the first Liston fight. Almost everyone had believed that Liston would
win, and many expected Ali to sustain serious damage*

17 "I know where I'm going, and I know the truth, and I don't have to be
what you want me to be. I'm free to be what I want"
Announcing his conversion to Islam at the press conference after beating Sonny Liston

18 "A rooster crows only when it sees the light. Put him in the dark and
he'll never crow. I have seen the light and I'm crowing"
On his membership of the Nation of Islam

19 "Cassius Clay is a slave name. I didn't choose it, and I didn't want it.
I am Muhammad Ali, a free name, and I insist people use it when speaking
to me and of me"

20 "People can't stand a blowhard, but they'll always listen to him"
Discussing the psychology of self-promotion with a journalist from Playboy *in 1964*

21 "I got the height, the reach, the weight, the physique, the speed,
the courage, the stamina, and the natural ability that's going to
make me great. Putting it another way, to beat me you got to be
greater than great"

22 "I am the astronaut of boxing. Joe Louis and Dempsey were just jet pilots. I'm in a world of my own"

23 "One of these days, they're liable to make the house I grew up in a national shrine"

24 "It's not bragging if you can back it up"

25 "Get up and fight, sucker!"
After knocking down Liston during their second fight

26 "All those people who blinked at that moment, they missed it"
On the punch that knocked down Sonny Liston during the rematch. The speed and angle of the punch meant that neither the audience nor the cameras – nor Liston – had seen it, and many thought the fight was a fix. It lasted just one minute, 42 seconds

27 "They can boo me, yell at me and throw peanuts at me – as long as they pay to get in"
On the advantage of notoriety

28 "It's nature to run from something that runs after you. And it's nature to chase something that runs away from you"
Talking about relations with the opposite sex. One writer later described Ali as "The pelvic missionary"

29 "My first wife"
Ali's answer when asked who his toughest opponent was. Sonji Ali's divorce settlement in 1966 cost her husband a total of $172,000

30 "Stay in college, get the knowledge, stay there till you are through. If they can make penicillin out of mouldy bread, they can sure make something out of you"
To a student who asked Ali whether he should stay in college

31 "I'll beat him so bad, he'll need a shoehorn to put his hat on"
Before fighting Floyd Patterson in 1965. Patterson had made the mistake of saying he wanted to "Reclaim the title for America" by wresting it from Ali and the other "Black Muslims"

32 "I am America. I am the part you won't recognise, but get used to me. Black, confident, cocky – my name, not yours. My religion, not yours. My goals, my own. Get used to me"

33 "Man, I ain't got no quarrel with them Viet Cong"

Ali had been talking to reporters at his home in Miami in February 1966 when he found out he had been reclassified as fit for army service. This reaction proved to be the defining moment in his career

34 "No Viet Cong ever called me nigger"

Ali's unrepentant answer to the fury caused by his earlier remark

35   **"Clean out my cell**
        And take my tail
        On the trail
        For the jail
        Without bail
        Because it's better in jail
        Watchin' television fed
        Than in Vietnam somewhere, dead"
        On the choice between joining the army
        and going to prison

36 "They maketh me fight out of the country. They leadeth me down the path of bad publicity. I shall be bewailed in the history of the sport forever. The sports fan shall follow me all the days of my life"

On being forced to fight George Chuvalo over the border in Canada

37 "You have to give him credit. He put up a fight for one-and-a-half rounds"

After beating British boxer Brian London by a knockout in round three

38 "I'm the greatest. And I'm knocking out all bums. And if you get too smart, I'll knock you out"

To a TV interviewer who asked if Ali was physically able to keep his mouth shut

39 "It's hard to be humble when you're as great as I am"

40 "I figured that if I said it enough, I would convince the world that I really was the greatest"

41 "It's something that will go down in history, like the left hook"
On the Ali shuffle

42 "I'm gonna have to be killed before I lose, and I ain't going to die easy"

43 "What's my name? What's my name?"
To opponent Ernie Terrell, who had refused to call him Muhammad Ali

44 "The only place they can take my title away from me is in the ring. And nobody can do it there, either"
Reaction to the news that the World Boxing Association were planning to strip him of his title for refusing to be drafted into the US Army

45 "Let the man that wins go to the backwoods of Georgia and Alabama or to Sweden or Africa. Let him stick his head in an elementary school; let him walk down a back alley at night. Let him stop under a street lamp where some small boys are playing and let him say: 'What's my name?' and see what they really say. Everybody knows me and knows I am the champion"
On plans to find a new heavyweight champion after his title had been revoked

46 "It was pretty bad. But I was great"
On the satirical musical Big Time Buck White, *in which Ali played a starring role*

47 "I hear you're talkin' around town that you can whup me. Well, here I is"
According to boxing writer George Plimpton, the words spoken by Ali to a truck driver who had stopped to replace a spare tyre. Ali reportedly drove off laughing

48 "You just keep whuppin' those guys in the ring, and I'll keep fighting Uncle Sam and one day we'll make a lot of money together"
Ali on the phone to future opponent Joe Frazier, as his lawyers fought to overturn the ban against him fighting

49 "Nobody has to tell me that this is a serious business. I'm not fightin' one man. I'm fightin' a lot of men, showing a lot of 'em here is one man they couldn't defeat, couldn't conquer... My mission is to bring freedom to 30 million black people"
On his comeback fight against Jerry Quarry in October 1970

50 "You took my title away. I'm gonna make you give it back!"
To Eddie Dooley, from the New York Athletic Commission. It had been Dooley's decision to deny Ali a licence to fight in the state after he had refused to be drafted. The WBA and the other states' boxing commissions quickly followed his lead

51 "I've never wanted to whup a man so bad. I'm gonna put some soul on his head. I tell you that the Beast is mine. And tonight he falls in nine"
Before the fight against Oscar Bonavena in December 1970. The fight lasted for 15 rounds, but ended when Bonavena was knocked down for the third time

52 "I hit Bonavena so hard it jarred his kinfolks all the way back in Argentina"
Recalling the Bonavena fight in an attempt to psych out Joe Frazier

53 "Fifteen referees. I want 15 referees to be at this fight because there ain't no one man who can keep up with the pace I'm gonna set except me. There's not a man alive who can whup me. I'm too fast. I'm too smart. I'm too pretty. I should be a postage stamp. That's the only way I'll ever get licked"
Before his first fight against Joe Frazier to regain the heavyweight championship in February 1971

54 "Joe's going to come out smokin'
But I ain't gonna be jokin'
I'll be pickin' and pokin'
Pouring water on his smokin'
This might shock and amaze ya
But I'm gonna destroy Joe Frazier"

55 "Frazier is so ugly he should donate his face to the US Bureau of Wildlife"

56 "I tripped over a left hook"
After being asked what went wrong in his fight against Frazier

57 "Ain't no reason for me to kill nobody in the ring"
Answering criticism that he had carried former sparring partner Jimmy Ellis for 12 gruelling rounds in July 1971

58 "I'm going to do to Buster what the Indians did to Custer"
Before fighting Buster Mathis in November 1971

59 **"So now I have to make a decision. Step into a billion dollars and denounce my people, or step into poverty and teach them the truth. Damn the money. Damn the heavyweight championship. Damn the white people. Damn everything. I will die before I sell out my people for the white man's money"**

On his reasons for refusing to sacrifice his principles to save his career

60 "I predict I'll knock him out in round five, because he's talkin' jive"

On Mac Foster, April 1972. Ali finally won on a points decision after 15 rounds

61 "No, I can beat this sucker"

Ali's response to trainer Angelo Dundee who wanted to stop his fight with Ken Norton in March 1973 after Ali's jaw had been broken in the second round. The fight carried on for another ten rounds before Norton was declared the winner. Responding to the upset, Ali called Norton "The Man Who Shot Liberty Valance"

62 "I took a nobody and created a monster. I put him on *The Dating Game*. I gave him glory. Now I have to punish him bad"

Before his rematch with Norton in September 1973. Ali won the fight in the 12th round

63 "It's just a job. Grass grows, birds fly, waves pound the sand. I just beat people up"

64 "Only a man who knows what it is like to be defeated can reach down to the bottom of his soul and come up with the extra ounce of power it takes to win when the match is even."

65 "You're always talking about, 'Muhammad, you're not the same man you were 10 years ago.' Well, I asked your wife, and she told me you're not the same man you was two years ago!"

Responding to a premature obituary by sports broadcaster Howard Cosell, who had predicted Ali would lose his fight to George Foreman in Zaire

66 "Howard Cosell was gonna be a boxer when he was a kid, only they couldn't find a mouthpiece big enough"

Another jibe at Cosell. For all his bluster, Cosell had often defended Ali. Asked about the decision to strip Ali of his title, he somberly reflected that: "They took away his title because he failed the test of political and social conformity"

67 "I've seen George Foreman shadow boxing and the shadow won"

68 "I'm so fast that last night I turned off the light switch in my hotel room and was in bed before the room was dark"

69   "I done wrassled with an alligator
      I done tussled with a whale
      Only last week I murdered a rock
      Injured a stone, hospitalised a brick
      I'm so mean I make medicine sick"
      Before the Rumble in the Jungle, October 1974

70   "There are two things that are hard to hit and see
      That's a spooky ghost and Muhammad Ali"

71 "I'm gonna fight for the prestige, not for me, but to
uplift my little brothers who are sleeping on concrete
floors today in America, black people who are living on welfare, black
people who can't eat, black people who
don't know no knowledge of themselves, black people
who don't have no future"
Before the Rumble in the Jungle

72 "I have a great one-two punch.
The one hits a lot, but the two hits a bunch"

73 "It's a divine fight. This Foreman – he represents
Christianity, America, the flag. I can't let him win... He
represents pork chops"
Ali on Foreman, during the pre-fight build-up

74 "If you even dream of beating me, you'd better wake up and apologise"

75 "Now you see me, now you don't.
George thinks he will, but I know he won't!"
On his tactics against Foreman. It proved to be a bluff. Ali spent most of the fight on the ropes while Foreman punched himself weary, a strategy Ali later called the "rope-a-dope"

76 "Come on George, show me something"
Reportedly whispered in George Foreman's ear during the Rumble in the Jungle. Ali taunted Foreman throughout the fight, saying "C'mon champ, you can do better than that. They told me you were a big hitter"

77   "It will be a killer
        And a chiller
        And a thrilla
        When I get the gorilla
        In Manila"

Before his third fight against Joe Frazier in 1975, dubbed the Thrilla in Manila

78 "You a boxer? What kind of boxes do you make?"

Joking with a middleweight sparring partner during pre-fight training in Manila

79 "Joe Frazier is so ugly that when he cries, the tears turn around and go down the back of his head"

80 "I always bring out the best in the men I fight, but Joe Frazier, I'll tell the world right now, brings out the best in me. I'm gonna tell ya, that's one helluva man, and God bless him"

After the Thrilla in Manila

"This is the legend of Muhammad Ali,
The greatest fighter that ever will be.
He talks a great deal and brags, indeed,
Of a powerful punch and blinding speed.
Ali fights great, he's got speed and endurance,
If you sign to fight him, increase your insurance.
Ali's got a left, Ali's got a right;
If he hits you once, you're asleep for the night"

82 "I am the onliest of boxing's poet laureates"

83 "I wasn't trying to knock him out at the beginning. I wanted all the 12,000 spectators to get into the arena"

On his February 1976 fight against Belgian heavyweight Jean-Pierre Coopman, who failed to live up to his nickname, 'The Lion of Flanders' and was knocked out in round five

84 "I like this place so much that I might go after your job"

After being invited to the White House by President Ford in 1976. Ten years earlier, Senator Richard Russell had predicted that "Cassius Clay will never be invited to the White House to see the President of the United States"

85 "[A] prize fight is like a war: the real part is won or lost somewhere far away from witnesses, behind the lines, in the gym, and out there on the road long before I dance under those lights"
In his autobiography, The Greatest: My Own Story

86 "Champions aren't made in gyms. Champions are made from something they have deep inside them – a desire, a dream, a vision. They have to have the skill and the will. But the will must be stronger than the skill"

87 "I won't miss fighting; fighting will miss me"
Discussing his retirement in 1979

88 "People don't realise what they had till it's gone. Like President Kennedy – nobody like him. Like The Beatles, there will never be anything like them. Like my man, Elvis Presley. I was the Elvis of boxing"

89 "Dundee told me: 'Go out and hit him, go out and hit him.' So I said, 'You go out and hit him. I'm tired."
After losing the last fight of his career to Trevor Berbick in 1981

90 "I'm the best. I just haven't played yet"
On his golf game

91 "He has two chances. Slim and none, and Slim's just left town"
Response to the question of whether an opponent had any chance of beating him

92 "The man who views the world at 50 the same as he did at 20 has wasted 30 years of his life"

93 "Me, whee!"
The shortest poem in English, quoted by Ali at Harvard when students asked him to recite one of his poems

94 "Will they ever have another fighter who writes poems, predicts rounds, beats everybody, makes people laugh, makes people cry, and is as tall and extra-pretty as me?"

95 "I have the best friend in the world, and that's Howard Bingham... And if you write that, I don't want Howard thinking I'm going soft, so write down that he's lucky I'm his friend too. And tell him I said that I'm the only person in the world who likes him"

Ali on the photographer who covered much of his career and became a personal friend

96 "When a man says 'I cannot,' he has made a suggestion to himself. He has weakened his power of accomplishing that which otherwise would have been accomplished"

97 "Boxing is a lot of white men watching two black men beat each other up"

98 "All I get is a day?"

On finding out that the mayor of Los Angeles had proclaimed a "Muhammad Ali Day"

99 "It wasn't the boxing. It was the autographs"

Joking about the reason for his illness

100 "Service to others is the rent you pay for your room here on earth"

"Maybe I was great in the ring, but outside of boxing, I'm just a brother like other people. I want to live a good life, serve God, help everybody I can. And one more thing. I'm still gonna find out who stole my bike when I was 12 years old in Louisville and I'm still gonna whup him. That was a good bike"

Talking to biographer Thomas Hauser. Ali was referring to the fact that he had taken up boxing as a boy so he could fight the person who'd stolen his bike

Muhammad
Ali

"I met the greatest!"

For pros and fans alike, an encounter with Ali
is a life-changing experience

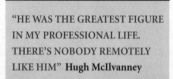

"HE WAS THE GREATEST FIGURE
IN MY PROFESSIONAL LIFE.
THERE'S NOBODY REMOTELY
LIKE HIM" **Hugh McIlvanney**

"I met The Greatest!"

AN ENCOUNTER WITH MUHAMMAD ALI ISN'T AN EVENT YOU FORGET IN A HURRY. CHARISMATIC, FUNNY, CHARMING AND GENUINELY INTERESTED IN OTHER PEOPLE, ALI HAS LEFT HIS IMPRESSION ON BOXING INDUSTRY PROFESSIONALS AND FANS ALIKE. HERE ARE SOME OF THEIR REMINISCENCES

DEREK WILLIAMS Boxing pundit, Sky Sports

Former European and Commonwealth Heavyweight Champion

met Ali in 1994, in a Soho (London) nightclub called **Moonlighting** – he wasn't partying of course. He was over on a promotional trip. It had been widely advertised that he would be dropping in, and such is the power of the man that they didn't serve alcohol that night, paying respect to his religious beliefs.

When he came in, with one of his daughters, hundreds of people stopped in amazement. There was the great **Muhammad Ali**! People began shaking...

The manager of the club called me over and introduced me to him. Ali looked happy to meet me, especially after he heard that I was a heavyweight boxer. He was very quiet but gracious.

It was a **momentous occasion** for me because Ali had influenced my career as a boxer from my childhood and people like me were children when Ali was at his greatest. Meeting him at that stage of his life didn't dampen the experience.

STEVE FARHOOD Boxing journalist

covered his last two fights, against Larry Holmes and Trevor Berbick, but my first and last personal encounter with Muhammad came in 1997.

The Ring magazine was about to celebrate its 75th anniversary and we were going to host a big gala in Atlantic City. The event was televised by **Classic Sports Network**, and part of the preparation was to tape a little message from Ali. We gave him every issue of *The Ring* in which he had appeared on the cover. No other boxer had been on the cover more than 15 times, but Ali had been featured **70-something times**, including being on the cover 11 months in a row in the 1970s. We had named the third Ali-Frazier fight as the greatest fight of *The Ring*'s 75 years.

And so I found myself with a cameraman, an audio guy and Ali in a hotel room in Manhattan. He did a cameo where he "attacked" the camera, shouting, "Joe Frazier, I'm going to get you!"

I was more than welcomed to do a private interview after we were done taping, and Ali and I walked into the bedroom of the suite. He was trembling, and there I was with pen and pad. It was an awkward and difficult moment because whatever I asked would have received minimal response, as he was unable to verbalise. After several questions I realised that it was difficult for both of us and we ended it there. It wasn't a particularly illuminating moment: rather a very awkward and unforgettable one.

BRIAN GANZ Ali fan

'␣ve met the great man three times, but two of them really stand out. The first time was when I was about 12 years old. My mother and I were driving down **Wilshire Boulevard** in Los Angeles. As I looked out of the car window, there he was: Muhammad Ali. I could not believe it! I went nuts. I told my mother to follow his car. We followed to him **Bob Big Boy**, which was famous for its soups; "The Greatest" loved his bean soup, I've heard. I ran in after him. He was very nice, joked around and signed a paper for me.

KEVIN MITCHELL Sports writer, *The Observer*

Three years ago I was in New York for a couple of days with **Don King**, to write about Muhammad. I didn't know he was actually going to be there. It was at the end of a rather unusual day, because we had already met **Louis Farrakhan**, the Nation of Islam leader, which was in itself rather unusual, and then Don King says, "I've got someone else that I want you to meet." So we went to the top floor of this hotel nearby in Manhattan, he opened the door – and there was Muhammad Ali.

It was totally unexpected. As everyone who meets him says, Ali does have a **presence** about him that can't be easily described – especially if you watched him at his peak and saw the athlete that he was, and then you see him face to face coping with his illness. It has an impact on you in that way. There's a lot of humanity about the man.

He has a repertoire, which is fairly well-known – he has a few stock jokes that he tells and he likes to do magic tricks. He trotted out his jokes, which we all laughed at because it would be rude not to. They weren't fantastic jokes, but they were reasonably funny.

We chatted – then, rather surreally, **Will Smith** who was playing him in the movie *Ali*, happened to ring up at that very minute. It was a bit odd.

"I met The Greatest!"

The thing about Ali that he has never lost is his sense of fun. He still has a lot of the little boy in him; he's pretty much a prankster. At one point, he and Don King were whispering something. It seemed pretty lewd, by what I could gather, because they were both laughing their heads off.

I didn't know how to say goodbye to him.

ANDY HALL Photographer

was there with Kevin Mitchell, to follow Don King around. I was so excited. I was 13 or 14 years old when the **Rumble in the Jungle** happened. I was living in Kenya at that time and the fight was the biggest thing happening in Africa.

Muhammad is still a big man: I could feel his muscles when I shook his hand and patted his arm (below). He was very chilled out, with his shirt unbuttoned, and slow in his movement and his speech, but every so often he would burst into life and say something that had us all in stitches.

Don King was holding court and I got the feeling Ali wanted to shut him up and divert all eyes back on himself.

Being there in a professional capacity didn't stop me from handing my camera to King and asking him to take a picture of **The Greatest** and me. I had this huge, cheesy grin on my face – I was dumbstruck.

Andy Hall gets up close and personal with The Greatest. Picture by Don King!

ANTHONY GEE Former boxing promoter

I grew up watching Ali and meeting him in the 1990s was one of the special moments in my life; it evoked all sorts of emotions. The first time I met him was at a hair and beauty show in London. I was there with **Lennox Lewis** and we all sat together, Ali was there with **Howard Bingham**. I shook his hand and we cracked a few jokes.

The next time we met was at the **Henry Cooper boxing gym**. He signed a couple of books for me. We spoke briefly. What I can remember is that he was very funny. He does a lot with his eyes. We had a laugh.

RON SHILLINGFORD Boxing writer and author of *No Glove, No Love*

E very kid with sporting ambitions has an idol and mine was unequivocally Muhammad Ali. No other black sports icon of the time compared. Not even Pelé, (Garfield) **Sobers** or (Arthur) **Ashe**.

For me, being short and timid, Ali was the embodiment of what I wanted to be: tall, handsome, articulate and a media star. I was so captivated, I used to rouse the rest of the household in the middle of the night to watch his fights.

I finally met my hero in 1986, at Witherspoon's training camp in Essex. **Frank Bruno** was getting ready to challenge **Tim Witherspoon** for the latter's world title and Ali was sitting at a table ringside, watching the sparring. As I hesitantly approached that hot, sunny afternoon, I swear he had an aura around him.

"Muhammad... Sorry to disturb you, but I've been a huge fan for years... can you sign this for me?"

He turned slowly, looked at me warmly then looked down at the iconic black

and white photo of himself, aged 13, in a boxing stance. He whispered: "What's your name?" I gave him a pen and he silently wrote with a shaky hand a long message on it that seemed to take an age.

"Thanks, Muhammad, I love you man," I said. We shook hands and I left, sweaty and shaking with excitement. His legacy is immeasurable. I truly feel blessed to have met him.

Ron Shillingford with Muhammad Ali: "He's still mightily impressive"

"I met The Greatest!"

RODNEY HINDS Journalist

I met him at **Sound Republic** in Leicester Square in London, two years ago (below). He was there to promote the video game **Knockout Kings**. When it was mentioned that he was going to be here, I said "I'm doing that job." I just wanted to meet the man who I regard as the greatest.

The first thing I noticed when I saw him was that everyone around him seemed to be in total awe of him – there was still quite a presence about him. Interestingly, **Lennox Lewis** was with him that evening and appeared to be so humble round him.

The meeting was very brief. It is very easy to get awestruck by the man, and admittedly I was overcome by events. I just said the basics like "Hello, how are you," as though it was my first day on the job. He is still mightily impressive despite the obvious fact he's slowed.

COLIN HART Reporter

He was one of the kindest, most gentle men I ever met. Of course the brash Clay/Ali was an act. If you were in a room, just two or three of you, which happened on many occasions during his career, he was a very quiet guy and very pleasant to talk to. But show him a notebook and pencil, show him a camera and he would play up to the media in the way we know and love.

On one occasion, I'd been to a fight in **Las Vegas** and was on my way with some media guys to **Atlantic City** to cover another bout. We had a day or two to spare, so we thought we'd hang out in LA before flying on. We were being a bit idle and someone said, "Ali lives here. Why don't we try to get in touch with him?"

It would come as a surprise to many people today that British boxing writers should have Ali's home number, but we did. **Jim Rosenthal** – now the presenter of Formula 1 racing on ITV but in those days a BBC radio commentator – had never spoken to Ali in his life, so we gave him the duty of calling. I remember Jim banging on my bedroom door and eight in the morning saying, "Get up! Ali wants to see us now!"

We jumped into two cabs and went to this address that Ali had given us. He lived off Wilshire Boulevard, an area where every **mansion** was bigger than the previous one, in a heavily guarded complex. The cabs drove into the complex and standing on the steps was Ali, in his "**uniform**": black shirt, black slacks and black shoes. We piled into this beautiful place he was living in and he gave us a tour of the premises, including his **trophy room**, which had to be seen to be believed.

He took us upstairs to the first level and we walked to a huge oak door at the end of the corridor. Ali turned round and put his finger to his lips, asking for quiet. He opened the door stuck his head in and began having a conversation with someone – it was Veronica, his third wife. She was in bed and he was saying, "Honey, get up – I want to show the British press the master bedroom!"

Could you imagine any world-class sportsman doing anything like that? It's like David Beckham saying, "Posh, get up…"

It makes you laugh, doesn't it? Veronica did get out of bed in the end, too…

KEN JONES Sports columnist, *The Independent*

I encountered Ali dozens of times throughout his career. One of the things I learned was that you had to work your way through things that he wanted to say and wait for something to come out of it. He would go off into flights of fancy and you had to wait for the storm of that to subside before getting down to some real stuff with him.

I actually met him in a lift in Lake Tahoe, Nevada, in 1972. **Reg Gutteridge** introduced me. I can remember being slightly awestruck. The strange thing was I had seen him in the flesh – I'd covered his fights against **Henry Cooper** – but to be in a confined space with him made you realise what presence he had.

I went to see him officially in Philadelphia in 1973, after the fight in which **Ken Norton** had broken his jaw. He was sitting at a table with **Howard Cosell**, who was trying to persuade him to do a television interview, which was ridiculous because he could only mumble due to his jaw being wired.

After a while he looked at me and said, "Come on." We went for a drive to downtown Philadelphia in his Rolls-Royce. We had a substantial conversation, in which he confessed to being silly in his training for the Norton fight, and he had been punished. He said he was going to regain the title and so on.

For the **Rumble in the Jungle** against George Foreman, **Hugh McIlvanney** and I stayed close to Ali in **N'Sele**, Zaire. We were the only media men there; the rest were in **Kinshasa** where the fight was being held, about 40 miles away.

About four or five hours after he had beaten Foreman, Hugh and I returned to N'Sele from Kinshasa. Hugh had some syndication work to do and once he'd finished that we went for a walk. It was very misty down by the river that night, but suddenly, as if by magic, there Ali was. He said to us, "You guys want to talk to me?"

We went into his bungalow and he was watching a pre-fight video of Foreman pounding the heavy bag awesomely. All of a sudden, he sat up and looked around the room and said, "I done fucked up a lot of minds."

We had never heard him swear before. It struck us that he had realised what he'd done. He had come off that tremendous high of the victory and suddenly it dawned on him that he had pulled off this amazing feat. That fight was to my mind the greatest sports event I've ever attended.

When he was preparing for his rematch against **Leon Spinks** in 1978, a few of us went to see him in a little house just outside New Orleans. It was the early hours of the morning and we walked up this street and turned in the gate. It was a very warm night and he was lying on a towel on the patio naked. He reached for another towel to cover him up. It was an odd sort of modesty that he had.

We were with him for 90 minutes or so. He chatted away, then he asked, "How did that carnival go in England?" He was referring to the **Notting Hill Carnival**.

HUGH McILVANNEY Journalist and writer

Y ou would come away from a talk with Muhammad just knowing that you had **pure gold**. It wasn't just that he was amusing: he also spread joy.

On one occasion we went to Chicago to see him and there were the five of us waiting for him. He came into the coffee shop and said, "I didn't give you permission to leave London." He drove us around Chicago and we got to stay with him all the time.

When he was training to fight **Joe Frazier** in 1971 he would do his roadwork around this golf course in Miami and be trailed in a Cadillac by this big, bad bodyguard called Reggie, who was from Chicago. He would often stop and talk to us – he wasn't at all that desperate about the running. He would say all kinds of things. "Do you think I could be president of the United States if I run?"

One day a little dog came yelping up, and Reggie's automatic response was to run over the dog. But Muhammad said "No!" He stroked the dog and said in a mock voice, "Reggie, this is just a bluff dog." That was just typical of him.

We would stand there and have all kinds of conversation with Muhammad, which would wander into theories about spaceships: he felt that the **black Muslim** movement had a link with a mothership that would be controlling Earth in the near future. You could never be quite sure how far his tongue was in his cheek, but he would give us some marvellous poetic monologues.

We were with him for five days during his preparations in Miami. There was a big Hollywood stake in the first Frazier fight; **Burt Lancaster** came down to Miami to help with publicity. The second time he fought **Henry Cooper** in 1966, the editor of *The Observer* newspaper, where I was working at the time, asked, "Do you think if you go across to America, you'll be able to get hold of him?"

I said, "I'll ring **Angelo [Dundee]**," who encouraged me to come over, like it was across the street. I was slightly wary because at the time he was jetting up to Chicago quite a lot to see **Elijah Muhammad**, but Angelo said to me, "Come! I'm here, the kid's here…"

I went there and spent two or three days alone with him. He had two Cadillacs, which were being used, so we went everywhere in cabs. We were just having fun.

While I was there we saw these two girls, and Ali said he had to speak to them. They talked, there was uproarious laughter and he came back to me and said, "Them two girls is prostitutes, but I've converted them some. They've stopped smoking and swearing but they're still prostitutes…"

He was the greatest figure in my professional life and I'm privileged that my prime coincided with that of Muhammad Ali. There's nobody remotely like him.

EMMANUEL STEWARD Trainer

The first time I met Muhammad Ali in person was in spring 1963; I had just won the **National Golden Gloves Tournament of Champions** in America. He was on his way to Denver to park outside the house of Sonny Liston and he came into Detroit. He stopped there to do some training and they charged people $10 just to watch him train. He had a big bus saying, "**The most colourful fighter in the world**" parked outside the gym. We were the only fighters training, and we grew to be friends.

There are two things that people overlook with Ali. First of all, he knows boxing. He was one of the most intelligent men I ever saw in boxing. Basically, he took rhythm and psychology and combined those two things. He was extremely clever, knowing how to get inside an opponent's mind. With those two main elements he went on to become one of the greatest fighters ever.

Secondly, he loved to box. People tend to think that he was just a pretty showman. He was extraordinarily tough, and just loved what he was doing. In my opinion he would have beaten any heavyweight that ever lived.

For his last fight against **Trevor Berbick** in Nassau, Bahamas, we shared the same gym, as my fighter **Thomas Hearns** was appearing on his undercard. Who would have thought it that after sharing a gym in the early 1960s, we would have been doing the same, 20 years after? That's the greatness and longevity of Ali.

Muhammad Ali

ephemera

From the classy to the brassy, Ali's is a life on sale in fight handbills,
used boxing boots – and signed Ovaltine tins

"IT'S JUST A JOB. GRASS GROWS,
BIRDS FLY, WAVES POUND THE
SAND. I BEAT PEOPLE UP"
Muhammad Ali

MUHAMMAD ALI IS ONE OF THE WORLD'S FEW REAL HEROES AND FOR TRUE FANS, OWNING A PIECE OF HIS PAST HAS AN IRRESISTIBLE LURE. THE ALI MEMORABILIA MARKET IS A STRANGE AND WONDERFUL THING, BUT MANY LONG TO POSSESS SOMETHING THAT BRINGS THEIR HERO THAT BIT CLOSER

As Ali has charted his course through life from amateur boxer to world heavyweight champion to icon, he's left a world of ephemera swirling in his wake. From the **robe** worn for the fight against **George Foreman** to cheap, plastic **action figures,** it's possible to reconstruct the highs and lows of the Ali story from what's been left behind.

The most valuable items of memorabilia are the **ring clothes** and **equipment** worn and used by Ali in his prime. He often gave them to members of his entourage or people who travelled to Deer Lake to watch him train, and much of it has made its way on to the **auction circuit** and the **Internet**. Original **fight posters** and **programmes** from his earlier fights can fetch thousands.

In stark contrast is the eclectic range of officially endorsed tat generated by some truly hopeless **business ventures** in the twilight of Ali's career, such as **share certificates** in Ali's failed **burger chain**, the "Rope-A-Dope" **skipping ropes** and the bottles of **Ali aftershave** available on eBay.

It's testament to the man's charisma that listening to **audio files of Ali's poetry** booming out from **websites** set up by diehard fans or glancing at one of the early **photographs** of him is enough to make you forgive the tawdry side. Photographs abound: for the truly dedicated, over 3,000 are collected in **GOAT** (see page 198), an 800-page, limited-edition tribute to Ali that weighs in at a hefty 75lb and has a correspondingly hefty £2,000 price tag.

Probably the best investment for anyone who wants to get to the heart of Ali is a good-quality biography. Writers such as **David Remnick** and **Norman Mailer** have done an excellent job of explaining why Ali's significance goes far beyond his achievements in the ring. Ali once told Remnick, "You don't own nothing, you're just a trustee in this life," which makes you wonder what he makes of the ephemera industry he's inspired. But the Ali story has never been about common sense, and for mere mortals who want to own a piece of it – no matter what it's worth – the pull of the Ali magic is just too strong.

Memorabilia

ALI COLLECTIBLES CAN BE FOUND TO SATISFY EVERY CRAVING AND BUDGET. SIGNED ITEMS AND RING CLOTHES ARE EASILY THE MOST EXPENSIVE, BUT THERE ARE BARGAINS OUT THERE IF YOU LOOK. BUYER BEWARE, HOWEVER: WHILE HUNTING FOR ALI MEMORABILIA NEEDN'T BE A DEPRESSING EXPERIENCE, SOME ONLINE SELLERS HAVE QUESTIONABLE MOTIVES, SUMMED UP BY ADS THAT INCLUDE EXPLOITATIVE LINES SUCH AS "HE MAY NOT BE SIGNING FOR MUCH LONGER." FOR DETAILS ON MORE REPUTABLE SITES, SEE "WHERE TO BUY" IN "ALI ON THE WEB," PAGE 254

Ring clothes: robes, gloves and boots

Items worn by Ali in fights and in training fetch the highest prices. There's also no shortage, on websites such as eBay, of more recently signed, unworn items such as shorts and gloves. $1,000 is the going rate and they're often authenticated by pictures of Ali at signing sessions, pen in hand, working his way through enormous piles of identical kit. You pays your money…

Fight robe $28,318

A full-length red satin robe with white trim and the words "Muhammad Ali" on the back in white letters. The robe was worn before the fight against Oscar Bonavena in December 1970, and has fared better than Ali's opponent, who was found dead outside a Las Vegas brothel six years later.

Fight-worn and autographed trunks $11,789

Autographed by Ali and, according to the website blurb, formerly part of the estate of Ali's assistant trainer Bundini Brown, these white Lonsdale shorts with a red stripe were worn in Ali's fight against Mac Foster in April 1971.

Fight shoes $9,260

White, size 13 fight shoes worn when Ali defended his title against Earnie Shavers at Madison Square Garden in September 1977. They're suitably battered and still have their original laces.

Training robe $6,112

A white terry-cloth robe worn during training for the fight against Larry Holmes with "Muhammad Ali" in black letters across the back. In the dubious prose of the online auctioneer, "Its strong use tells a tale of desire and unrelenting will that was the man as it is toned from the heavy sweat and determination it had absorbed."

Head protector $3,281
A black leather Everlast head protector worn by Ali during training for the fight with Larry Holmes (Ali's penultimate professional bout, in Las Vegas in 1980), and signed by Ali.

Training glove $2,783
One red training glove, worn by Ali during his preparation for the Rumble in the Jungle, in Zaire. It's signed by Cassius Clay Sr, Bundini Brown and finally by Ali with the prophetic words "Muhammad Ali – the title will be mine! The Mummy will fall – 1974."

Fight gloves $18,723
The gloves worn by the then Cassius Clay during his first professional fight. Signed at the post-fight press conference, the right glove is signed "Cassius Marcellus Clay" and the left is signed by Ali's opponent, Tunney Hunsaker.

Muhammad Ali and Joe Frazier-signed boxing gloves $1,199
Pair of unworn red Everlast gloves, one signed by Ali and the other by Frazier, with the apparently rare inscription "Smokin' Joe Frazier," presented with pictures from each bout the two fought against one another and some explanatory text.

Protective cup $1,150
1970s vintage black leather protective cup worn during training and possibly during fights, this was given to Eddie "Bossman" Jones, one of Ali's sparring partners during the preparation for the Rumble in the Jungle.

Piece of Ali's robe $199.99
Comes with a certificate of authenticity and a picture of Ali meeting The Beatles. The size of each individual piece of fabric on offer, together with the fact this piece is number 156 of 200, suggests that the original garment must have been roughly the size of Texas.

Photographs, prints and posters

PHOTOGRAPHER NEIL LEIFER SAID OF ALI, "HE MADE YOUR JOB A SUCCESS JUST BY SHOWING UP" AND ALI IS THE SUBJECT OF SOME CLASSIC SPORTS PHOTOGRAPHY. ALMOST ALL OF IT IS STILL AVAILABLE, FROM CHEAP, MASS-PRODUCED POSTERS AND ART PRINTS TO LIMITED-EDITION REPRINTS SIGNED BY THE PHOTOGRAPHER OR BY ALI HIMSELF

Ali vs Williams by Neil Leifer *New York Times Store* $1,140
An 11in x 14in print of one of the most famous sports photographs of all time: Leifer's dizzying aerial view of the ring with Cleveland Williams spreadeagled on the canvas and Ali celebrating in the opposing corner. Signed by Leifer, and part of a limited edition of 350.

Jaw X-ray *Webgalleria* $895
Arguably the most unusual Ali image available, this X-ray of his jaw was taken after it had been broken during the fight against Ken Norton in March 1973, and has been signed by Ali as well as Norton.

Muhammad Ali Center limited-edition autographed print *Ali Center* $650
One of a limited edition of promotional posters signed by Ali and sold in aid of the Muhammad Ali Center in Louisville, Kentucky.

Ali negative *Lelands* $201
Oddly poignant 2.5in square colour negative of a shirtless Ali with a white dove perching on an outstretched finger.

Black and white training photograph *eBay* $400
Unframed 14in x 18in gelatin silver print of a photograph taken by Morris Lane of Ali training in San Juan, Puerto Rico, in 1976. A tight head shot of Ali, with his face framed by his Everlast headguard, it's a rare instance of a limited edition that justifies the name – there are only 19 others.

Ali by Bill Peronneau *eyestorm* $600
Rare silver gelatin print of one of the "Cabin Series" of photographs, taken in 1974 by photo journalist and well-known documenter of the Civil Rights movement, Bill Peronneau, who had been invited up to Ali's cabin in the

Pocono Mountains. The beautiful print shows Ali in an unusually reflective mood, sitting in a rocking chair in a rustic cabin.

Agency photograph of Ali and baby daughter Laila *eBay* $69.95
Black and white archive photograph from the Associated Press Agency.

Ali and Elvis *eBay* $40
This black and white 16in x 20in print of Elvis and Ali squaring up to each other in a Vegas hotel suite, with Ali in a jewelled robe, is a staple of online Ali memorabilia sales. Dubious "signed" versions cost around four times more.

Ali and Bundini Brown art print *AllPosters.com* $23.99
A 24in x 32in print of Bundini Brown talking to Ali in the ring. The back of Bundini's t-shirt sports the immortal line "Float like a butterfly, sting like a bee," while Ali stares menacingly over his shoulder at an unseen opponent.

Ali training poster *AllPosters.com* $8.99
Famous shot of Ali sparring with the camera in 24in x 34in poster format, with the quote "The fight is won or lost far away from witnesses…" in the bottom left.

Autographs

ALI HAS PROBABLY SIGNED MORE AUTOGRAPHS THAN ANY OTHER CELEBRITY. ORIGINAL CASSIUS CLAY SIGNATURES ARE THE MOST SOUGHT AFTER; FIGHT PHOTOGRAPHS CO-SIGNED BY HIS MORE ILLUSTRIOUS OPPONENTS ALSO COMMAND A HIGH PRICE. SOME BARGAIN ITEMS ARE BEST APPROACHED WITH SENSIBLE TREPIDATION, AND NEVER HAS THE PHRASE "CAVEAT EMPTOR" BEEN MORE RELEVANT THAN FOR SOMEONE CONTEMPLATING ONE OF THE NET'S "BARGAIN" $4 ALI SIGNATURES

Handwritten letter to Odessa Clay *Lelands* $10,297
Written by Ali to his mother from Frankfurt on the eve of his fight against Karl Mildenberger in September 1966. In it, Ali promises that he'll try to call after the fight and advises his mother not to worry. It's signed "Cassius" – although he had changed his name two years before. It's this anomaly that explains the hefty price tag.

Replica championship belt *Lelands* $5,149
Green leather WBC belt identical to the one presented to Ali after his fight with Floyd Patterson in November 1965, signed by both Ali and Patterson.

Photograph of Frazier and Ali *Grandstand Sports* $1,699
16in x 20in black and white photograph of Ali dodging Frazier's left hook, signed by both fighters.

Photograph of Cassius Clay with Joe Louis *Webgalleria* $1,295
Joe Louis attempting to interview the then Cassius Clay in the ring immediately after the first Liston fight, although the signature, "Cassius Clay", is a recent one. Ali sometimes signs his old name on pictures of himself taken

before his conversion to Islam. It's surprising, given the importance he attached to changing his name, but unusual enough to raise the price $200–$300.

Superman vs Ali comic *Webgalleria* $750
One-shot comic produced by American publisher DC Comics in 1978 and signed by Ali, with a cover that shows Ali and Superman facing each other in the ring in front of a crowd of real and fictional stars. Ali wins, apparently. A guest slot for Spider-Man was ruled out for legal reasons.

Limited edition Fossil watch
www.boxing-memorabilia.com $645
Fossil watch from 1994 in a wooden presentation case. It comes with a certificate of authenticity and, more importantly, an autographed print of Neil Leifer's photograph of Ali standing over a dazed Sonny Liston.

Islamic information pamphlet *History for Sale* $549
Ali signs pamphlets as a way of spreading the word about Islam, recognising that they're less likely to get thrown away unread if they've been signed by the three-times world heavyweight champion. A number are available on the Internet, with prices ranging from $100 upwards.

Book of photographs by Wilfrid Sheed *eBay* $350
Hardback signed and dated by Ali on the set of biopic *The Greatest* in 1976.

Programme *History for Sale* $249
Programme from *Esquire*'s "Tribute to 50 Who Made the Difference" event held at the Lincoln Center in New York in November 1983 and signed "Muhammad Ali '83".

Matchbook *History for Sale* $129
Probably signed around 1968, according to the site blurb, this might not be as impressive as a glossy photograph of Ali and Joe Frazier, but it's a way of owning a vintage Ali signature without blowing the mortgage.

Fight posters, programmes and tickets

THE RULE OF THUMB IS THAT ITEMS FROM ALI'S EARLIER FIGHTS TEND TO FETCH THE HIGHEST PRICES. SOUVENIRS FROM KEY EVENTS SUCH AS THE THRILLA IN MANILA AND THE RUMBLE IN THE JUNGLE ARE EQUALLY SOUGHT AFTER, WHILE THE PRESENCE OF SIGNATURES OF BOTH ALI AND AN OPPONENT SUCH AS FRAZIER OR FOREMAN CAN ALSO INCREASE THE PRICE DRAMATICALLY

Muhammad Ali vs Jerry Quarry programme *SP Boxing* $1,500
The programme issued for Ali's first fight after he was stripped of the heavyweight title, signed by Ali and Quarry.

Muhammad Ali vs Cleveland Williams poster *Web Galleria* $1,400
Original on-site poster from what is widely seen as Ali's greatest fight. Signed by Ali, it's also available with Williams's signature, which pushes the price up to $2,095. According to the poster, the most expensive seat on the night cost a modest $50, a level of generosity likely to give Don King a heart attack.

Thrilla in Manila flyer *www.boxing-memorabilia.com* $995
A flyer used to promote the third fight between Ali and Joe Frazier, held in the Araneta Coliseum in the Philippines in 1975 and billed on the flyer as "Super Fight III." Printed in lurid green and red, the flyer might not win any design awards, but it's still a rare piece of boxing history.

Muhammad Ali vs George Foreman poster *Lelands* $813
Promotional poster for the closed circuit broadcast of the Rumble in the Jungle in 1974, created by sports artist LeRoy Neiman. Ali and Foreman

emerge from a blaze of blues and greens above the evocative line "World Heavyweight Championship Fight – 15 Rounds Direct from Kinshasa, Zaire – Tuesday October 29."

Muhammad Ali vs Earnie Shavers *Webgalleria* $595
Reproduction of the original on-site poster signed by Ali and Shavers, who is advertised as "The hardest punching heavyweight in the world."

Muhammad Ali vs George Chuvalo programme *Lelands* $380
Red and white four-page programme sold at Ali's first meeting with Chuvalo in Toronto in 1966.

Muhammad Ali vs Brian London poster *Lelands* $230
Classic boxing poster with both fighters' names in giant block type, advertising Ali's fight against Brian London at Earl's Court in London in 1966. Striking a patriotic note, the poster reproduces former Ali opponent Amos Johnson's suggestion that "London may be too tough and strong for Clay." London barely survived three rounds.

Muhammad Ali vs Joe Frazier poster *A&R Collectibles* $99
An original poster created by Italian artist Piatti to advertise the closed-circuit showing of the first Ali-Frazier fight in Harlem. An abstract rendering of a boxer's head in the shape of a glove with some suitably 1970s-era typography, it's one of the more distinctive and artistically interesting fight posters. A signed version will set you back $1,500.

Muhammad Ali vs Ernie Terrell ticket *eBay* $29.99
An unused ticket issued for a bout that was never fought. Ali finally fought Terrell the following year, inflicting a severe beating for Terrell's refusal to call him "Muhammad Ali."

Larry Holmes vs Muhammad Ali poster *eBay* $24.99
LeRoy Neiman's poster for Ali's fight against Larry Holmes in October 1980 at Caesar's Palace. As the poster says, the fight was dubbed "The Last Hurrah" which, unfortunately, it wasn't.

Quirky stuff

SOME TRULY WEIRD AND WONDERFUL ALI MEMORABILIA CAN BE FOUND ON THE INTERNET. A QUICK TRAWL BROUGHT IN THIS TYPICAL HAUL...

Deer Lake training bell *Lelands* $4,025
Brass ring bell used at Ali's training camp at Deer Lake, fully working and complete with the original cord and handle.

Original artwork *eBay* $2,495
One of a range of prints from paintings by Ali, all signed and dated 1979. With subjects including fighter planes and boats, it's not quite Picasso.

Original Ali water bottle *eBay* $1,310
Brown glass bottle wrapped in white boxing tape signed by Bundini Brown and inscribed with "M. Ali," "Ali Only" and "Ali" in black marker.

Autographed "Louisville Slugger" baseball bat *www.webgalleria.com* $750
Demonstrating that no connection is too tenuous for the memorabilia market, Ali signed 94 of these famous baseball bats made in his home town.

Mego Muhammad Ali action figure *www.gasolinealleyantiques.com* $235
You saw his fights, you've read the books, now play with the plastic replica. Or rather, leave it in its box to appreciate in value. This action figure from 1976 comes complete with robe, trunks, gloves and punching action. Guaranteed to sting like a bee and float in the bath.

Muhammad Ali life mask *eBay* $39.99
"It's like having Ali right there with you," writes the creator, rashly assuming that you expect Ali to be gold instead of black. The version with eyes costs an extra $20, but it's the stuff of which nightmares are made.

Champburger share certificate *www.scripophily.net* $79.95
A certificate for 100 shares in Ali's ill-fated burger chain. That anyone would use Ali's name to front such a spectacularly naff franchise speaks volumes about the criminal abuse of his goodwill and his finances, and the fact that these certificates are now changing hands for $80 speaks volumes about what happened to Champburger.

Muhammad Ali signature cologne *www.rotmanauction.com* $70
Unused 1.7cl bottle of scent in its original black, red and gold box. Offers you
the chance to smell like the champ, assuming he would ever wear 20-year-old
cologne bought over the Internet.

Desktop clock *eBay* $13.99
CD-sized desktop clock picture of Ali in mid-fight. As one of the testimonials
says with uncanny accuracy, "They're like photos that tell the time."

"Rope-A-Dope" skipping rope *eBay* $12.99
Sports history's most grimly inevitable cash-in, the Rope-A-Dope skipping
rope has "autographed" wooden handles and the unopened packaging even
has a picture of Ali skipping, for anyone unsure how to use it.

eBay's six most valuable items

eBay IS HOME TO SOME TOP-DOLLAR ALI MEMORABILIA. YOU CAN BID FOR
SIGNED PIECES OF CLASSY ARTWORK, GLOVES AND TRUNKS WORN BY THE MAN
HIMSELF, OR A LIFESIZE REPLICA FOR YOUR LIVING ROOM…

Signed limited-edition LeRoy Neiman art print $4,900
Leading sports artist Neiman, who also painted Joe DiMaggio and Babe Ruth,
met Clay in his dressing room before his fight against Billy Daniels in 1962,
sketching the young fighter on the rubdown table. This colourful print, signed by
artist and subject, captures the theatrical flair and sheer athletic vitality of The
Greatest. "He was fast with his rhetoric and swift with his fists," says Neiman,
"and the intent of the painting and print is to emphasise his boundless energy."

Authentic worn boxing trunks $3,000
Made Expressly For Muhammad Ali, says the label of these white satin Everlast
trunks with black trim. "As a young boy my dad took me to see him train in
Miami," claims the seller. "One day he brought me into ring and showed me how
to throw punches and play boxed with me. Muhammad Ali and my dad became
good friends over the years. He gave these trunks to my dad to give to me."

Gordon Parks 1966 photographic print $2,400
A silver 14x11 print of the famous black-and-white photograph of Ali sitting in
his ring corner with his head bowed and hands bound, ready for another session,

Ephemera

PROFILE **An expert's guide to the market** MUHAMMAD ALI MEMORABILIA

WE ASKED DAVID CONVERY, SPORTING MEMORABILIA SPECIALIST AT AUCTIONEERS CHRISTIE'S, FOR A FEW WORDS OF ADVICE TO HELP YOU SPOT WHETHER THAT PHOTOGRAPH YOU'RE ABOUT TO BUY ON EBAY – THE ONE OF ALI AND ELVIS PLAYING GOLF WITH MARILYN AND JFK – IS ALL THAT IT SEEMS...

Ali's autograph is particularly easy to copy. The most recent examples are almost straight lines with a few vertical strokes, so if you get the opportunity, try to look at the paper from behind. If there's no indentation, it's likely that the signature is a mass-produced copy.

Certificates of authenticity, shortened to "COA", aren't worth the paper they're printed on. Desktop printing technology makes it easy to create a reasonably convincing document in next to no time, and a certificate from John Doe in Nowheresville, Idaho, is unlikely to impress future buyers when it's time to sell.

Items signed "Cassius Clay" don't necessarily mean they date back to before 1964, which is when Ali changed his name. Ali is increasingly signing memorabilia as "Muhammad Ali aka Cassius Clay".

Memorabilia is not necessarily a good investment. Ali is a prolific signer of autographs, so the quantity of memorabilia on the market means that prices are comparatively low. One-off items, such as the gloves worn for a particular fight, are a better bet.

Memorabilia with a story behind it has the greatest value. In 2001, Christie's sold the gloves Ali had worn in his 1966 fight against Henry Cooper. Cooper famously knocked Ali down with his left hook, but Ali's trainer Angelo Dundee bought Ali some time by pointing out a split in the gloves and Ali went on to win. The gloves fetched £37,500.

Items from reputable collections are often the best bet – and fetch the highest prices. In 1997, Christie's auctioned 348 lots of Ali memorabilia – more than 3,000 pieces – from a private collection assembled by Los Angeles businessman Ronnie Paloger, for over $1.3 million.

Don't get carried away. It's easy to convince yourself that you've found a bargain, especially if you're looking on the Internet, but the chances are that the item you're about to buy is worth a lot less than you think. Bear in mind, too, that Ali retains most of the items relating to his career, so if it looks too good to be true, it almost certainly is.

was taken in training in Florida in 1966 by the award-winning artist, writer, composer and film-maker Gordon Parks, who later directed the movie *Shaft*.

Original signed Muhammad Ali artwork $1,499

Drawn and autographed by The Greatest himself, this simple framed one-off piece of art bears the inscription, "Spread the word around the world, tell both friend and foe, I'm fighting now for freedom, let my people go."

Signed 1963 'prophecy' glove $999

This authenticated item was signed by Clay in training in 1963 with the words "Next Heavyweight Champion of the World." Months later, he fulfilled the prophecy by defeating Sonny Liston. "The signature and prophecy are penned against the burgundy background of the lightly scuffed glove and a tad light, but are eminently readable and historically significant," according to the billing.

Lifesize Muhammad Ali sculpture $860

This 6ft replica – based on the *Sports Illustrated* cover depicting Ali towering over Sonny Liston – was sculptured from resin by Jack Dowd. "Like a theatrical performance, my sculpture is more focused and more intense than life."

Ali on the Web

FOR SOMEONE WHOSE CAREER GENERATED REAMS OF STATISTICS, FILLED BOOKS WITH QUOTES AND WHOSE LIFE HAS TAKEN ON GREATER SIGNIFICANCE THAN THAT OF ANY SPORTSMAN BEFORE OR SINCE, ALI HAS NOT BEEN WELL SERVED BY THE INTERNET – UNLESS YOU'RE LOOKING TO SPEND SOME MONEY WITH ONE OF THE HUNDREDS OF ONLINE MEMORABILIA SELLERS

Official websites

The official Muhammad Ali site is competent enough, but you can't help thinking that, given the resources available, it's a bit disappointing.

The websites of the BBC, *New York Times* and *The Courier-Journal*, Lousiville's local paper, all have pages that display Ali-related material from their archives to good effect – but strangely, it's the Adidas site – **www.adidas.com** – that provides a genuinely spine-tingling Ali moment. Here, visitors can view the advert which uses archive footage and technology to enable the Ali of 40 years ago to spar with his daughter Laila. The pride and defiance in Laila's voice as she says, "Rumble, young girl, rumble," is so powerful, it's easy to forget that it's all about selling trainers.

Muhammad Ali *www.ali.com*
Ali's official site features news, a brief biography (by Gregory Allen Howard, author of the screenplay for *Remember The Titans*), some background information and his fight record, as well as the chance to view testimonies, many of which are genuinely moving, by fans talking about how Ali has influenced their lives.

The Muhammad Ali Center *www.alicenter.org*
The Shockwave-based intro is a lesson in how to open a Web page with maximum impact, flashing up pictures of Ali over a pounding score. The purpose of the site is to publicise the Ali Center, which will open in 2005 to provide a focal point for the celebration of Ali's life and the promotion of his ideals. The online shop has some genuinely worthwhile merchandise, and it's all for a good cause.

Howard Bingham *www.howardbingham.com*
Bingham got an F (for "fail") from his photography tutor at college in Los Angeles and was advised to try something else for a living. Despite this, he stuck to his guns and became Ali's photographer and a close friend. His official site is informative and well laid-out, but doesn't show nearly enough of his photographs.

Websites about Ali

The Courier-Journal
www.courier-journal.com/ali/index.html
The local paper in Louisville, Ali's home town, is justly proud of its favourite son and has dedicated a subsection of its site to him. The page is updated with news stories about Ali, but it's the chance to view the newspaper's extensive archives of articles about Ali – with contemporary photographs – dating back to the start of his career as a flyweight in 1954, that really makes it worth a visit.

Ali at 60 *news.bbc.co.uk/sport1/hi/boxing/specials/ali_at_60*
This BBC site, created to celebrate Ali's 60th birthday, gathers together an impressive range of information, with video and audio clips from the fights and a library of articles on Ali and different aspects of his life.

The New York Times *www.nytimes.com/books/98/10/25/specials/ali.html*
A selection of photographs and articles on Ali from the *Times*'s own archives.

International Boxing Hall of Fame *www.ibhof.com/ali.htm*
Ali's entry on the International Boxing Hall of Fame website.

Photography online

Ali Through The Lens of Howard Bingham *www.kodak.com/go/Ali*
A fantastic site that tells the story of the making of the Michael Mann film, but also the history of Ali, using Howard Bingham's photographs. Many include audio files with Bingham explaining the significance of the images, and talking about his relationship with Ali. The presentation of each menu as a sepia-toned fight poster is a great touch.

  The Sports Illustrated covers
www.sportsillustrated.cnn.com/centurys_best/boxing/gallery/ali/main/index.html
A viewable list of all 35 covers of the American sports magazine that have featured Ali, charting his journey from the "Cassius Invades Britain" cover of June 1963 to the present day.

Articles about Ali online

Muhammad Ali by George Plimpton
www.time.com/time/time100/heroes/profile/ali01.html
Written for *Time* magazine's list of the 100 most important people of the 20th century, this article is literate but accessible, informed but readable and warmed by genuine affection for its subject.

The Myth of Muhammad *www.salon.com/oct96/books961104.html*
A review of Davis Miller's *The Tao of Muhammad Ali* from *Salon* that makes
some interesting points about the dangers of mythologising Ali.

Fans' websites

Ring King *www.ring-king.co.uk*
Guided tour of one fan's Muhammad Ali memorabilia collection. It doesn't
reveal how much he paid for each item, but it's an interesting insight into
what's available – even if the signed boarding card might be taking the casual
viewer's interest too much for granted.

Float Like a Butterfly *www.float-like-a-butterfly.de*
Excellent site created by German fan Johannes Ehrmann, with a brief biog
of Ali, descriptions of classic bouts and a useful range of career statistics as
well as a thorough list of quotes and poems, some of them available as MP3s.

Where to buy memorabilia online

Lelands *www.lelands.com*
A superb site. The online auctions held in May and December each year
always include a fascinating array of memorabilia, even though these tend
to include more expensive items like fight-worn gloves and robes. At least
there's a searchable archive of past auctions that gives anyone without a spare
$20,000 the chance to indulge in some window shopping.

Web Galleria *www.webgalleria.com*
Reportedly the biggest range of Ali memorabilia on sale anywhere. The
majority of the stock seems to have been signed recently, although there is
a selection of fight-worn and training equipment and an eclectic array of
original endorsed products – the official Ali afro comb, anybody? The
vintage-poster section contains some superb originals.

History for Sale *www.historyforsale.com*
Reputable site that specialises in autographed items. There's normally an array

of signed letters, notes and cards, and although none of them are cheap, there are generally a few items for the more modest budget.

Grandstand Sports

www.grandstandsports.com/gsm/p_Muhammad_Ali_1.asp
Well laid-out site with a variety of Ali memorabilia, including signed ring clothes and photographs.

Notable and Notorious

www.notableandnotorious.com/muhammadali.htm

Not the most attractive site, nor the most reassuring name, but there's a good range of memorabilia, particularly signed photographs.

SP Boxing *www.spboxing.com*

Useful resource for paper ephemera such as fight programmes and photographs, many of them signed.

eBay *www.eBay.com*

As diverse a range of Ali memorabilia as you'd expect from the world's favourite online auction site, ranging from value-free tat sold by dissembling con men to more worthwhile items such as limited-edition prints and curios.

Where to buy books, posters and photographs online

Sportspages *www.sportsbooksdirect.co.uk*

The online version of the UK-based sports bookshop. It sells books on Ali, including some titles that are not readily available elsewhere, as well as books on boxing history and anthologies of boxing writing.

All Posters *www.AllPosters.com*

Sells Ali posters and art prints. The stock includes Flip Schulke's famous shot of Ali pretending to train underwater and a poster version of Andy Warhol's screenprint, as well as an excellent range of other Ali action images and portraits in mono and colour.

PROFILE The magic of MUHAMMAD ALI

Ali is the master of the cheap magic trick. For anyone else, making handkerchiefs and coins disappear would seem at best corny and at worst bizarre, but thanks to Ali's guileless charm, it's become an essential part of his public appearances.

He was already performing magic tricks for local children shortly after he moved to Miami to train at Angelo Dundee's gym, and as the journalists who have served as his captive audience will tell you, Ali's repertoire has remained remarkably unchanged ever since.

The disappearing handkerchief is Ali's signature trick, and cheerfully ignoring his own rule, "never do a trick twice," he has performed it for everybody from Bill Clinton to the crowds of children he met when he visited Brixton in London.

Performing tricks also gives Ali the opportunity to send up people who make the mistake of taking him too seriously. Ali once asked Rick Reilly, from *Sports Illustrated*, if he would believe in Islam if Ali could make a glass levitate.

"He quieted his shakes," Reilly wrote afterwards, "stared hard at the glass and then announced, 'April Fools!'"

The Islamic religion preaches against deceit, so Ali makes a point of explaining how his tricks are done – even the disappearing handkerchief trick, in which the handkerchief disappears into a fake finger.

Asked by a journalist from *Esquire* why he bothered learning the tricks if he was only going to give away the secret to his audience afterwards, Ali explained the reason is, "To prove to them how easily they can be deceived." As always with Ali, the answer might not be entirely serious – and as with his magic tricks, it's just possible that the joke's on us.

Amazon *www.amazon.com*
The best for reasonably priced Ali books, DVDs and music. The zShops offer a good way of tracking down more obscure or out-of-print titles.

New York Times Store *www.nytimes.com/nytstore/photos/personalities*
The *Times* sells five of Neil Leifer's classic photographs of Ali, including the aerial view of the Cleveland Williams fight and Ali raging at a prone Sonny Liston. The photographs are limited editions, and prices are increasing as they sell out, so you'll need your credit card. Or a generous loan.

The music of Ali

"I'm gonna go and play me some **soul music**, man," Ali tells a group of journalists at one point during **When We Were Kings**, the documentary about his fight with George Foreman in Zaire, "a bit of **James Brown**."

Music was a big part of the promotion for the fight, with James Brown, **B.B. King** and **The Spinners** all being flown out to Africa for the accompanying festival. However, it's likely that Ali would have been just as happy listening to **Chubby Checker**. Early rock 'n' roll has long been a favourite of Ali's, and his friend Howard Bingham once observed that he was never interested in famous people, with one exception: "Old rock stars. Ali loved **Fats Domino**, **Little Richard**, Jackie Wilson, **Sam Cooke**, **Lloyd Price**, Chubby Checker, all those guys. He still does."

When the 16-year-old Ali met **Lloyd Price**, singer of *Personality* and *Stagger Lee*, he told Price, "I love your music and I'm gonna be famous like you." Price replied, "Kid, you're dreaming," but years later he became part of Ali's entourage – and has the dubious honour of being the person who introduced him to **Don King**. **Little Richard** was reportedly Ali's favourite singer, attending his lavish 50th birthday celebration in 1992, and Ali also struck up an unlikely rapport with **Elvis**.

According to Thomas Hauser, Ali had admired Elvis "intensely" since he was 14, once describing himself as the "Elvis of boxing." Elvis responded by presenting Ali with a robe bearing the legend "The People's Champion," which Ali wore before his defeat against Ken Norton.

A singer who made a more direct connection with Ali's developing political sensibilities was **Sam Cooke**. Cooke wrote **A Change is Gonna Come**, which became synonymous with the **Civil Rights** movement and the two became friends during the early 1960s – the 2003 documentary *Sam Cooke – Legend* shows some rare footage of Cooke, who died after a still-mysterious shooting in 1964, and Ali singing together at Columbia Records in New York.

Cooke helped Ali record a song called *The Gang's All Here*, recently reissued on Sony's *I Am The Greatest*, an album featuring early examples of Ali's poetry, first released in 1963 as part of the build-up for the Liston fight. The reissue also includes Ali's rendition of **Ben E. King's** *Stand By Me*.

Ali recorded two other spoken-word albums later in his career. **Ali and His Gang Vs Mr Tooth Decay**, released in 1976, was a bizarre homily, aimed at children, on the evils of sugary foods, and is the only time Ali, **Howard Cosell** and **Frank Sinatra** appeared on the same record. The sleeve artwork seems to have been drawn under the influence of the kind of pharmaceuticals that inspired the follow-up, **The Dope King's Last Stand.** Grammy-nominated in 1977, it co-starred **President Carter**, **Pat Boone** and **Billie Jean King**…

Ali has also been the subject of several musical tributes. **The Fugees** contributed *Rumble in the Jungle* to the superb *When We Were Kings* soundtrack. Most recently, **Faithless'** album *Outrospective* includes the song *Muhammad Ali*. Most of his fans will identify with the lines, "Accept these humble words of praise, and my gratitude for those glorious days."

PROFILE 10 things you didn't know about MUHAMMAD ALI

His favourite **hobby** is magic, but his other great passion is **highlighting contradictions in the Bible**. According to his biographer David Remnick, Ali carries with him a long list of inconsistencies that he's found in the Old and New Testaments.

Black is his favourite colour.

He's afraid of **flying**, but on one flight played a practical joke by announcing over the intercom, "This is the captain speaking. We're having problems with one engine and we're gonna crash."

At **school**, he achieved his highest grade in **metalwork**. His "Scholastic Zeal" was rated "Average," and when he sat the US Army IQ test he received a rating of 78.

Roses are his favourite flowers.

The **Quran** is his favourite book. As a devout Muslim, Ali consults the Quran

regularly and prays five times a day. Before fights, Ali would stand in his corner and make **Dua**, the Muslim gesture of supplication used with both palms of both hands, or in Ali's case, gloves, facing upwards.

Ice cream is his favourite food.

He was sentenced to **10 days in prison** in Dade County, Florida, in 1968 for driving without a valid licence.

He can't **swim**, but he still convinced *Life* photographer Flip Schulke that he **trained underwater**. Schulke was inspired to take a series of photographs of Ali in sparring poses below the surface of a hotel pool, and *Life* made them the subject of a five-page feature.

Sylvester Stallone wrote the screenplay that became *Rocky* after watching Ali pulverise part-time liquor salesman Chuck "The Bayonne Bleeder" Wepner.

Ali and food

"Some people can eat and not gain weight, but if I just look at food, my belly gets bigger," Ali once told an interviewer, forgetting that his weight gain may have had something to do with the one dish he's always had a weakness for – ice cream

Ali and **ice cream** go back a long way. Writer **Peter Manseau** noted that an early *Sports Illustrated* article on Ali patronisingly located him somewhere on an ideological spectrum between **Malcolm X** and **vanilla ice cream** – "black radicalism on the one hand, white innocence on the other" – and when Ali was banned from boxing he dismissed fears about money worries by saying that he and wife could "still afford to go out to eat ice cream."

Despite the fact he made a bizarre spoken-word album in 1976 in which he and **Frank Sinatra** warned children off unhealthy sugary foods, Ali still has his sweet tooth. A journalist from *Esquire* remembers Ali, whose speech has been affected by Parkinson's Syndrome, acting out a complicated **mime** to tell the staff of a restaurant that he wanted to order a piece of pie for dessert, and drawing two big circles in the air to represent two scoops of ice cream.

During his fighting career, Ali's diet was the responsibility of one woman – Lana Shabazz. Ali met Shabazz when she was working at a Muslim restaurant in Manhattan. "I'd feed him **lamb shanks**, **string beans**, **rice**, **carrots**," she told Ali's biographer Thomas Hauser. "He had a big appetite. As often as not, he'd eat two plates of food." Boxing publicist Irving Rudd remembered that Shabazz also made "a hell of a **pecan pie**."

One of Ali's more unusual food associations also involves an item of memorabilia worth hunting down. In 1971, not long after his losing bout with Joe Frazier at Madison Square Garden, Ali undertook a promotional tour of several UK cities (as well as taking the tour to Nigeria) on behalf of the malt drink **Ovaltine**, visiting the factories at Norwich and Kings Langley, as well as local supermarkets (the site of the Norwich visit even boasts a blue plaque to mark the occasion), where he **signed Ovaltine tins** for fans. Quite a few of these tins must still be tucked away in cupboards across the UK…

In a recent interview with for the Muslim website **www.soundvision.com**, Ali revealed that his favourite dish is "Chicken and rice, or lamb and rice if I'm in a Muslim country," before adding the inevitable: "also ice cream."

Muhammad
Ali
in pictures

In his prime he was the most recognisable man on the planet.
These images chart the story of a legend

The Clay dynasty in March 1964:
Seated (left to right) are aunts Louise Clay, Eva Wadell and Coretta Clay, grandmother Edith Clay and cousin Gillie Plunkett
Standing (left to right) are aunt Mary Turner, brother Rudy Clay, father Cassius Clay Snr, Cassius Clay Jnr and mother Odessa Clay

Cassius and his brother Rudolph assist their 99-year-old great-grandmother, Betsy Jane

Rudolph beefs up the Olympic hopeful's stomach muscles with a medicine ball, January 1960.

"The Australian got the bronze, the Pole got the silver and they gave me the pretty gold medal. That was my biggest thrill"

In fact Clay defeated the Russian (1956 Olympic Middleweight champion Gennadiy Shatkov) on the way to the final. With Clay on the winners' podium at the 1960 Olympics are (left to right): Giulio Saraudi (Italy) and Anthony Madigan (Australia) – joint bronze winners, and the Pole Zbigniew Pietrzykowski – silver medallist

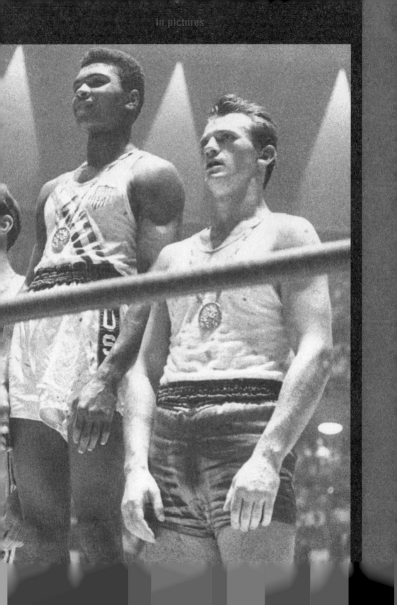

Sweet dreamer? Don't you believe it. This 17-year-old already has his eye fixed firmly on ring glory

The impish Clay fooled *Sports Illustrated* and *Life* photographer Flip Schulke into believing he trained by punching underwater. In fact he couldn't swim, but he emptied his lungs, sank down and assumed this classic stance for *Life* magazine, 8 September 1961

November 1960.Clay used his
first advance of $10,000 from the
Louisville sponsorship group of
local businessmen to buy his
mother a brand new pink Cadillac

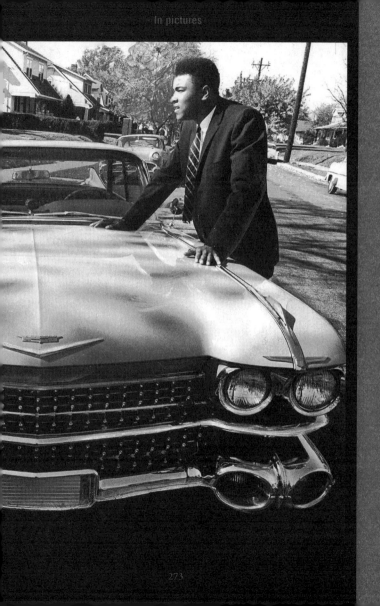

"Float like a butterfly, sting like a bee
His hands can't hit what his eyes can't see"
Angelo Dundee raises his protege's arm
after his sixth straight professional victory,
against Lamar Clark in Louisville, 1961

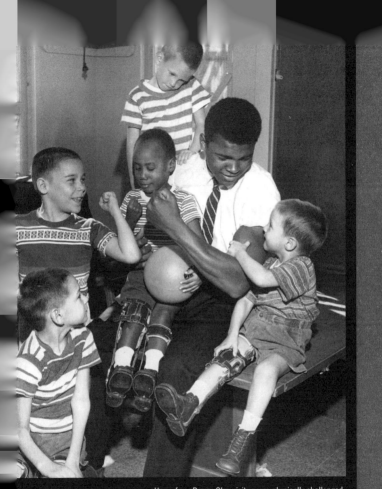

Home from Rome, Clay visits some physically challenged

"I AM THE GREATEST!"
In February 1964, The Beatles were taken to Ali's training camp in Miami. There, photographer Harry Benson recalls, Clay ordered them around, shouting "Who's the most beautiful?" and "I am the greatest!" Despite their game mugging, The Beatles were not best pleased

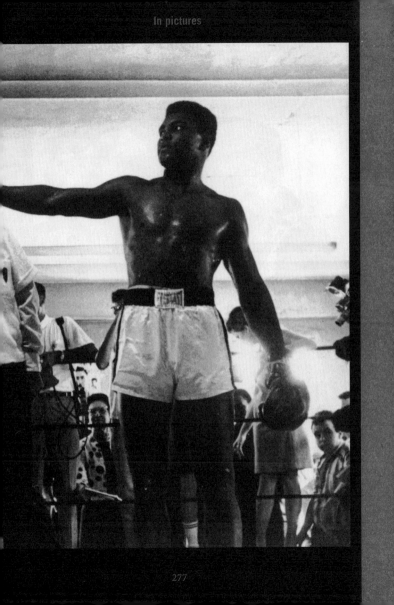

Cassius Clay and Malcolm X in Harlem, February 1964, just before his first clash with Sonny Liston. Clay announced his membership of the Nation of Islam – and his new name Muhammad Ali – the day after his famous victory

"Clay was standing over me, right? To get up I have to use one hand and one knee. Now you can tell what a normal guy will do but there's no telling what a nut will do. And Clay is definitely a nut"
Muhammad Ali orders Sonny Liston to his feet after scoring a knockdown in the first minute of their title rematch, May 1965

"I said I was the greatest, not the smartest"
Clay takes one of the tests that resulted in his '1Y'
classification by the Miami Draft Board in January
1964. Giving him instructions is Lt Reno Diorio

"The on'liest way you can get the title is in the ring. The on'liest way you can lose it is in the ring. I have the real belt – traditionally – that Jack Johnson and Joe Louis had"

November 1964 – Ali displays the world heavyweight belt that would be taken from him in 1967, along with his boxing licence. Note the sign on the wall behind him

"I turned down millions of dollars in sponsorship and endorsements because of my religious beliefs before the draft ever came up" Muhammad Ali poses for *Esquire's* April 1968 front cover. A reworking of 15th-century Italian painter Andrea del Castagno's *The Martyrdom of St Sebastian*, the picture is a comment on Ali's treatment after his faith-based refusal to be drafted for Vietnam

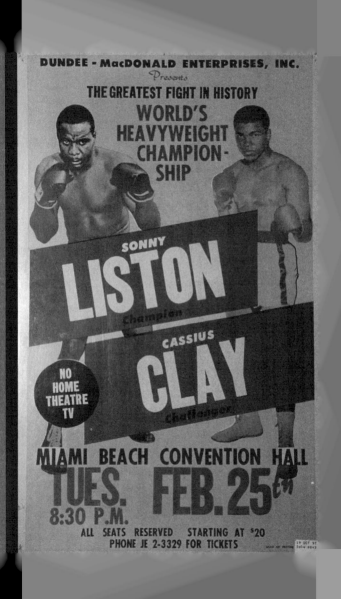

"I'm the most recognised and loved man that ever lived, cuz there weren't no satellites when Jesus and Moses were around, so people far away in the villages didn't know about them"

"This is the story of Cassius Clay
The most colourful fighter in the world today
This brash young fighter is something to see
And the heavyweight championship is his destiny"
Brother Rudolph raises Clay's hand as he shows
off his Olympic gold medal to a crowd at his
former high school in Louisville, 1960

"I won't miss boxing.
Boxing will miss me"
The most famous name in boxing returns to
the ring after three-and-a-half years in exile

"My right hand was trembling with Parkinsons, my left was trembling with fear, but somehow I got the thing lit"
Muhammad Ali lights the Olympic flame for the 1996 Olympic Games in Atlanta

AND STILL THE GREATEST

Muhammad Ali celebrates his
50th birthday, January 1992

Muhammad

ALI

the record books

The Athlete of the Century and how he got there:
Ali's bout by bout record

"I'M NOT THE GREATEST,
I'M THE DOUBLE GREATEST!
NOT ONLY DO I KNOCK 'EM
OUT, I PICK THE ROUND"

MUHAMMAD ALI WAS THE FIRST BOXER TO CAPTURE A WORLD
HEAVYWEIGHT CHAMPIONSHIP ON THREE SEPARATE OCCASIONS.
AND THAT'S ONLY ONE EXTRAORDINARY ASPECT OF AN EXTRAORDINARY
PROFESSIONAL CAREER, WHICH IS DETAILED BELOW, FIGHT BY FIGHT

Muhammad Ali Right-handed; height 6ft 3in; weight 186-236lbs

Born 17 January 1942; Louisville, Kentucky
Formerly Cassius Marcellus Clay (until 26 February 1964)
Nicknames 'The Louisville Lip', 'The Greatest'

Amateur record 138 bouts: 131 wins, 7 losses

1956 Novice title, Louisville, Kentucky
1959 Intercity Golden Gloves Champion
1959 National AAU Light Heavyweight Champion
1960 Intercity Golden Gloves Champion
1960 National AAU Light Heavyweight Champion
1960 Olympic Light Heavyweight Champion

Professional record 61 bouts: 56 wins (37 by KO/TKO), 5 losses

Undisputed World Heavyweight Champion 1964-67, 1974-78, 1978-79

Professional ring record by fight (World title opponents in bold)

KO – knockout; TKO – technical knockout; D – decision

Year	Date	Opponent	Venue	Result
1960	29 Oct	Tunney Hunsaker	Louisville	Win D 6
	27 Dec	Herb Siler	Miami Beach	Win TKO 4
1961	17 Jan	Tony Esperti	Miami Beach	Win TKO 3

Professional ring record by fight continued

KO – knockout; TKO – technical knockout; D – decision

1961	7 Feb	Jim Robinson	Miami Beach	Win TKO 1
	21 Feb	Donnie Fleeman	Miami Beach	Win TKO 7
	19 Apr	Lamar Clark	Louisville	Win KO 2
	26 Jun	Duke Sabedong	Las Vegas	Win D 10
	22 Jul	Alonzo Johnson	Louisville	Win D 10
	7 Oct	Alex Miteff	Louisville	Win TKO 6
	29 Nov	Willi Besmanoff	Louisville	Win TKO 7
1962	10 Feb	Sonny Banks	New York	Win TKO 4
	28 Mar	Don Warner	Miami Beach	Win TKO 4
	23 Apr	George Logan	Los Angeles	Win TKO 4
	19 May	Billy Daniels	New York	Win TKO 7
	20 Jul	Alejandro Lavorante	Los Angeles	Win KO 5
	15 Nov	Archie Moore	Los Angeles	Win KO 4
1963	24 Jan	Charlie Powell	Pittsburgh	Win KO 3
	13 Mar	Doug Jones	New York	Win D 10
	18 Jun	Henry Cooper	London	Win TKO 5
1964	25 Feb	**Sonny Liston**	Miami Beach	Win TKO 7
	Wins Heavyweight Championship of the World			

1965	25 May	**Sonny Liston**	Lewiston, ME	Win KO 1
	22 Nov	**Floyd Patterson**	Las Vegas	Win TKO 12
1966	29 Mar	**George Chuvalo**	Toronto	Win D 15
	21 May	**Henry Cooper**	London	Win TKO 6
	6 Aug	**Brian London**	London	Win KO 3
	10 Sep	**Karl Mildenberger**	Frankfurt	Win TKO 12
	14 Nov	**Cleveland Williams**	Houston	Win TKO 3
1967	6 Feb	**Ernie Terrell**	Houston	Win D 15
	22 Mar	**Zora Folley**	New York	Win KO 7

28 Apr 1967 *Refuses induction into the US army. Is stripped of World Heavyweight title and barred from fighting while he appeals against a five-year prison sentence for draft evasion*

1970	26 Oct	Jerry Quarry	Atlanta	Win KO 3
	7 Dec	Oscar Bonavena	New York	Win TKO 15
1971	8 Mar	**Joe Frazier**	New York	Loss D 15
	26 Jul	Jimmy Ellis	Houston	Win TKO 12
	17 Nov	Buster Mathis	Houston	Win D 12
	26 Dec	Jurgen Blin	Zurich	Win KO 7
1972	1 Apr	Mac Foster	Tokyo	Win D 15
	1 May	George Chuvalo	Vancouver	Win D 12

Professional ring record by fight continued

KO – knockout; TKO – technical knockout; D – decision

1972	27 Jun	Jerry Quarry	Las Vegas	Win TKO 7
	19 Jul	Al 'Blue' Lewis	Dublin	Win TKO 11
	20 Sep	Floyd Patterson	New York	Win TKO 7
	21 Nov	Bob Foster	Stateline, NV	Win KO 8
1973	14 Feb	Joe Bugner	Las Vegas	Win D 12
	31 Mar	Ken Norton	San Diego	Loss D 12
	10 Sep	Ken Norton	Los Angeles	Win D 12
	20 Oct	Rudi Lubbers	Jakarta	Win D 12
1974	28 Jan	Joe Frazier	New York	Win D 12
	30 Oct	**George Foreman**	Kinshasa	Win KO 8
		Regains Heavyweight Championship of the World		
1975	24 Mar	**Chuck Wepner**	Cleveland	Win TKO 15
	16 May	**Ron Lyle**	Las Vegas	Win TKO 11
	30 Jun	**Joe Bugner**	Kuala Lumpur	Win D 15
	1 Oct	**Joe Frazier**	Manila	Win TKO 14
1976	20 Feb	**Jean-Pierre Coopman**	San Juan	Win KO 5
	30 Apr	**Jimmy Young**	Landover, MD	Win D 15
	24 May	**Richard Dunn**	Munich	Win TKO 5

1976	28 Sep	**Ken Norton**	New York	Win D 15
1977	16 May	**Alfredo Evangelista**	Landover, MD	Win D 15
	29 Sep	**Earnie Shavers**	New York	Win D 15
1978	15 Feb	**Leon Spinks**	Las Vegas	Loss D 15
	Loses Heavyweight Championship of the World			
	15 Aug	**Leon Spinks**	New Orleans	Win D 15
	Regains Heavyweight Championship of the World			
1979	27 Jun	Announces his retirement		
1980	2 Oct	**Larry Holmes**	Las Vegas	Loss TKO 11
1981	11 Dec	Trevor Berbick	Nassau	Loss D 10
	12 Dec	*Retires from professional boxing*		

Notable exhibitions

Spar – sparring session; Exh – exhibition

1961	6 Feb	Ingemar Johansson	Miami Beach	Spar 2
1972	1 Jul	Lonnie Bennett	Los Angeles	Exh 2
	1 Jul	Eddie Jones	Los Angeles	Exh 2
	1 Jul	Billy Ryan	Los Angeles	Exh 2
	1 Jul	Charley James	Los Angeles	Exh 2
	1 Jul	Rudolph Clay (his brother, later Rahaman Ali)	Los Angeles	Exh 2

Notable exhibitions

Spar – sparring session; Exh – exhibition

1976	25 Jun	Antonio Inoki	Tokyo	Exh, draw 15
1977	29 Jan	Peter Fuller	Boston	Exh 4
	29 Jan	Walter Haines	Boston	Exh 1
	29 Jan	Jerry Houston	Boston	Exh 2
	29 Jan	Ron Drinkwater	Boston	Exh 2
	29 Jan	Matt Ross	Boston	Exh 2
	29 Jan	Frank Smith	Boston	Exh 1
	2 Dec	Scott LeDoux	Chicago	Exh 5
1978	14 Jul	Lyle Alzado	Denver	Exh 8

Notable awards

15 September 2000
Muhammad Ali is made a United Nations Messenger of Peace. His citation notes that he has raised more than $50m for charities around the world, and that he was instrumental in freeing more than a dozen US hostages from Iraq in 1990, days before the Gulf War broke out.

December 2000
Ali tops numerous 'Athlete of the Century' polls, including that of *Time* magazine. In the UK, he is voted BBC Sports Personality of the Century.

31 May 2002
The Muhammad Ali Boxing Reform Act is passed by the US Congress. The Act states:
The purposes of this Act are –
(1) to protect the rights and welfare of professional

boxers by preventing certain exploitative, oppressive and unethical business practices they may be subject to on an interstate basis;

(2) to assist State boxing commissions in their efforts to provide more effective public oversight of the sport;

(3) to promote honorable competition in professional boxing and enhance the overall integrity of the industry.

The Muhammad Ali Center

The $40m Ali centre is scheduled to open in 2005. Based in Ali's hometown of Louisville, Kentucky, the centre is designed to promote his legacy, and to teach and inspire people to be their best and fulfill their dreams. The centre will draw on six themes of his life (conviction, confidence, dedication, respect, spirituality and giving) in telling his life story. For more info see www.alicenter.org or call (001) 502-584-9254.

Rough Guides travel...

Rough Guides are available from good bookstores worldwide. New titles are published every month. Check www.roughguides.com for the latest news.

...music & reference

Also! More than 120 Rough Guide music CDs are available from all good book and record stores.
Listen in at www.worldmusic.net

**HOW WOULD 'THE GREATEST'
LIKE TO BE REMEMBERED?**

"As a man who never sold out his people.
But if that's too much then just a good
boxer, and I won't even mind if you don't
mention how pretty I was."
-MUHAMMAD ALI